UNDERSTANDING AND USING

ENGLISH GRAMMAR

Second Edition

TEACHER'S GUIDE

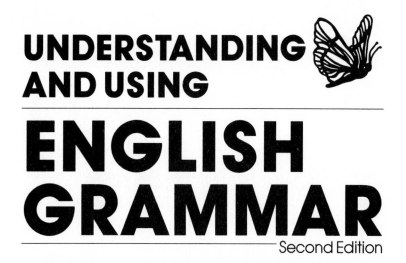

UNDERSTANDING AND USING

ENGLISH GRAMMAR

Second Edition

TEACHER'S GUIDE

Barbara F. Matthies
Betty Schrampfer Azar

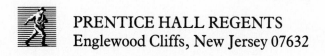

PRENTICE HALL REGENTS
Englewood Cliffs, New Jersey 07632

Publisher: *Tina B. Carver*
Managing editor, production: *Sylvia Moore*
Editorial/production supervisor: *Janet Johnston*
Prepress buyer: *Ray Keating*
Manufacturing buyer: *Lori Bulwin*
Scheduler: *Leslie Coward*
Cover supervisor: *Marianne Frasco*
Cover designer: *Joel Mitnick Design*
Interior designer: *Ros Herion Freese*
Page makeup: *Mary Fitzgerald*

© 1993 by PRENTICE HALL REGENTS
A Division of Simon & Schuster
Englewood Cliffs, New Jersey 07632

Printed in the United States of America

10 9 8 7 6 5 4 3 2 1

ISBN 0-13-928565-2

ISBN 0-13-943994-3 (VOL.A)
ISBN 0-13-944018-6 (VOL.B)

Prentice-Hall International (UK) Limited, *London*
Prentice-Hall of Australia Pty. Limited, *Sydney*
Prentice-Hall Canada Inc., *Toronto*
Prentice-Hall Hispanoamericana, S.A., *Mexico*
Prentice-Hall of India Private Limited, *New Delhi*
Prentice-Hall of Japan, Inc., *Tokyo*
Simon & Schuster Asia Pte. Ltd., *Singapore*
Editora Prentice-Hall do Brasil, Ltda., *Rio de Janeiro*

Contents

Preface

This *Teacher's Guide* is intended as a practical aid to teachers. You can turn to it for notes on the content of a unit and how to approach the exercises, for suggestions for classroom activities, and for answers to the exercises in the main text and to the Guided Study practices in the workbooks.

General teaching information can be found in the introduction. It includes:

- the rationale and general aims of *Understanding and Using English Grammar*
- classroom techniques for presenting charts and using exercises
- suggestions on the use of the workbook in connection with the main text
- comments on differences between American and British English
- a key to the pronunciation symbols used in this *Guide*

The rest of the *Guide* contains notes on charts and exercises.

The notes about the charts may include:

- suggestions for presenting the information to students
- points to emphasize
- common problems to anticipate
- assumptions underlying the contents
- additional background notes on grammar and usage

The notes that accompany the exercises may include:

- the focus of the exercise
- suggested techniques as outlined in the introduction
- possible specialized techniques for particular exercises
- points to emphasize
- problems to anticipate
- assumptions
- answers
- expansion activities
- item notes on cultural content, vocabulary, and idiomatic usage. (Some of these item notes are specifically intended to aid any teachers who are non-native speakers of English.)

Introduction

General Aims of *Understanding and Using English Grammar*

The principal aim of *Understanding and Using English Grammar* is, simply put, to provide review and reinforcement of basic English structures and, upon this foundation, to enable the students to expand their performance repertoire in all skill areas. The text seeks to apprise English language students of certain grammatical features of high frequency and utility in English. As learners become aware of these structures, they begin to see and hear them more easily. This can lead, in turn, to more success in using the structures naturally and appropriately in their own speaking and writing, especially if they are provided with numerous practice opportunities. The exercises provide practice in listening, speaking, reading, and writing skills, since grammar underlies all of them.

The text depends upon a partnership with a teacher, for the teacher animates and directs the students' language-learning experiences. In practical terms, the aim of the text is to support teachers by providing a substantial base of material to be used creatively according to their needs and preferences.

Classroom Techniques

Following are some techniques that have proven useful. *Suggestions for Presenting the Grammar Charts* are discussed first. Next are some notes on *Degrees of Teacher and Student Involvement*. Then *Techniques for Exercise Types* are outlined.

Suggestions for Presenting the Grammar Charts

A chart is a concise visual presentation of the structures to be covered in one section of a chapter. Some charts may require particular methods of presentation, but generally any of the following techniques can be used.

Technique #1: Use the examples in the chart and your own examples to explain the grammar in your own words, and answer any questions about the chart. Elicit other examples of the target structure from the learners. Then go to the accompanying exercise immediately following the chart.

Technique #2: Elicit oral examples from the students before they look at the chart in the textbook. To elicit examples from the students, ask leading questions whose answers will include the target structure. (For example, for the present progressive, ask: "What are you doing right now?") You may want to write the elicited answers on the chalkboard and relate them to the examples in the chart. Then proceed to the exercises.

Technique #3: Assign the chart and accompanying exercise(s) for out-of-class study. In class the next day, ask for and answer any questions about the chart, and then immediately proceed to the exercises. (With advanced students, you might not need to deal thoroughly in class with every chart and exercise. With intermediate students, it is usually advisable to clarify charts and do most of the exercises.)

Technique #4: Lead the students through the accompanying exercise prior to discussing the chart. Use the material in the exercise to discuss the focus of the chart as you go along. At the end of the exercise, call attention to the examples in the chart and summarize what was discussed during the exercise.

Technique #5: Before presenting the chart in class, give the students a short written quiz on its content. Have the students correct their own papers as you review the answers. The quiz should not be given a score; it is a learning tool, not an examination. Use the items from the quiz as examples for discussing the grammar in the chart.

Presentation techniques often depend upon the content of the chart, the level of the class, and the students' learning styles. Not all students react to the charts in the same ways. Some students need the security of thoroughly understanding a chart before trying to use the structure. Others like to experiment more freely with using new structures; they refer to the charts only incidentally, if at all. Given these differing learning strategies, you should vary your presentation techniques and not expect students to "learn" or memorize the charts. The charts are just a starting point for class discussion and a point of reference.

Demonstration can be very helpful to explain the meaning of structures. You and the students can act out situations that demonstrate the target structure. Of course, not all grammar lends itself to this technique. For example, the present progressive can easily be demonstrated ("I *am writing* on the board right now."). However, the use of gerunds as the objects of prepositions ("instead *of writing*" or "thank you *for writing*") is not especially well suited to demonstration techniques.

In discussing the target structure of a chart, use the chalkboard whenever possible. Not all students have adequate listening skills for "teacher talk," and not all students can visualize and understand the various relationships within, between, and among structures. Draw boxes and circles and arrows to illustrate connections between the elements of a structure.

The students need to understand the terminology, but shouldn't be required or expected to give detailed definitions of terms, either in class discussion or on tests. Terminology is just a tool, a useful label for the moment, so that you and the students can talk to each other about English grammar.

Most students benefit from knowing what is going to be covered in the following class session. The students should be assigned to read the charts at home so that they can become familiar with the target structure and, it is to be hoped, come to class with questions.

For every chart, try to relate the target structure to an immediate classroom or "real-life" context. Make up or elicit examples that use the students' names, activities, and interests. The here-and-now classroom context is, of course, one of the grammar teacher's best aids.

Degrees of Teacher and Student Involvement

Most of the exercises in the text are intended to be teacher-led, but other options are group work, pair work, and student-led work.

TEACHER-LED EXERCISES

In an eclectic text such as this, many approaches are possible, based on various sound theories of language learning and teaching. The teacher plays many roles and can employ a wide variety of techniques.

In essence, all exercises in the main text are teacher-led. Even so, there is a wide range of possible teacher involvement: from lecturing on "rules" to eliciting deductive understandings, from supplying answers to eliciting responses, from being the focus of the students' attention to being solely an initiator and facilitator. Consider the students' goals and the time that is available, then decide whether to focus a lot of attention on every item in an exercise or to go through it quickly and spend time on related activities. It is beneficial for students to push hard and work intensively on English grammar, but it is also beneficial for the students to spend relaxed time in class exchanging ideas in structure-oriented conversations or similar pursuits.

GROUP WORK AND PAIR WORK

Many, but not all, exercises in the text are suitable for group or pair work. Suggestions for such alternatives are included in the comments on the exercises in the Chapter Notes in this *Guide*.

Exercises done in groups or pairs may often take twice as much time as they would if teacher-led, but it is time well spent if you plan carefully and make sure that the students are speaking in English to each other. There are many advantages to student–student practice.

When the students are working in groups or pairs, their opportunities to use what they are learning are greatly increased. They will often explain things to each other during pair work, in which case both students benefit. Obviously, the students in group work are often much more active and involved than in teacher-led exercises.

Group and pair work also expands the students' opportunities to practice many communication skills at the same time that they are practicing target structures. In peer interaction in the classroom, the students have to agree, disagree, continue a conversation, make suggestions, promote cooperation, make requests, be sensitive to each other's needs and personalities, and the like—exchanges that are characteristic of any group communication, in the classroom or elsewhere.

In addition, group and pair work helps to produce a comfortable learning environment. In teacher-centered activities, students may sometimes feel shy and inhibited or may experience stress. They may feel that they have to respond quickly and accurately and that *what* they say is not as important as *how* they say it, even though you strive to convince them to the contrary. If you set up groups that are noncompetitive and cooperative, the students usually tend to help, encourage, and even joke with each other. This encourages them to experiment with the language and to speak more.

Students should be encouraged to monitor each other to some extent in group work, especially when monitoring activities are specifically assigned. (But perhaps you should remind them to give some *positive* as well as corrective comments to each other in order to maintain good feelings.) You shouldn't worry about "losing control" of the students' language production, and they shouldn't worry about learning each other's mistakes. Not every mistake needs to be corrected, but you can take some time at the end of an exercise to call attention to mistakes that you heard frequently as you listened in on the groups.

WAYS OF USING EXERCISES FOR GROUP OR PAIR WORK

1. Divide the class into groups of two to six, usually with one student as leader. You may appoint the students to the groups or sometimes let them divide themselves. You may appoint a leader or let the students choose one. Leadership can be rotated. Be sure that the leader understands what to do, and set a reasonable time limit for finishing the activity.

2. For ORAL (BOOKS CLOSED) exercises, only the leader has his/her text open. If these exercises are used for pair work, one student has an open text and the other doesn't. Halfway through an exercise, the pair may change roles.

3. For ORAL or some other types of exercises, the students can discuss completions, transformations, etc., among themselves prior to, or instead of, class discussion. You can move about the classroom answering questions as necessary.

4. For exercises that require writing in the textbook, each group should produce one set of answers that all (or at least a majority) of the members agree are correct. The leader can present the group's answers for class discussion or hand in a collaborative paper for your correction and sometimes even for a grade. Similarly, pairs of students can compare their answers prior to class discussion and come to an agreement on the correctness.

STUDENT-LED EXERCISES

Once in a while you may wish to ask a student to assume the teacher's role in some of the ORAL or ORAL (BOOKS CLOSED) exercises; the student conducts the exercise by giving the cues and determining the appropriateness of the response, while you retire to a corner of the room. It is helpful, but not essential, for you to work with the student leader outside of class in preparation for his/her role as teacher. Usually, a student-led oral exercise will take twice as much class time as a teacher-led exercise, but if the time is available, it can be a valuable experience for the student-teacher and fun for the entire class.

Techniques for Exercise Types

Some of the exercises in the text have specific labels: ORAL (BOOKS CLOSED), ORAL, WRITTEN, ORAL/WRITTEN, ERROR ANALYSIS, PREPOSITIONS, PHRASAL VERBS, PRETEST. It is important to note that the "oral" and "written" labels on particular exercises are only suggestions to the teacher. If you deem it appropriate, you can have the students write out an oral exercise or discuss a written exercise.

Exercise: ORAL (BOOKS CLOSED)

a. For exercises of this type, which range from simple manipulation to open-ended communicative interaction, the students have their books closed. These exercises are not intended as fast-paced drills to be completed without interruption. Their pace should allow ample time for the students to understand and respond as well as enough time for short spontaneous conversations to occur. These exercises provide a good opportunity for the students to develop their listening and speaking skills while expanding their ability to use the target structures. With their books closed, they can concentrate on what you and others are saying and can practice speaking without relying on written words.

b. Be flexible in handling these exercises. You don't have to read the items aloud as though reading a script from which there should be no deviation. Modify the format to make it more workable for your particular class. Try to add more items spontaneously as they occur to you. Change the items in any way to make them more relevant to your students. (For example, if you know that some students plan to watch the World Cup soccer match on TV, include a sentence about that.) Omit irrelevant items. Sometimes an item will start a spontaneous discussion of, for example, local restaurants or current movies or certain experiences the students have had. These spur-of-the-moment dialogues are very beneficial to the students. Encourage and facilitate the discussion, and then, within a reasonable length of time, bring attention back to the grammar at hand.

c. To initiate an ORAL (BOOKS CLOSED) exercise, give the class an example or two of the format. Sometimes you will want to give explicit oral directions. Sometimes you will want to use the chalkboard to write down key words to help the students focus on the target structure or consider the options in their responses.

d. Repeat a cue in ORAL (BOOKS CLOSED) exercises as often as necessary. Start out with normal spoken English, but then slow down and repeat as needed. You may want to write on the board, do a pantomime, demonstrate, draw a picture—whatever may help the students understand what you're saying. One of your goals is to convince students that they *can* understand spoken English. They shouldn't feel failure or be embarrassed if they don't understand a spoken cue immediately. If an exercise is too difficult for your class as a whole or for particular students, let them do it with their books open.

e. In general, ORAL (BOOKS CLOSED) exercises follow a chart or an open-book exercise. First, students should build up their understanding of the structure and practice using it. Then they will feel more confident during these oral exercises, which for many students are riskier and far more difficult than open-book work.

Essentially, in the ORAL (BOOKS CLOSED) exercises, the teacher is saying to the students, "Okay, now you understand such-and-such [for example, word order in noun clauses], so let's play with it a bit. With any luck, you'll be happily surprised by how much you already know. Mistakes are no big problem. They're a natural part of learning a new language. So just give it a try and let's see what happens."

f. Sometimes ORAL (BOOKS CLOSED) exercises precede a chart or open-book exercises. The purpose of this order is to elicit student-generated examples of the target structure as a springboard to the discussion of the grammar. If you prefer to introduce any particular structure to your students orally, you can always use an ORAL (BOOKS CLOSED) exercise prior to the presentation of a chart and written exercises, no matter what the given order is in the textbook.

Exercise: ORAL

Exercises of this type are intended to be done with books open but require no writing and no preparation. In other words, the students can read what is in the text, but they don't have to write in their books. You don't have to assign these exercises ahead of time; they can be done directly in class. These exercises come in many forms and are often suitable for group or pair work.

Exercise: ORAL/WRITTEN

This label indicates that the material can be used for either speaking practice or writing practice. Sometimes it indicates that the two are combined: e.g., a speaking activity may lead to a writing activity.

Exercise: WRITTEN

In this type of exercise, the students should use their own paper and submit their answers to you. Some of the WRITTEN exercises require sentence completion, but most are designed to produce short, informal compositions. In general, the topics or tasks concern aspects of the students' lives in order to encourage free and relatively effortless communication as they practice their writing skills. While a course in English rhetoric is beyond the scope of this text, many of the basic elements are included and may be developed and emphasized according to your purposes.

For best results, whenever you make a writing assignment, let your students know what you expect: "This is what I suggest as content. This is how you might organize it. This is how long I expect it to be." It is always a good idea for you to sit down and write an assignment yourself before discussing it with the class. If at all possible, give your students composition models, perhaps taken from good compositions written by previous classes, perhaps written by you, perhaps composed as a group activity by the class as a whole (e.g., you write on the board what the students tell you to write, and then you and the students revise it together).

In general, WRITTEN exercises should be done outside of class. All of us need time to consider and revise when we write. The topics in the exercises are structured so that plagiarism should not be a problem. Use in-class writing if you want to appraise the students' unaided, spontaneous writing skills. Tell your students that these written exercises are simply for practice and that— even though they should always try to do their best—mistakes that occur will be considered only as opportunities for learning.

Encourage the students to use their dictionaries whenever they write. Point out that you yourself never write seriously without a dictionary at hand. Discuss the use of margins, indentation of paragraphs, and other aspects of the format of a well-written paper.

Ask your students to use lined paper and to write on every other line, so that you and they have space to make corrections. APPENDIX 3 presents a system for marking errors so that students may make their own corrections and so that you may mark papers quickly and efficiently. (See p. xviii of this *Guide* for information about using APPENDIX 3.)

Exercise: ERROR ANALYSIS

For the most part, the sentences in this type of exercise have been adapted from actual student writing and contain typical errors. ERROR ANALYSIS exercises focus on the target structures of a chapter but may also contain miscellaneous errors that are common in student writing at this level, such as omission of final -*s* on plural nouns or capitalization of proper nouns. The purpose of including them is to sharpen the students' self-monitoring skills.

ERROR ANALYSIS exercises are challenging and fun, a good way to summarize the grammar in a chapter. If you wish, tell the students they are either newspaper editors or English teachers; their task is to locate all mistakes and write corrections.

The recommended technique is to assign an ERROR ANALYSIS for in-class discussion the next day. The students benefit most from having the opportunity to find the errors themselves prior to class discussion. These exercises can, of course, be handled in other ways: seatwork, written homework, group work, pair work.

Some teachers object to allowing students to see errors written in a textbook. However, there is little chance that any harm is being done. Students look at errors all the time in their own writing and profit from finding and correcting them. The benefits of doing ERROR ANALYSIS exercises far outweigh any possible (and highly unlikely) negative results. Point out that even native speakers or highly proficient non-native speakers—including you yourself—have to scrutinize, correct, and revise what they write. This is a natural part of the writing process.

Exercise: PREPOSITIONS

Exercises of this type focus on prepositions that combine with verbs and adjectives. The intention is that the students simply make their "best guess" according to what "sounds right" to them when completing each item, then get the correct answers from class discussion and learn the ones they missed. They can refer to the list of combinations in APPENDIX 2 if they want to.

To reinforce the prepositions in an exercise, you can make up quick oral reviews (books closed) by rephrasing the items and having the students call out the prepositions. For example:

Text entry: I subscribe __*to*__ several magazines.
Made-up oral reinforcement exercise:
　　TEACHER: "I like to read magazines. I subscribe . . . ."
　　STUDENTS call out: "to"
　　TEACHER: "Good. Subscribe **to**. I subscribe **to** several magazines."

Text entry: Do you believe __*in*__ ghosts?
Made-up oral reinforcement exercise:
　　TEACHER: "I'm not convinced that ghosts exist. What about you? Do you believe . . . ."
　　STUDENTS call out: "in"
　　TEACHER: "Right. Believe **in**. Do you believe **in** ghosts?"

Exercise: PHRASAL VERBS

These contain two- and three-word verbs and can be handled in the same ways as the PREPOSITIONS exercises, adding increased emphasis on discussion of the phrases as vocabulary items.

As with the PREPOSITIONS exercises, the PHRASAL VERBS exercises are interspersed throughout the text at the ends of chapters. The intention is that the students review and/or learn a few of the most common of these expressions at a time. The scope and length of the text do not allow for an intensive treatment of the hundreds of phrasal verbs in the English language.

The term "adverb particle" is not used in the text, as it is deemed a possible source of confusion and unnecessary for the students' purposes.

Exercise: PRETEST

The purpose of these exercises is to let the students discover what they do and do not know about the target structure in order to get them interested in a chart. Essentially, PRETEST exercises illustrate a possible teaching technique: quiz the students first as a springboard for presenting the grammar in a chart.

Additional Techniques

Most of the exercises in the textbook do not have specific labels. The following section outlines additional techniques not only for labeled exercises but also for other activities.

The majority of the exercises in the text require some sort of completion, transformation, combination, discussion of meaning, or a combination of such activities. They range from those that are tightly controlled and manipulative to those that encourage free responses and require creative, independent language use. The techniques vary according to the exercise type.

FILL-IN-THE-BLANKS AND CONTROLLED COMPLETION EXERCISES

The label "fill-in-the-blanks" refers to those exercises in which the students complete the sentences by using words given in parentheses. The label "controlled completion" refers to those exercises in which the students complete sentences using the words in a given list. Both types of exercises call for similar techniques.

Technique A: A student can be asked to read an item aloud. You can say whether the student's answer is correct or not, or you can open up discussion by asking the rest of the class if the answer is correct. For example:

TEACHER: "Juan, would you please read Number 2?"
STUDENT: "Diane *washes* her hair every other day or so."
TEACHER (to the class): "Do the rest of you agree with Juan's answer?"

The slow-moving pace of this method is beneficial for discussion not only of grammar items but also of vocabulary and content. The students have time to digest information and ask questions. You have the opportunity to judge how well they understand the grammar.

However, this time-consuming technique doesn't always, or even usually, need to be used, especially with more advanced classes.

Technique B: You, the teacher, read the first part of the item, then pause for the students to call out the answer in unison. For example:

Text entry: Diane (*wash*) _____ her hair every other day or so.
TEACHER (with the students looking at their texts): "Diane . . . ."
STUDENTS (in unison): "washes" (plus possibly a few incorrect responses scattered about)
TEACHER: ". . . washes her hair every other day or so. *Washes.* Do you have any questions?"

This technique saves a lot of time in class and is slow-paced enough to allow for questions and discussion of grammar, vocabulary, and content. It is essential that the students have prepared the exercise by writing in their books, so it must be assigned ahead as homework.

Technique C: With an advanced class for whom a particular exercise is little more than a quick review, you can simply give the answers so the students can correct their own previously prepared work in their textbooks. You can either read the whole sentence ("Number 2: Diane washes her hair every other day or so") or just give the answer ("Number 2: washes"). You can give the answers to the items one at a time, taking questions as they arise, or give the answers to the whole exercise before opening it up for questions. As an alternative, you can have one of the students read his/her answers and have the other students ask him/her questions if they disagree.

Technique D: Divide the class into groups (or pairs) and have each group prepare one set of answers that they all agree is correct prior to class discussion. The leader of each group can present their answers.

Another option is to have the groups (or pairs) hand in their set of answers for correction and possibly a grade.

It's also possible to turn these exercises into games wherein the group with the best set of answers gets some sort of reward (perhaps applause from the rest of the class).

Of course, you can always mix Techniques A, B, C, and D—with the students reading some aloud, with you prompting unison response for some, with you simply giving the answers for others, with the students collaborating on the answers for others. Much depends on the level of the class, their familiarity and skill with the grammar at hand, their oral-aural skills in general, and how flexible or limited your available classtime is.

Technique E: When an exercise item has a dialogue between speakers A and B, ask one student to be A and another B and have them read the entry aloud. Then, occasionally, say to A and B: "Without looking at your text, what did you just say to each other?" (If necessary, let them glance briefly at their texts before they repeat what they've just said in the exercise item.) The students may be pleasantly surprised by their own fluency.

OPEN COMPLETION EXERCISES

The term "open completion" refers to those exercises in which the students use their own words to complete the sentences.

Technique A: Exercises where the students must supply their own words to complete a sentence should usually be assigned for out-of-class preparation. Then in class, one, two, or several students can read their sentences aloud; the class can discuss the correctness and appropriateness of the completions. Perhaps you can suggest possible ways of rephrasing to make a sentence more idiomatic. Students who don't read their sentences aloud can revise their own completions based on what is being discussed in class. At the end of the exercise discussion, you can tell the students to hand in their sentences for you to look at, or merely ask if anyone has questions about the exercise and not have the students submit anything to you.

Technique B: If you wish to use an open completion exercise in class without having previously assigned it, you can turn the exercise into a brainstorming session in which students try out several completions to see if they work. As another possibility, you may divide the students into small groups and have each group come up with completions that they all agree are correct and appropriate. Then use only these completions for class discussion or as written work to be handed in.

Technique C: Some open completion exercises are designated WRITTEN, which usually means the students need to use their own paper, as not enough space has been left in the textbook. It is often beneficial to use the following progression: (1) assign the exercise for out-of-class preparation; (2) discuss it in class the next day, having the students make corrections on their own papers based on what they are learning from discussing other students' completions; (3) then ask the students to submit their papers to you, either as a requirement or on a volunteer basis.

TRANSFORMATION AND COMBINATION EXERCISES

In transformation exercises, the students are asked to change form but not substance (e.g., to change the active to the passive, a clause to a phrase, or a question to a noun clause).

In combination exercises, the students are asked to combine two or more sentences or ideas into one sentence that contains a particular structure (e.g., an adjective clause, a parallel structure, a gerund phrase).

In general, these exercises, which require manipulation of a form, are intended for class discussion of the form and meaning of a structure. The initial stages of such exercises are a good opportunity to use the chalkboard to draw circles and arrows to illustrate the characteristics and relationships of a structure. Students can read their answers aloud to initiate the class discussion, and you can write on the board as problems arise. Another possibility is to have the students write their sentences on the board. Also possible is to have them work in small groups to agree upon their answers prior to class discussion.

DISCUSSION-OF-MEANING EXERCISES

Some exercises consist primarily of you and the students discussing the meaning of given sentences. Most of these exercises ask the students to compare the meaning of two or more sentences (for example, *You should take an English course* vs. *You must take an English course*). One of the main purposes of discussion-of-meaning exercises is to provide an opportunity for summary comparison of the structures in a particular unit.

The basic technique in these exercises is for you to pose questions about the given sentences and then let the students explain what a structure means to them (which allows you to get input about what they do and do not understand). Then you summarize the salient points as necessary. Students have their own inventive, creative way of explaining differences in meaning. They shouldn't be expected to sound like grammar teachers. Often, all you need to do is listen carefully and patiently to a student's explanation, and then clarify and reinforce it by rephrasing it somewhat.

PRONUNCIATION EXERCISES

A few exercises focus on pronunciation of grammatical features, such as endings on nouns or verbs and contracted or reduced forms.

Some phonetic symbols are used in these exercises to point out sounds that should not be pronounced identically; for example, /s/, /əz/, and /z/ represent the three predictable pronunciations of the grammatical suffix spelled -s or -es. It is not necessary for students to learn a complete phonetic alphabet; they should merely associate each symbol in an exercise with a sound that is different from all others. The purpose is to help students become more aware of these final sounds in the English they hear to encourage proficiency of use in their own speaking and writing.

In the exercises on spoken contractions, the primary emphasis should be on the students' hearing and becoming familiar with spoken forms rather than on their production of these forms. The students need to understand that what they see in writing is not exactly what they should expect to hear in normal, rapid spoken English. The most important point of most of these exercises is that the students listen to your oral production and become familiar with the reduced forms.

Language learners are naturally conscious that their pronunciation is not like that of native speakers of the language. Therefore, some of them are embarrassed or shy about speaking. In a pronunciation exercise, they may be more comfortable if you ask groups or the whole class to say a sentence in unison. After that, individuals may volunteer to speak the same sentence. The learners' production does not need to be perfect, just understandable. You can encourage the students to be less inhibited by having them teach you how to pronounce words in their languages (unless, of course, you're a native speaker of the students' language in a monolingual class). It's fun—and instructive—for the students to teach the teacher.

SEATWORK

It is generally preferable to assign exercises for out-of-class preparation, but sometimes it's necessary to cover an exercise in class that you haven't been able to assign previously. In ''seatwork,'' you have the students do an unassigned exercise in class immediately before discussing it. Seatwork allows the students to try an exercise themselves before the answers are discussed so that they can discover what problems they may be having with a particular structure. Seatwork may be done individually, in pairs, or in groups.

HOMEWORK

The textbook assumes that the students will have the opportunity to prepare most of the exercises by writing in their books prior to class discussion. Students should be assigned this homework as a matter of course.

The use of the term "written homework" in this *Guide* suggests that the students write out an exercise on their own paper and hand it in to you. How much written homework you have the students do is up to you. The amount generally depends upon such variables as class size, class level, available classtime, your available paper-correcting time, not to mention your preferences in teaching techniques.

Most of the exercises in the text can be handled through class discussion without the necessity of the students' handing in written homework. By combining the *Workbook* with the main text, students can regularly do homework that they can correct themselves. Most of the written homework to be handed in that is suggested in the text and in the chapter notes in this *Guide* consists of activities that will produce original, independent writing.

CORRECTING WRITING ERRORS

APPENDIX 3 in *Understanding and Using English Grammar* (pp. A29–A30 in the back of the text) presents a system for marking errors in students' written work. It uses a numbering scheme for the purpose of signaling errors. This system is quite flexible, intended only to give the students hints when they set about correcting their own writing.

Some of the numbers have multiple uses. For example, 2 (Wrong Form) can signal that an adjective has been used instead of an adverb, a noun instead of an adjective, a gerund instead of an infinitive, incorrect *has being done* instead of *has been done*, incorrect *would has* instead of *would have*, etc. Other numbers have more limited uses. For example, 13 is intended only for run-on sentences or comma splices.

Some errors could be marked by either of two numbers. For example, *to*, as in *The weather is to cold*, could be marked by either 3 (Wrong Word) or 8 (Spelling). The word *beautifuls*, as in *I saw some beautifuls pictures*, could be marked by either 1 (Singular-Plural) or 2 (Wrong Form). Simply choose the number that you think will give the student the best help in correcting and learning from the mistake in that context.

For some errors, it is necessary to use two numbers in the same circle. For example, the word *intresting*, as in *I am intresting in that subject*, could be marked by both 8 (Spelling) and 2 (Wrong Form).

Write the full correction for any error that you are sure the student would be unable to correct himself/herself. When necessary, write a more idiomatic phrase. Use 12? (Meaning Not Clear) when you want the student to find a different way to express what s/he is trying to say, or when the handwriting is illegible.

Using the numbers soon becomes automatic, and marking papers proceeds quickly and efficiently.

Reviewing the corrections made later by the students also proceeds smoothly, especially if they have written the original composition on every other line, have left adequate margins, and have used a pen or pencil of a different color to make the corrections. Compositions with numerous errors should be rewritten entirely.

You may wish to add numbers to the list to specify particular problems with structure or style. For example, 14 could suggest Parallel Structure; 15 could denote Repetitiveness. The numbers given in APPENDIX 3 have been distilled from many to a few through years of experimentation, but the system is still adaptable.

Using the *Workbook*

The *Workbook* contains two kinds of exercises: Selfstudy and Guided Study. The answer key for the Selfstudy Practices is found at the end of the *Workbook* on perforated pages. Encourage your students to remove this answer key and put it in some sort of folder. It's much easier for the students to correct their own answers if they make their own answer key booklet. The answers to the Guided Study Practices are in this *Guide*.

The *Workbook* mirrors the main text. Exercises are called "exercises" in the main text and "practices" in the workbook to minimize confusion when you make assignments. Each practice in the *Workbook* has a content title and refers the students to appropriate charts in the main text.

In the chapter notes in this *Guide*, you will find the notation "◇ **WORKBOOK**" followed by the practices that can be assigned at or near that point in the lesson.

SELFSTUDY PRACTICES (ANSWERS GIVEN IN THE *WORKBOOK*)

Answers to the Selfstudy Practices are included in the *Workbook* so that students can immediately check their understanding and accuracy. The primary purpose of the Selfstudy Practices is to give the students ample opportunity to understand and use the target structures on their own. They should be encouraged to bring any questions about the Selfstudy Practices to class.

Selfstudy Practices can be assigned by you or, depending upon the level of maturity or sense of purpose of the class, simply left for the students to use as they wish. They may be assigned to the entire class or only to those students who need further practice with a particular structure. They may be used as reinforcement after you have covered a chart and exercises in class or as introductory material prior to discussing a chart in class.

In addition, the students can use the Selfstudy Practices to acquaint themselves with the grammar of any units not covered in class. Earnest students can use the *Workbook* to teach themselves.

GUIDED STUDY PRACTICES (ANSWERS NOT GIVEN IN THE *WORKBOOK*)

Answers to the Guided Study practices are given only in this *Teacher's Guide* for two reasons: (1) because many of the answers depend on students' creativity and require the teacher's judgment, and (2) so that some of the practices can be used as supplementary teaching materials for class use, written homework, individualized instruction, or possibly as quizzes.

PRACTICE TESTS IN THE *WORKBOOK*

Each chapter in the *Workbook* has Practice Test A (Selfstudy) and Practice Test B (Guided Study). You may wish to use one as a "pretest" and the other as a "post-test," or simply use both of them as summary review material upon finishing a chapter.

The practice tests are not really intended as "tests." They are simply another exercise type, to be used as a teaching tool like any other exercise. The students should simply be encouraged to do their best and learn from their mistakes.

You may, however, wish to have the students take a practice test in class under time-pressure conditions for experience in taking that kind of test. (Allow 30 seconds per item.) You could also have the students time themselves if they do the practice test at home.

Notes on American vs. British English

Students are often curious about differences between American and British English. They should know that the differences are minor. Anyone who has studied British English (BrE) should have no trouble adapting to American English (AmE), and vice versa.

DIFFERENCES IN GRAMMAR

Many of the differences in grammar are either footnoted in the main text or mentioned in the chart notes in this *Guide*. For example, the footnote to Chart 5-18 contains the information that BrE uses a plural verb with *government* whereas AmE uses a singular verb. Similarly, the notes in this *Guide* for Chart 2-11 contain the information that *don't let's* is considered incorrect in AmE but is acceptable informal usage in BrE. Teachers need to be careful not to inadvertently mark usage differences as errors; rather, they should simply point out to the students that a difference exists between two equally correct varieties of English.

Differences in article and preposition usage in certain common expressions follow. These differences are not noted in the text; they are given here for the teacher's information. The symbol Ø denotes that "nothing" is used there.

AmE	BrE
be in *the* hospital	be in *Ø* hospital
be at *the* university (be in *Ø* college)	be at *Ø* university
go to *a* university (go to *Ø* college)	go to *Ø* university
go to *Ø* class/be in *Ø* class	go to *a* class/be in *a* class
in *the* future	in *Ø* future (OR in *the* future)
did it *the next* day	did it *Ø* next day (OR *the* next day)
haven't done something *for/in* weeks	haven't done something *for* weeks
ten minutes *past/after* six o'clock	ten minutes *past* six o'clock
five minutes *to/of/til* seven o'clock	five minutes *to* seven o'clock

DIFFERENCES IN SPELLING

Variant spellings can be noted but should not be marked as incorrect in the students' writing. Spelling differences in some common words follow.

AmE	BrE
jewelry, traveler, woolen	jewellry, traveller, woollen
skillful, fulfill, installment	skilful, fulfil, instalment
color, honor, labor, odor	colour, honour, labour, odour
realize, analyze, apologize	realise, analyse, apologise
defense, offense, license	defence, offence, licence (n.)
theater, center, liter	theatre, centre, litre
check	cheque (bank note)
curb	kerb
forever	for ever/forever
jail	gaol
program	programme
specialty	speciality
story	storey (of a building)
tire	tyre
spilled, dreamed, burned	spilt, dreamt, burnt (See the footnote to Chart 1-11.)

DIFFERENCES IN VOCABULARY

Differences in vocabulary usage usually do not significantly interfere with communication. Students should know that when American and British speakers read each other's literature, they encounter only very few differences in vocabulary usage. A few differences between AmE and BrE follow.

AmE	BrE	AmE	BrE
attorney, lawyer	barrister, solicitor	fired/laid off	made redundant
bathrobe	dressing gown	living room	sitting room, drawing room
can (of beans)	tin (of beans)	raise in salary	rise in salary
cookie, cracker	biscuit	rest room	public toilet, WC (water closet)
corn	maize	schedule	timetable
diaper	nappy	sidewalk	pavement, footpath
driver's license	driving licence	sink	basin
drug store	chemist's	soccer	football
elevator	lift	stove	cooker
eraser	rubber	truck	lorry, van
flashlight	torch	trunk of a car	boot of a motorcar
gas, gasoline	petrol	be on vacation	be on holiday
hood of a car	bonnet of a motorcar		

Key to Pronunciation Symbols

THE PHONETIC ALPHABET (Symbols for American English)

CONSONANTS

Most consonant symbols are used phonetically as they are in normal English spelling. However, a few additional symbols are needed, and some other letters are more restricted in their use as symbols. These special symbols are presented below. (Note that slanted lines indicate that phonetic symbols, not the spelling alphabet, are being used.)

/Θ/ (Greek theta) = voiceless *th* as in "**th**in," "**th**ank"
/δ/ (Greek delta) = voiced *th* as in "**th**en," "**th**ose"
/ŋ/ = *ng* as in "si**ng**," "thi**n**k" (but not in "danger")
/š/ = *sh* as in "**sh**irt," "mi**ss**ion," "na**t**ion"
/ž/ = *s* or *z* in a few words like "plea**s**ure," "a**z**ure"
/č/ = *ch* or *tch* as in "wa**tch**," "**ch**ur**ch**"
/ǰ/ = *j* or *dge* as in "**j**ump," "le**dge**"

The following consonants are used as in *conventional spelling:*

/b, d, f, g, h, k, l, m, n, p, r, s, t, v, w, y, z/

Spelling consonants that are **not** used phonetically in English: c, q, x

VOWELS

The 5 vowels in the spelling alphabet are inadequate to represent the 12–15 vowel sounds of American speech. Therefore, new symbols and new sound associations for familiar letters must be adopted.

Front	**Central**	**Back** (lips rounded)
/i/ or /iy/ as in "**b**ea**t**"		/u/, /u:/, or /uw/ as in "**b**oo**t**"
/ɪ/ as in "**b**i**t**"		/ʊ/ as in "**b**oo**k**"
/e/ or /ey/ as in "**b**ai**t**"		/o/ or /ow/ as in "**b**oa**t**"
		/ɔ/ as in "**b**ough**t**"
/ɛ/ as in "**b**e**t**"	/ə/ as in "**b**u**t**"	
/æ/ as in "**b**a**t**"	/a/ as in "**b**o**t**her"	

GLIDES: /ai/ or /ay/ as in "**b**i**t**e"
/ɔi/ or /ɔy/ as in "**b**oy"
/au/ or /aw/ as in "ab**ou**t"

British English has a somewhat different set of vowel sounds and symbols. You might want to consult a standard pronunciation text for that system.

UNDERSTANDING AND USING

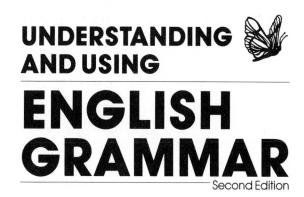

ENGLISH GRAMMAR

Second Edition

TEACHER'S GUIDE

Notes and Answers: Main Text

Chapter 1: **VERB TENSES**

ORDER OF CHAPTER	CHARTS	EXERCISES	WORKBOOK
First day of class talking/writing		Ex. 1 → 2	
Overview of verb tenses	1-1 → 1-5	Ex. 3 → 4	Pr. 1 → 3
Spelling of *-ing* and *-ed* forms	1-6	Ex. 5 → 9	Pr. 4
Simple present/present progressive	1-7 → 1-10	Ex. 10 → 14	Pr. 5 → 7
Simple past/past progressive	1-11 → 1-14	Ex. 15 → 23	Pr. 8 → 17
Cumulative review and practice		Ex. 24 → 25	
Present perfect/ present perfect progressive	1-15 → 1-16	Ex. 26 → 37	Pr. 18 → 24
Past perfect/past perfect progressive	1-17 → 1-18	Ex. 38 → 41	Pr. 25 → 29
Cumulative review and practice		Ex. 42 → 44	
Future time	1-19 → 1-25	Ex. 45 → 51	Pr. 30 → 38
Cumulative review and practice		Ex. 52 → 65	Pr. 39 → 44 Pr. Tests A & B

General Notes on Chapter 1

• OBJECTIVE: This chapter begins with an overview of all twelve of the English verb tenses. The intention is for the students to understand that somewhat logical relationships do exist among the tenses, i.e., that there is some predictability to the tense system in English.

• APPROACH: Students using this text are probably somewhat familiar with all the verb tenses (with the possible exception of the future perfect and future perfect progressive, two little-used tenses). In presenting the initial charts in this chapter, you can help the learners understand the overall patterns in the English tense system (that all progressive tenses indicate that an activity is/was/will be in progress, for example, or that all perfect tenses indicate that one activity occurs before another activity or time). Then as you concentrate on each tense in turn as you proceed through the chapter, you can refer to Chart 1-5 to put each tense within the framework of English verb tenses. For example, you can relate the use of the past progressive *(I was sitting in class at this time yesterday)* to the present progressive *(I am sitting in class right now)*.

• TERMINOLOGY: The text calls all twelve of the verb forms in Chart 1-5 "tenses." Some other analyses of the English verb system may propose that there are only two tenses: past and non-past. They may use the term "aspect" for the perfective and progressive forms.

In this text, the term "tense" is deemed useful to both you and the students because it is a relatively easy and traditional term to use pedagogically to identify twelve verb forms that have particular meanings and uses within a relational system. Whatever these twelve forms are called, the only important consideration for the student is their meaning and use. In sum, it is helpful for purposes of teacher-student communication for the students to learn the "names" of the "tenses," but one should never lose sight of the fact that almost all grammar labels are simply a means to an end, not an end in themselves, in the ESL/EFL classroom.

☐ EXERCISE 1, p. 1. *Getting to know each other the first day of class.*

TECHNIQUE: *Oral, teacher-led; followed by pair work.* *

First, ask students to suggest questions for topics in the list. Try to elicit idiomatic questions—forms that a native speaker of English would normally use in this situation.

Next, divide the class into pairs, if possible mixing language groups in a multilingual class or mixing proficiency levels in a monolingual class. Discuss two ways to conduct the interview: (1) Student A completes the entire interview of Student B, then Student B conducts an interview of Student A; or (2) Students A and B take turns asking about each topic.

Give the class 10 to 15 minutes for the interviews. Then ask each student to introduce his/her interviewee, giving the person's name and interesting comments about him or her. Either the student or you should write the interviewee's name on the chalkboard. The rest of the class should be encouraged to write down the names of their classmates as a way to start getting to know each other.

As followup to the in-class activity, you could ask the students to write the information from their interviews in a short composition (in class or out of class) and hand it in.

EXPANSION ACTIVITY: Assign pairs or small groups of students to go someplace together before or during the next class period and write a report of their experiences. (They could go to an eating place near the school, to a park, to a particular landmark in the city. Remind them to use only English.) You may also wish to have the students use their experiences for oral reports. If you assign the students different places to go, the subsequent oral reports can serve to provide the class as a whole with information about their surroundings.

ASSUMPTIONS: This exercise assumes that students know how to ask and answer basic questions in English. (You may wish to give a "short course" in question word order if the need arises during class discussion, but primarily this first exercise in class is not intended to focus on any particular grammar. You may, however, wish to refer the students to Appendix 1, Unit B (Questions) if problems such as word order arise, or use that unit as a followup to this exercise.) This exercise also assumes that the students don't know each other. If all the students are already acquainted, they could pretend to be famous persons being interviewed by television or newspaper reporters and make up entirely different questions.

---

* See the INTRODUCTION: *Classroom Techniques* (pp. ix–xviii) for descriptions of possible techniques to use in the various kinds of exercises: *written, oral (books closed), fill-in-the-blanks, completion,* etc., and ways of handling teacher and student involvement: *teacher-led, student-led, group work, pair work.*

POSSIBLE ANSWERS:

1. What is your name? [Compare with "What do you call yourself?" or "How are you called?", grammatically correct but idiomatically inappropriate questions.]
2. How do you spell your (last) name?/How do you spell that? [Discuss cultural naming systems: What is a first name, middle name, last name, given name, surname, maiden name?]
3. Where are you from? / What country are you from? / What is your hometown? / Where were you born?
4. Where are you living? / Where do you live?
5. How long have you been living in (name of this city or town)/living here? How long do you plan to be/are you planning to be/are you going to be in (name of this city or town)/be here?
6. Why did you (decide to) come here?
7. [If a student]: What is your major/your field of study? / What are you studying?
   [If an employee]: What kind of work do you do? / What do you do for a living?
8. What do you like to do in your spare time? / Do you have any hobbies?
9. How are you getting along?
10. How do you like living here?/What do you think of (name of this city or town)?

□ **EXERCISE 2, p. 1.** *Using present, past, and future tenses in writing.*

TECHNIQUE: *Written.* *

Discuss what you want the composition to contain before the students begin writing—for example: basic biographical information (name, place of origin, family, education and/or work, etc.); places of residence, travel, and other activities in the past two years; plans for the immediate future (school, work, places of residence, etc.).

ALTERNATIVE: Instead of an autobiography, each student could write a biography of the person s/he interviewed or another person in the class. This would require an additional interview session concerning present, past, and future activities.

◇ **WORKBOOK:** You may wish to have the students do Practice Test A (Chapter 1) at this point, or save Test A for summary review at the end of the chapter.

□ **EXERCISE 3, p. 1.** *Oral survey of verb tenses.*

TECHNIQUE: *Oral (books closed), teacher-led.* *

This is not a drill or a test. It is a launching pad, so to speak. If you wish, you can use this exercise to introduce almost all the essential information contained in Charts 1-1 through 1-5 by discussing each item in detail and presenting the diagram of tenses that appears in the following charts. Or you can simply use this exercise as a quick run-through of the tenses prior to your presentation of Charts 1-1 through 1-5.

Do the exercise with books open if your class seems to be having a lot of difficulty understanding and remembering what you are saying when you give them the cues. Otherwise, begin now to get your students used to handling oral interaction without depending upon reading what is written in the text.

EXPECTED QUESTIONS: **1.** A: What do you do every day before you come to school?
2. A: What did you do last night?   **3.** A: What have you done/have you been doing since you got up this morning? [Even though the present perfect progressive is possible, try to elicit the present perfect in item 5 so that you can compare its use with that of the present perfect progressive in item 6.]   **4.** A: What are you doing right now (at exactly 9:17 A.M.)?
5. A: What were you doing at exactly (9:17 A.M.) yesterday?   **6.** A: What have you been doing for the past five minutes?   **7.** A: What will you do/are you going to do tomorrow?
8. A: What will you be doing/are you going to be doing at exactly (9:23 A.M.) tomorrow?
9. A: What had you done by the time you got to class today?   **10.** A: What will you have done

---

* Throughout this *Teacher's Guide*, see the INTRODUCTION for descriptions of suggested techniques, pp. ix–xviii.

by the time you go to bed tonight?   [Suggestion: Continue the exercise by repeating the cues in random order, perhaps changing the wording slightly. Also, the past perfect progressive and the future perfect progressive are not included in this exercise. You may add them if you wish.]

CHARTS 1-1 through 1-5: OVERVIEW OF VERB TENSES

• The purpose of these charts is to help the students understand the relationships in form and meaning among verb tenses. Discuss the examples, explain the diagrams, summarize tense forms and meanings, and ask for additional examples from the class.

• Not all possible uses of each tense are included in these charts. Tense information is expanded in the individual charts for each tense later in the chapter.

• In Chart 1-5, point out the tense relationships both vertically and horizontally, especially for the progressive, perfect, and perfect progressive forms and meanings.

• Perhaps make a wall chart or transparency of Chart 1-5 for reference during class discussions throughout the time spent on Chapter 1.

• See the INTRODUCTION to this *Guide* (pp. ix–x) for suggestions for presenting the grammar charts.

☐ **EXERCISE 4, p. 8.** *Oral survey of verb tenses.*

TECHNIQUE: *Oral (books closed), teacher-led.*
    As problems occur, lead a discussion of verb tenses that summarizes the information in the preceding charts. Call attention to time expressions such as *right now, since, before, by the time.* Show how the meanings of these expressions are related to the meanings of the verb tenses.
    ALTERNATIVE: *Pair work or group work.*

◇ **WORKBOOK:** Practices 1, 2, 3.

☐ **EXERCISE 5, p. 8.** *Spelling of -ing and -ed forms.*

TECHNIQUE: *Pretest.*
    Follow the example: say the word, then a complete sentence, then the word again. Students write only the word on their papers.
    At the end, they can correct their own or each other's papers as you or the students write on the chalkboard. Discuss spelling rules as the papers are being corrected. The order of this exercise mirrors the order of the spelling rules presented in Chart 1-6.
    ALTERNATIVE: You may wish to tell the students to correct their own papers by referring to Chart 1-6 before you discuss the answers with the class.

POSSIBLE SENTENCES: [Use sentences about yourself and your students whenever possible. These sentences are here just in case you need them.]   **1.** Hoped. Maria **hoped** to finish her work early last night. Hoped.   **2.** Dining. I was **dining** with Ali when Kim called. Dining.
3. Stopped. My clock **stopped** at noon yesterday. Stopped.   **4.** Planning. Olga has been **planning** her vacation for weeks. Planning. [and so on]   **5.** It **rained** last Thursday.
6. We've been **waiting** for a letter for weeks.   **7.** I've been **listening** to your pronunciation this week.   **8.** What **happened** after class yesterday?   **9.** Your spelling is **beginning** to improve.   **10.** Do you remember what **occurred** on July 8th?   **11.** Pierre is **starting** to enjoy living here.   **12.** The teacher **warned** the students not to be late for class.   **13.** Everyone **enjoyed** Somchart's party last weekend.   **14.** Hiroshi was **playing** loud music at midnight.
15. How long have you been **studying** English?   **16.** Ms. Lee **worried** about her exams.
17. My great-grandfather **died** many years ago.   **18.** Carlos was **lying** on the floor when I walked into the room.

CHART 1-6: SPELLING OF *-ING* AND *-ED* FORMS

• Briefly discuss the spelling rule illustrated by each group of examples so that the students become familiar with the content of the chart and can use it for later reference as needed.

• Discuss this chart in conjunction with giving the correct answers to Exercise 5.

☐ EXERCISES 6 → 9, p. 10.   *Spelling practice of -ing and -ed forms.*

        TECHNIQUE: *Seatwork.*

            Complete one exercise at a time. Give students a few minutes to write the answers, then have them check their own work or each other's. Either students or the teacher can supply answers, preferably written on the chalkboard.

            Even if the students don't know the meaning of some of the words in these exercises, they should be able to spell the forms correctly. After the students have written the correct forms, supply vocabulary definitions for the class as necessary.

            ALTERNATIVES: *Pair or group work. Written homework.*

EX. 6 ANSWERS: **2.** hiding   **3.** running   **4.** ruining   **5.** coming   **6.** writing   **7.** eating   **8.** sitting   **9.** acting   **10.** patting   **11.** opening   **12.** beginning   **13.** earning   **14.** frying   **15.** dying   **16.** employing

EX. 7 ANSWERS: **2.** trying, tried   **3.** staying, stayed   **4.** taping, taped   **5.** tapping, tapped   **6.** offering, offered   **7.** preferring, preferred   **8.** gaining, gained   **9.** planning, planned   **10.** tying, tied   **11.** helping, helped   **12.** studying, studied   **13.** admitting, admitted   **14.** visiting, visited   **15.** hugging, hugged   **16.** raging, raged

EX. 8 ANSWERS: **1.** bored   **2.** jarred   **3.** jeered   **4.** intensified   **5.** sobbed   **6.** looted   **7.** pointed   **8.** ripened   **9.** referred   **10.** destroyed

EX. 9 ANSWERS: **1.** raiding   **2.** riding   **3.** bidding   **4.** burying   **5.** lying   **6.** arguing   **7.** taming   **8.** teeming   **9.** trimming   **10.** harming

◇ WORKBOOK: Practice 4.

CHARTS 1-7 and 1-8: SIMPLE PRESENT AND PRESENT PROGRESSIVE

• Now that the students have covered preliminary material on the English tense system and spelling of *-ing* and *-ed* forms, the text focuses on each tense in more detail.

• Throughout the rest of Chapter 1, the exercises contain questions, negatives, contractions, and midsentence adverbs. These topics are assumed to be primarily review at this level, but the students still need work with them. You may wish to refer your students to Appendix 1 for more information about these topics, or fit the Appendix 1 units into your class instruction as you see the need and find the time.

□ **EXERCISE 10, p. 12.** *Simple present vs. present progressive.*

        TECHNIQUE: *Fill-in-the-blanks.* *

        ANSWERS: **1.** is washing   **2.** washes   **3.** usually sits . . . is sitting   **4.** am trying
        5. Do you always lock   **6.** am still waiting   **7.** is shining   **8.** shines . . . wakes
        9. is snowing . . . doesn't snow   **10.** isn't going . . . attends . . . usually has . . . is working

□ **EXERCISE 11, p. 12.** *Using present progressive.*

        TECHNIQUE: *Oral.*

        Students write one action on a piece of paper. You collect those papers and redistribute them around the class. If the class is very large, this can be done in small groups. A student, without saying anything, performs the action on his/her piece of paper, and another person describes the activity using the present progressive. This is a lively technique for involving several language skills while using English to describe something that is actually happening.

CHART 1-9: NONPROGRESSIVE VERBS

• The key point is the difference between ''states'' and ''activities.'' No verb is inherently ''nonprogressive.'' The intention of this chart and its terminology is simply to inform the students that certain common verbs are usually not used in the progressive.

• In the list of nonprogressive verbs, even the verbs without asterisks can, usually only in fairly rare circumstances, be used in the progressive. The text, however, concentrates only on the usual, most frequent use of these words. (For example: ''I am loving being on vacation'' is possible. The more usual usage of *love:* ''I love [not *am loving*] my family very much.'')

• The list of nonprogressive (i.e., stative) verbs is by no means complete. For the most part, it stresses only those verbs used in the exercises. A few other verbs you may or may not wish to mention as being nonprogressive when used to describe ''states'' are *amaze, astonish, concern, equal, exist, impress, involve, lack, measure, please, regret, resemble, satisfy, sound, surprise, wish.*

◇ **WORKBOOK:** Practice 5.

□ **EXERCISE 12, p. 14.** *Nonprogressive verbs.*

        TECHNIQUE: *Fill-in-the-blanks.*

        ANSWERS: **2.** doesn't belong   **3.** It's beginning . . . don't have . . . is wearing   **4.** don't own . . . wear [habitual activity]   **5.** I'm looking . . . is writing . . . is biting . . . is scratching . . . is staring . . . seems . . . is thinking . . . . What do you think Ahmed is doing?   **6.** is fixing [i.e., repairing] . . . needs   **7.** often tutors . . . is helping . . . doesn't understand . . . are working/ have been working   **8.** am looking . . . looks . . . has . . . isn't having   **9.** is standing . . . Are you talking about the woman who is wearing . . . ? I'm not talking about her. I mean . . . is wearing . . . I don't know. I don't recognize her.   **10.** A: . . . What do you hear? What am I doing? B: I believe you are rubbing . . . . A: . . . Are you listening carefully? B: Aha! You're rubbing . . . . [Follow item 10 with a game in which students close their eyes and make guesses about noises. Have one or several students close their eyes while another student makes a noise of some kind, e.g., writing on the chalkboard, tapping a foot, opening/closing a window or door, closing a book, snapping fingers, blowing, etc. Keep the focus of the game on the use of the present progressive.]

---

* See the INTRODUCTION, pp. xv–xvi, for several suggestions for handling a fill-in-the-blanks exercise.

□ **EXERCISE 13, p. 16.** *Using present tenses for description.*

TECHNIQUE: *Written homework.*
   To introduce this assignment, have the class brainstorm ideas for a sample composition that might begin with "I am sitting in my English class" as a way of explaining to them what you want them to write at home.

◇ **WORKBOOK:** Practice 6.

CHART 1-10: USING THE PRESENT PROGRESSIVE WITH
               ALWAYS

• Note the word order for the students: *always* occurs immediately before the main verb.

• The structure in this chart may not be especially significant in a student's overall language usage ability, but it's fun and can be used to point out that a grammatical form can, in and of itself, convey a speaker's emotional attitude. This chart and the following exercise are also good places for students to practice conveying emotion in speech through sentence stress and intonation.

□ **EXERCISE 14, p. 16.** *Using* always *with the present progressive.*

TECHNIQUE: *Transformation; teacher-led, oral.*
   Encourage the students to be a bit theatrical as they produce their sentences. Model some of the sentences for the students: say the sentences with annoyance or disgust in your voice, emphasizing the word *always*. Use some gesture of annoyance such as rolling your eyes upward and lifting your eyebrows while saying *always*, or making some forceful gesture with your hands and arms. Students should repeat your sentence with the same voice and gestures. In some sentences, use *constantly* or *forever* instead of *always* for variation.
   Item 8 is a dialogue for completion. (See the INTRODUCTION for ways of handling completion exercises.) Encourage the students to use voice and gestures to show annoyance.

◇ **WORKBOOK:** Practice 7.

CHART 1-11: REGULAR AND IRREGULAR VERBS

• Review the terminology.

• The list on pp. 18–19 is for reference. Ask the students to look through it to see if they have any questions about vocabulary or pronunciation. Define and pronounce as necessary.

◇ **WORKBOOK:** Practice 8.

□ **EXERCISE 15, p. 20.** *Pronunciation of* -ed.

TECHNIQUE: *Oral, teacher-led.*
   For items 1 through 24, students repeat after you. Discuss the difference between voiceless and voiced sounds. (The voiceless sounds in English are the consonants /p t k h f θ s č š/. Other consonants and all vowels are voiced.) To explain voiced vs. voiceless sounds, have the students put their hands to their throats so they can feel their voice box vibrate when they make the /v/

sound but not when they make the /f/ sound. Point out that their teeth and lips are in exactly the same position for both sounds. Other voiceless/voiced pairs that you can similarly demonstrate are /t/ and /d/, /s/ and /z/, /p/ and /b/.

For items 25 through 35, ask a student to read one sentence aloud. You may then ask the student to tell you which pronunciation was attempted for each past tense verb, or ask the rest of the class what they heard.

ALTERNATIVE: *Group work* for items 25 through 35, in which students monitor each other.

ANSWERS: **25.** jumped /pt/, shouted/təd/ **26.** lasted /təd/ **27.** flooded /dəd/, inundated /təd/ **28.** tapped /pt/ **29.** described /bd/ **30.** demanded /dəd/ **31.** departed/ təd/, landed /dəd/ **32.** pushed /št/, pulled /ld/ **33.** handed /dəd/ **34.** tooted /təd/ **35.** asked /kt/

☐ **EXERCISES 16 → 19, pp. 20–23.** *Review of simple past of irregular verbs.*

TECHNIQUE: *Oral (books closed), teacher-led.*

The exercises should go at a fast pace, almost like a game. Responses can be individual or the whole class together. Students should be encouraged to respond as quickly as possible rather than to formulate their answers in their mind's eye first. A mistake is nothing more than a learning opportunity. Tell them just to open their mouths and see what happens. (This encouragement is especially pertinent for those cultural groups that tend to write what they want to say in their minds before they speak and judge themselves harshly if they err.) They may be surprised by how much they already know. And while they're practicing irregular verbs, they're also building fluency.

ALTERNATIVE: *Group work.* After you set the pace and demonstrate the format, the students can continue in small groups with leaders asking the questions. Only the leaders have their texts open. The leaders are responsible for monitoring the responses.

Exercises 16 → 19 can be done over several class periods, not all at one time. They can also be repeated at a later time, after a few days or weeks, for review. They are good for the last five minutes of a class period. They can also be used as oral test items.

SUGGESTION: If you wish, include some regular verbs: Did you *wait* for the bus this morning? Did you *watch* TV last night? Did you *open* the window? etc.

EX. 16 ANSWERS: **1.** Yes, I drank some coffee before class. **2.** Yes, I brought my books to class. **3.** . . . forgot my . . . . **4.** shook **5.** caught **6.** drove **7.** lost **8.** found **9.** wound **10.** . . . understood what you said. **11.** . . . told my friend . . . . **12.** spread [no change in form] **13.** fell **14.** hurt [no change in form] myself **15.** flew **16.** wore **17.** hung **18.** ate **19.** took **20.** rode **21.** swore to tell [This refers to a formal promise, as in a court of law.] **22.** Yes, I forgave you. **23.** wrote **24.** No! The dog bit me! [a little humor!]

EX. 17 ANSWERS: **1.** No, someone else made a mistake. **2.** broke **3.** stole **4.** took **5.** drew **6.** swept **7.** taught **8.** dug **9.** fed **10.** hid your book from you. **11.** blew **12.** threw **13.** tore **14.** built **15.** spoke to [Add a person's name in the blank space.]

EX. 18 ANSWERS: **1.** Yes, I gave you some money. **2.** stood **3.** chose [Comment on the spelling and pronunciation of *choose* and *chose*.] **4.** ran [If the class does not meet in the morning, substitute another time word.] **5.** slept **6.** heard **7.** withdrew **8.** woke up [*Waked* is also possible.] **9.** swam **10.** went **11.** bent **12.** sent **13.** sang [Be sure the pronunciations of *sang* and *song* are different.] **14.** stuck **15.** ground **16.** struck **17.** lit [*Lighted* is also acceptable.] **18.** meant **19.** held **20.** spoke to [Add someone's name.]

EX. 19 ANSWERS: **1.** Yes, class began at . . . [Add the correct time.] **2.** rose **3.** cut [no change in form] **4.** bled **5.** grew **6.** stung **7.** rang **8.** froze **9.** quit [no change in form; *quitted* also possible in British English] **10.** fought **11.** crept **12.** shot **13.** fled **14.** won **15.** slid **16.** swung **17.** blew up **18.** burst [no change in form] **19.** broadcast [no change in form] **20.** knew

◇ **WORKBOOK:** Practices 9 through 13.

☐ **EXERCISE 20, p. 23.** *Special attention in a few troublesome verbs.*

> TECHNIQUE: *Discussion; seatwork.*
>
> Discuss the chart. (If necessary, refer students to Appendix 1, Unit A-1, for further information about transitive and intransitive verbs.) Then do the exercise entries as brief seatwork, followed by discussion of correct answers.
>
> *ANSWERS:* **1.** raised **2.** rises **3.** sat **4.** set **5.** lay **6.** lying **7.** laid **8.** lie **9.** lies **10.** hung.

◇ **WORKBOOK:** Practice 14.

CHARTS 1-12 and 1-13: SIMPLE PAST AND PAST PROGRESSIVE

• Suggestion: In your presentation, compare the tenses in some of the example sentences with other tenses. For example:

> I **stood** under a tree when it **began** to rain. vs. I **was standing** under a tree when it **began** to rain. vs. I **had stood** under a tree when it **began** to rain. vs. I **had been standing** under a tree for several minutes when it **began** to rain. vs. I **will stand** under a tree when it **begins** to rain. vs. I **will be standing** under a tree when it **begins** to rain. [Demonstrate these various relationships by using an imaginary tree and rain.]

• This chart is the first place the word ''clause'' is mentioned. You may wish at this point to explain that a clause is a structure that has a subject and a verb, and make the distinction between a main (independent) clause and a dependent clause. Students will concentrate on complex sentences in later chapters. Adverb clauses of time are in Chapter 8. You may wish to refer the students to Charts 8-4 and 8-5, but at this point it is usually sufficient simply to refer to ''*when* clauses'' and ''*while* clauses.'' The text assumes that the students are quite familiar with sentences containing basic adverb clauses of time with subordinating conjunctions such as *when, while, before,* and *after.* For the time being, keep the focus on verb tenses, with minimal attention to complex sentence structure.

• Note in (i) and (j): In sentences with *when,* the progressive usually occurs in the main clause. In sentences with *while,* the progressive usually occurs in the ''*while* clause.'' (Sometimes *when* has the same meaning as *while,* and the progressive is used in a ''*when* clause'':e.g., *When* [i.e., *while*] *I was walking home last night, I suddenly remembered that it was my wife's birthday.)*

☐ **EXERCISES 21 & 22, pp. 24–27.** *Simple past vs. past progressive.*

> TECHNIQUE: *Fill-in-the-blanks.*
>
> Exercises 21 and 22 are similar. One can be done in class and the other assigned for out-of-class preparation for the next class.
>
> In Exercise 22, some items are dialogues between Speakers A and B. Two students can read a dialogue aloud. Then you can ask them to repeat it with their books closed. This is a good technique to use occasionally for improving fluency.
>
> *EX. 21 ANSWERS:* **2.** didn't want to . . . was raining **3.** called . . . wasn't . . . was studying **4.** did not hear . . . was sleeping **5.** was shining . . . was blowing . . . were singing **6.** were arguing . . . walked **7.** opened . . . found **8.** were not . . . were playing **9.** was climbing . . . tripped . . . fell . . . didn't hurt **10.** was reading . . . fell . . . closed . . . tiptoed **11.** was snowing . . . was shining . . . were shoveling [also spelled: shovelling] . . . was lying **12.** was shoveling [shovelling] . . . brought
>
> *EX. 22 ANSWERS:* **1.** almost had . . . was driving . . . saw . . . was coming . . . stepped . . . swerved . . . just missed **2.** decided . . . were starving **3.** finally found . . . was already . . .

were talking busily/were busily talking . . . were speaking . . . were conversing . . . were just sitting . . . chose . . . sat . . . walked . . . stopped   **4.** A: Did you hear . . .   B: wasn't listening . . . was thinking   **5.** B: was waiting   **6.** B. was she wearing   **7.** B: stepped . . . was running . . . stung   **8.** A: Did you break . . .   B: slipped . . . was crossing

---

CHART 1-14: USING EXPRESSIONS OF PLACE WITH PROGRESSIVE TENSES	

- The point is that prepositional phrases of place can have two positions: (1) the neutral position at the end of the clause or (2) the focus position, which emphasizes the place, between *be* and the main verb.

- The neutral position is used in answer to "What?" questions because the focus is then on the activity. The focus position is used in answer to "Where?" questions.

☐ **EXERCISE 23, p. 27.**   *Expressions of place with progressive verbs.*

TECHNIQUE: *Transformation; teacher-led, oral.*

Items 1 through 5 require only a change in position. You or a student can read the sentence, then another student can say the changed sentence. Or a student can simply give the transformation.

For more advanced groups, items 1 through 5 can be given an expanded form. Two or four students can be Speakers A and B or A, B, C, and D.

   1. A: *What's Sally doing?*
       B: *She's listening to music in her room.*
   A or C: *Where's Sally?*
   B or D: *She's in her room, listening to music.*

Items 12 through 16 can be done with books closed. Make the items more interesting by using names of familiar persons in place of the names in the book. Make up additional oral cues by asking questions about familiar persons: Where is (*name of a school administrator*) now, and what is s/he doing? Where were you last night at nine, and what were you doing? etc.

POSSIBLE ANSWERS: **2.** Roy is on the couch taking a nap.   **3.** Anita was in England (last month) attending a concert (last month). [Either position for the expression of time is acceptable.] **4.** The teacher is at her desk . . . .   **5.** . . . because they were at the park playing . . . . **7.** He's upstairs _____ing . . . .   **8.** She's in her office _____ing . . . .   **9.** She's in the kitchen _____ing . . . .   **10.** He was at home _____ing . . . .   **11.** He was in New York _____ing . . . .   **13.** . . . I was in _____ lying in the sun.   **14.** We are _____ studying . . .   **15.** . . . because he was _____ hiding from . . . .   **16.** . . . she was _____ trying to . . . . [Note that the expression of place cannot come between *was* and *supposed* because that is not a progressive tense form.]

◇ **WORKBOOK:** Practices 15, 16, 17.

☐ **EXERCISE 24, p. 28.**   *Describing past activities.*

TECHNIQUE: *Pantomime.*

A pantomime is performed silently. Ideas are communicated by gestures and movements, not by words. Individual students choose incidents to pantomime. They need to think for a while about how they will perform.

Demonstrate a pantomime yourself or select a volunteer. Then ask a student to describe what happened using past verbs. Other students can then add details that were missed. Your task is to focus attention on the correct use of verb tenses because, in the excitement of describing the details, students may tend to slip into present or uninflected forms. The grammar focus should be on consistent use of past verbs. You may wish to let other errors go by unremarked.

☐ **EXERCISE 38, p. 40.** *Pronunciation of the auxiliary verb* had.

TECHNIQUE: *Oral, teacher-led.*

ITEM NOTES: [Items 1 and 2 show the contractions with pronouns. Other items require students to supply the spoken contractions.] **3.** "children-/əd/" **4.** "roommates-/əd/" **5.** [No contraction is possible because "had" is the main verb.] **6.** "flood-/əd/" **7.** Where'd [spoken as a single syllable /wɛrd/, but note that "d" before "y" in "you" becomes /ǰ/— "Where-/ǰu/"] **8.** Who'd [hu:d]

☐ **EXERCISES 39 & 40, pp. 40-41.** *The simple past and past perfect.*

TECHNIQUE: *Fill-in-the-blanks.*

EX. 39 ANSWERS: **1.** . . . had been/was [Both are possible because the word "before" shows the relationship between the two events.] . . . became **2.** felt . . . took/had taken [Both are a possible with "after."] **3.** had already given . . . got **4.** left . . . had collected **5.** was . . . had stopped

EX. 40 ANSWERS: **1.** had already begun . . . got . . . quietly took **2.** roamed . . . had become . . . appeared **3.** had never seen [possibly *never saw* in very informal English] . . . visited **4.** had already boarded . . . got **5.** saw . . . had not seen [before I saw her yesterday] . . . did not recognize . . . had lost [before I saw her yesterday]

◇ **WORKBOOK:** Practices 25, 26, 27.

☐ **EXERCISE 41, p. 41.** *The present perfect progressive and past perfect progressive.*

TECHNIQUE: *Fill-in-the-blanks.*

ANSWERS: **1.** have been studying **2.** had been studying **3.** had been daydreaming **4.** have been sleeping **5.** had been standing

◇ **WORKBOOK:** Practice 28.

☐ **EXERCISE 42, p. 42.** *Review of present and past verbs.*

TECHNIQUE: *Discussion of meaning.* *

ANSWERS: **2.** Gloria [Riding her bicycle was in progress at the time the rain stopped, meaning she began to ride her bike before the rain stopped. Paul rode his bicycle after the rain stopped: the "*when* clause" happens first when both clauses contain the simple past.] **3.** Dick [Ann went to the store after she had run out of food. Dick went to the store while running out of food was in progress.] **4.** Mr. Sanchez ["taught for nine years," simple past, indicates that the activity was completed in the past; "has taught for nine years" means he is still teaching, i.e., the activity is not completed.] **5.** Alice [George walked to the door only after the doorbell rang. Alice knew someone was coming to ring her doorbell because she began to walk toward the door before the bell rang.] **6.** Joe [Maria finished eating before I arrived. Joe ate after I got there, so he was the one who was still hungry.] **7.** Carlos [similar to item 4] **8.** Jane [Sue's lying in the sun was still in progress when she applied lotion.] **9.** Mr. Fox [Mr. Fox's waving was already in progress when I looked across the street.]

---

* See the INTRODUCTION, p. xvii, for suggestions for handling discussion-of-meaning exercises.

□ **EXERCISE 43, p. 43.** *Past time narrative.*

> TECHNIQUE: *Oral (books closed), teacher-led or group work.*
> Have the students read the example before they close their books. The stories may get a little silly, but the students should have fun.

□ **EXERCISE 44, p. 44.** *Past time narrative.*

> TECHNIQUE: *Written group work.*
> Each person in the group is to begin a story. In a group of six people, six different stories will be circulating at the same time.
> A time limit (2–3 minutes per contribution) is advisable unless you wish to make this an activity that takes up an entire class period.
> After the stories are written and you are discussing them in class, you may or may not wish to bring up the possibility of using present tenses in a narrative. For example: *Let me tell you about Pierre's day yesterday. He gets in trouble as soon as his alarm clock rings. When he hears the alarm and gets out of bed, he steps on a snake! Would you believe that? He's nearly frightened to death, but the snake slithers away without biting him. Etc.* The text doesn't deal with this use, but you might want to explore it with an advanced class.

◇ **WORKBOOK:** Practice 29.

CHART 1-19: SIMPLE FUTURE/*BE GOING TO*

• This chart merely introduces the two basic forms for expressing the future. It does not show their differences in function or meaning; see Chart 1-20.

• Model "gonna" for the students. Don't rush them to use it in their speech, and remind them that good enunciation is important to second-language learners and that normal contracted speaking will occur naturally as they gain experience with the language. Point out that "gonna" is not used in writing.

□ **EXERCISE 45, p. 44.** *Pronunciation of contracted* will.

> TECHNIQUE: *Oral, teacher-led.*
> Contraction of *will* is natural in conversation; this exercise gives students practice in hearing these forms and trying to produce them themselves. Most of the personal pronoun contractions are pronounced as a single syllable: *I'll* /ayl/, *you'll* /yul/, *he'll* /hiyl/, *she'll* /šiyl/, *we'll* /wiyl/, *they'll* /ðeyl/. Other words add a syllable for the contraction: *it'll* /ɪtəl/, *that'll* /ðætəl/, etc.
>
> ANSWERS: [Items 1 to 4 show the commonly written contracted forms. In other items, the forms are not usually written but should be spoken in this exercise.] **6.** weather'll **7.** Mary'll **8.** Bill'll **9.** children'll **10.** Who'll [This is sometimes a written form, also. It is pronounced as one syllable /hu:1/.] **11.** Where'll **12.** long'll **13.** Nobody'll **14.** That'll **15.** What'll

---

CHART 1-20: *WILL* VERSUS *BE GOING TO*

• Students often ask about the difference between *will* and *be going to* even though in their own independent production they may only rarely make the mistake of using one where the other is required.

□ **EXERCISE 46, p. 46.** Will *and* be going to.

TECHNIQUE: *Fill-in-the-blanks, teacher-led or group work.*

Most of the items are dialogues between Speaker A and Speaker B. Students can work out the answers in small groups, then speak the dialogues in a natural manner. You may wish to encourage them to experiment with contractions when they speak.

ANSWERS: *PART I* [Note that there is no difference in meaning between *will* and *be going to* in these sentences.] **2.** will be/is going to be . . . will come/is going to come **3.** B: I'll probably see/I'm probably going to see **4.** will be/is going to be **5.** A: will not/won't/is not going to be . . . Who'll be/Who's going to be **B.** will/is going to teach . . . I'll/I'm going to be . . . you'll/you're going to be
PART II [Note that there is a difference in meaning here between *will* and *be going to: will* expresses "willingness" and *be going to* expresses "a prior plan."] **8.** I'll get **9.** I'll turn **10.** A: I'm going to enroll . . . I'm going to take **11.** B: I'll make . . . That will **12.** B: I'll get **13.** B: I'm going to be **14.** A: I'm going to place **15.** B/C/D: I'll do it! **16.** B: I'm going to erase

◇ **WORKBOOK:** Practices 30 and 31.

> **CHART 1-21: EXPRESSING THE FUTURE IN TIME CLAUSES**
>
> • The focus is on verb usage in complex sentences containing dependent (subordinate) adverbial clauses, called "time clauses" here. The structure of sentences with these clauses is discussed more thoroughly in Chapter 8.
>
> • Learners naturally feel that it is logical to use the future tense in the time clause as well as in the main clause. Point out that that is not traditional in English usage. There are certain patterns and systems within a language, but a language should not be expected to be completely logical.

□ **EXERCISE 47, p. 48.** *Using future and simple present with time clauses.*

TECHNIQUE: *Fill-in-the-blanks, teacher-led.*

Keep attention focused on the time clause. Problems may occur because students try to use future verbs instead of the simple present there.

In items 7 and 8, the verbs "plan," "hope," and "intend" are used. These words refer to a *present* condition, a thought or feeling *at this moment* about a future activity. Therefore, they are in a present, not in a future, tense form. Plans, hopes, and intentions occur in the present but concern future activities.

ANSWERS: **2.** eat [*Have eaten* is also correct, but try to keep the focus on the two choices in the directions: *will/be going to* or the simple present.] . . . will probably take/am probably going to take **3.** get . . . I'll call/I'm going to call **4.** watch . . . I'll write/I'm going to write **5.** I'll wait/I'm going to wait . . . comes **6.** stops [or *has stopped*] . . . I'll walk/I'm going to walk **7.** graduate . . . intend [present tense because now it is my plan] . . . will go/am going to go . . . get **8.** are you going to stay/will you stay . . . plan . . . hope . . . are you going to do/will you do . . . leave . . . I'll return/I'm going to return . . . get [Point out the parallel structure, in which the subject and auxiliary don't need to be repeated after *and*.] I'll be . . . return . . . get

□ **EXERCISE 48, p. 49.** Will/be going to *and the simple present.*

      TECHNIQUE: *Oral, teacher-led.*

      POSSIBLE ANSWERS: **2.** [simple present . . . future]   **3.** [Future . . .simple present]
      4. [future . . . simple present]   **5.** [simple present . . . future]   **6.** [future . . . simple
      present]   **7.** [simple present . . . future]

◇ **WORKBOOK:** Practices 32, 33, 34.

CHART 1-22: PRESENT PROGRESSIVE/SIMPLE PRESENT FOR FUTURE TIME

• The present progressive, meaning future time, must relate to a plan or intention.

• The simple present, meaning future time, is limited to scheduled events.

• This use of present verbs to mean future time is common, especially in conversational English. The difficulty for students is to learn the limitations of this use.

□ **EXERCISE 49, p. 50.** *Understanding future time and tense relationships.*

      TECHNIQUE: *Discussion of meaning, teacher-led or group work.*

      ANSWERS: **4.** in the future   **5.** in the future   **6.** now   **7.** in the future   **8.** habitually
      9. in the future   **10.** in the future   **11.** habitually   **12.** A: now B: now A: in the future
      [*Do you want* asks about a present plan for a future activity.]   **13.** A: in the future B: in the
      future   **14.** in the future   **15.** in the future   **16.** in the future   **17.** in the future   **18.** in
      the future

CHART 1-23: FUTURE PROGRESSIVE

• Relate the examples to similar sentences with the present progressive and past progressive.

• In the exercises in the text, the future progressive is associated with an activity that will be in progress at a specific moment of future time. However, as in (d), the future progressive is also used to express predicted activities that will be in progress at a vague or nonspecific future time: *I'll be seeing you!* OR *I'll be waiting to hear from you.* OR *Just wait. Before you know it, the baby will be talking and walking.*

□ **EXERCISE 50, p. 52.** *Using the future progressive.*

      TECHNIQUE: *Fill-in-the-blanks.*

      ANSWERS: **1.** will be attending   **2.** arrive . . . will be waiting   **3.** get . . . will be shining . . .
      will be singing . . . will still be lying   **4.** B: will be lying A: will be thinking   **5.** will be
      staying   **6.** will be doing . . . will be attending . . . studying [Point out the ellipsis, the omission
      of the subject and auxiliary verb, in parallel structure.]   **7.** is . . . will probably be raining
      8. will be visiting

◇ **WORKBOOK:** Practice 37.

- These are the two most infrequently used tenses in English.

- Relate these tenses to perfects and perfect progressives in the present and the past.

☐ **EXERCISE 51, p. 53.** *Future perfect and future perfect progressive.*

TECHNIQUE: *Fill-in-the-blanks.*

ANSWERS: **1.** have been . . . had been . . . will have been   **2.** get . . . will already have arrived   **3.** got . . . had already arrived   **4.** have been sitting . . . had been sitting . . . will have been sitting   **5.** will have been driving   **6.** will have been living/will have lived   **7.** get . . . will have taken   **8.** will have been running   **9.** will have had . . . dies   **10.** will have been

◇ **WORKBOOK:** Practice 38.

☐ **EXERCISE 52, p. 54.** *Expressing future time.*

TECHNIQUE: *Oral, teacher-led or group work.*
    Have the students brainstorm ideas about the future. If necessary, ask provocative leading questions. You may wish to have one student ask another a question about a given topic. You may wish to divide the students into groups and just let them talk, with no written or oral reports.
    ALTERNATIVE: Divide the class into small groups. Assign one topic to each group, or allow them to choose a topic. Give them about 10 minutes to develop a presentation of their ideas. Then ask one person in each group to give the information to the class orally.
    ALTERNATIVE: Assign one topic to each student and ask for an oral presentation of ideas. As a followup, students can write their paragraphs and hand them in to you.
    In previous exercises, such as the descriptions of the pantomimes, you have stressed to the students the importance of being consistent in tense usage; for example, if you begin to tell a story in the past tense, stay in the past tense and don't slip into the present. Now, however, point out that a paragraph of sentences on a single topic may *require* a mixing of past, present, and future.

- -

NOTE: The rest of Chapter 1 provides practice with all the verb tenses. When students have to choose the appropriate tense(s) according to context and meaning, it is important that they have opportunities to discuss their choices and understand their difficulties. One of your many roles is to help them become sensitive monitors and effective editors.
    Now that the foundation for verb tense usage has been laid, the students need guided practice and, most important, lots of out-of-class language experiences as the complex process of adult second language acquisition proceeds. You may wish to tell your students that they shouldn't expect to become instant experts in verb tense usage after studying this chapter, but that you expect their development to be excellent and their ultimate goal eminently reachable. (Sometimes students equate second language learning with other academic pursuits. They may feel that once they study a chapter in mathematics or chemistry, they are now masters of the information it contains—and expect the same results in a second language class. You may wish to discuss with your students the many ways in which the study of a second language is different from other courses of study.)

- -

□ **EXERCISE 53, p. 55.** *Review of verb tenses.*

TECHNIQUE: *Discussion of meaning.*

It is not important for the students to name or define the verb tenses. The important lesson is for them to understand and attempt to explain the meaning of each sentence, noting the differences among similar sentences with different verb tenses.

If you have a wall chart or transparency of Chart 1-5, this might be a good time to bring it out again.

ANSWERS:

1. (a) frequently, repeatedly, again and again. (b) at this moment, right now.

2. (a) right now. (b) at this time on a past day. (c) at this time on a future day, or at a specific point of future time.

3. (a) completed before now. (b) completed before another event or time in the past. (c) a plan to complete in the future before another event or time.

4. (a), (b), and (c) have the same meaning. (d) means that the teacher's arrival was a signal for the students to leave immediately. (e) means that the students had started to leave shortly before the teacher arrived, but they had not yet gone.

5. (a) The waiting began two hours ago and is still in progress at present. (b) The waiting began two hours before another event or time in the past. (c) The waiting will have been in progress for two hours by the time another event occurs; the waiting may begin in the future or may have begun in the past.

6. (a) not finished yet. (b) finished at an unspecified time before now. (c) at a specific time in the past (. . . "last night," "last weekend," etc.).

7. (a) in progress recently, but not yet completed. (b) completed, but no date or time is specified.

8. (a) and (b) are the same: You come, then I will begin to study. (c) and (d) are the same: Studying begins before you come and is in progress upon your arrival. (e) Studying will be completed before you come. (f) The studying will have been in progress for two hours by the time another event occurs; the studying may begin in the future or may have begun in the past.

9. (a) completed activity [He probably works in another place now.] (b) present activity that began two years ago.

10. All four sentences mean the same.

□ **EXERCISE 54, p. 56.** *Review of verb tenses.*

TECHNIQUE: *Oral (books closed), teacher-led.*

Approach each item conversationally; add extra words, rephrase the questions, put the questions in relevant contexts. These questions are in the text merely to suggest ideas as you engage the students in an oral review of verb tenses.

In items where there are several related questions, ask a question and wait for the response, then follow that answer with the next question to the same student. Don't stop for corrections or explanations until the item (the conversation) is completed.

Short answers are natural in conversations. However, in this exercise students are practicing verb tenses, so they should answer in complete sentences. Students easily understand that this exercise is a sort of "grammar game," especially an item such as #15.

ALTERNATIVE: This exercise can be done in pairs or small groups. At this point, the students can simply monitor each other and check with you as necessary.

POSSIBLE ANSWERS: **1.** We've been studying verb tenses. We've studied the present perfect tense. We studied it two weeks ago. **2.** We'll have studied adjective clauses, gerunds, and many other grammatical structures. **3.** Yes, I had. [British: Yes, I had done.] We studied some tenses last year. **4.** We'll have been studying it for about three weeks. **5.** I was practicing English. After that, I went to the next class. **6.** I'm answering your question. I've been doing that for about 30 seconds. **7.** I'm probably going to be sitting in this room again. **8.** I'll be sleeping. Last night at midnight I was sleeping. **9.** I'll be living in my own home. I was living in another city.   **10.** I've been to the zoo. I went there last month.   **11.** I eat, study, and listen to the radio.   **12.** Since I came here, I've done a lot of grammar homework.   **13.** I've flown across the Pacific two times, climbed mountains, and written songs. I flew twice last year, climbed in 1986, and wrote a song last month.   **14.** I've given some roses to my mother-in-law.   **15.** [review of all tenses]

☐ **EXERCISE 55, p. 56.**   *Review of verb tenses.*

TECHNIQUE: *Fill-in-the-blanks.*

ANSWERS: **1.** is studying [Check the spelling: *yi*] . . . is also taking . . . begin   **2.** had already eaten . . . left . . . always eats . . . goes [Check for *s* endings.] . . . don't usually/usually don't . . . go . . . usually get . . . go [no *will* in the time clause] . . . am going to eat [also possible: *will eat*]   **3.** called . . . was attending   **4.** will be attending   **5.** got . . . was sleeping . . . had been sleeping   **6.** is taking . . . fell . . . has been sleeping   **7.** started . . . has not finished . . . is reading   **8.** has read . . . is reading . . . has been reading . . . intends . . . has read . . . has ever read.   **9.** eats [no *will* in the time clause] . . . is going to go/will go . . . will have eaten . . . goes [no *will* in the time clause]

◇ **WORKBOOK:** Practices 39, 40, 41.

☐ **EXERCISES 56 & 57, pp. 58–59.**   *Review of verb tenses.*

TECHNIQUE: *Pair work.*
    Make sure the students understand the format.
    The main point of this exercise is to practice verb tenses, and the intention is that at least some of the exercise items develop into short natural dialogues between classmates.
    You may wish to walk around the room and listen to the exchanges, but don't interrupt. Answer individual questions, but make longer explanations to the class only after the exercise is completed.
    A and B should exchange roles for Exercise 57.

☐ **EXERCISE 58, p. 59.**   *Using verb tenses in speaking and writing.*

TECHNIQUE: *Pair work.*
    When you make this assignment, announce a time limit (perhaps 5 minutes) so that the stories are not long. This is not a dictation exercise, so Student A should listen to Student B's complete story, *then* report it in a written paragraph. Both students should tell their stories to each other first; then they can both write at the same time.

☐ **EXERCISE 59, p. 59.**   *Using verb tenses in speech.*

TECHNIQUE: Only a few students each day should speak. Thus, the exercise can continue over several days. Students who are not speaking should be instructed to take notes in order to practice their listening skills. They can note questions to ask for additional information. They can also note problems with verb tenses or pronunciation. These notes can be used for discussion after the speaker is finished.
    Remind students of the time limit. During the reports, you may wish to appoint one student as a timekeeper.
    As preparation for this exercise, you may wish to bring a newspaper article to class and have the class work together in making a 2–3 minute summary so that the students will understand exactly what you expect. The article may also be used for a discussion of verb forms; you can discuss the verb forms that the students have already studied and point out the forms that they are going to study later (e.g., modals, sequence of tenses in noun clauses, gerunds and infinitives, passives).

TECHNIQUE: *Fill-in-the-blanks.*

Students can perform some of these dialogues dramatically, with appropriate gestures and emotional voices. This can be great fun. You might want to assign the dialogues to be memorized by pairs of students and then presented to the class without their looking at their books.

ANSWERS: **1.** I'm listening   **2.** A: Have you met . . . . B: I've never had . . . .   **3.** A: are you doing . . . . B: I'm trying . . . . A: will/are going to electrocute   **4.** A: He's lying . . . . B: see . . . certainly looks   **5.** A: Are you taking . . . ["Econ 120" is the name of a course in the Economics Department.] B: I'm not . . . . A: Have you ever taken . . . B: I have. A: did you take . . . was . . . is he . . . B: is   **6.** B: was yawning . . . flew A: don't believe . . . You're kidding!   **7.** A: . . . went B: I've seen . . . saw . . . It's good, isn't it? [commenting on the general quality of the written work, not on last night's production]   **8.** A: had never been B: were you doing [at that time, last month] A. were driving [Driving to Washington was in progress when A was in B's hometown.]   **9.** A: was . . . haven't received . . . need . . . don't have B: do you need A: I'll pay [indicating willingness rather than a prior plan] . . . get [no *will* in a time clause]   **10.** A: She's not . . . B: I'll be sitting . . . .

TECHNIQUE: *Fill-in-the-blanks.*

ANSWERS: **1.** has never flown [*And he has* is a signal that the man is still living, so the present perfect is needed.]   **2.** I've been waiting . . . hasn't arrived   **3.** are . . . reach   **4.** will already have left/will have already left . . . get [time clause]   **5.** are having . . . has been [Upper 90s Fahrenheit = 35°–37° Celsius.]   **6.** went . . . got . . . were dancing . . . were talking . . . was standing . . . had never met [before last night.] . . . introduced   **7.** was lying [possibly *lay*] . . . heard . . . got . . . looked . . . had just backed [*Back into* means to hit something while moving backwards.]   **8.** am planning . . . I'm going to go/I'll go . . . leave [time clause] . . . I'll go/I'm going to go . . . is studying . . . has been living . . . knows . . . has promised [at no specific time in the past] . . . have never been . . . am looking [possibly *look*]   **9.** was sitting . . . got . . . was sitting . . . tried . . . was lecturing . . . had been hiccupping [Also possible: *had hiccupped*; *hiccup* is also spelled *hiccough*.] . . . raised . . . excused   **10.** has been raining . . . has dropped . . . is [Low 40s Fahrenheit = 4°–6° Celsius.] . . . was shining . . . changes . . . wake [time clause] . . . will be snowing

TECHNIQUE: *Fill-in-the-blanks.*

Students in pairs can work out the answers. Then one pair can read the whole exercise aloud to the class. Other students should note any errors but should not interrupt the dialogue. At the end, discussion can always clear up the mistakes.

ANSWERS: **(1)** Are you studying . . .   **(2)** Yes, I am. Are you?   **(3)** I've been . . . was studying [possibly *studied*]   **(4)** . . . are you taking   **(5)** I'm taking . . . are you taking   **(6)** I'm studying . . . need . . . take [time clause]   **(7)** have you been   **(8)** I've been . . . arrived . . . I've been studying . . . lived/was living   **(9)** speak . . . Did you study/Had you studied . . . came   **(10)** studied [possibly *had studied*] . . . spent . . . picked . . . was living [possibly *lived*]   **(11)** are . . . came . . . had never studied . . . started   **(12)** do you plan/are you planning   **(13)** I'm not . . . return . . . will have been   **(14)** hope/am hoping

TECHNIQUE: *Fill-in-the-blanks.*

ALTERNATIVE: Students in pairs or individually can work out the answers, then write the letter (without the numbers). When they finish, they can exchange letters and look for each other's mistakes. (Copying from a text is usually more beneficial for lower- or mid-level students than for advanced students, who make few copying mistakes and generally find it busywork.)

This exercise is intended as a model for the student writing in the assignment that follows in Exercise 64.

ANSWERS: (2) received   (3) have been trying   (4) have been   (5) have had   (6) has been staying   (7) have spent/have been spending   (8-9) have been   (10) went . . . watched   (12) have barely had [also possible: *have had barely*, in which case *barely* modifies *enough*]   (13) is . . . am sitting   (14) have been sitting   (15) leaves/will leave/is leaving/is going to leave   (16) have decided [possibly *decided*]   (17) am writing   (18) am getting   (19) will take/am going to take . . . get   (21) are you getting   (22) are your classes going

☐ **EXERCISE 64, p. 66.** *Using verb tenses in writing.*

TECHNIQUE: *Homework. Alternative: seatwork.*

You may wish to require the students to use each of the 12 tense forms at least once. That sometimes results in occasional forced sentences, but the students generally find it challenging and fun.

◇ **WORKBOOK:** Practices 42 and 43.

☐ **EXERCISE 65, p. 66.** *Recognizing errors.*

TECHNIQUE: *Error analysis.* ★

Not all of the mistakes are verb tense; some involve capital letters, singular-plural agreement, and pronoun usage. All the mistakes are typical of many learners at this level of proficiency and are the kinds of errors they should be on the alert for in their own writing.

ANSWERS: **1. have been** living . . . **G**rand **A**venue . . . **S**eptember   **2. was** in . . . **N**ew **Y**ork **C**ity [A noun is capitalized when it is part of the name of a particular place.] . . . week**s**   **3. has** changed . . . time**s** [Compare: *city* is not capitalized in this sentence because it is not part of a name.]   **4.** shout**s** . . . make**s**   **5.** when I **arrive**   **6.** ever **told** . . . parents **teach**   **7.** thing**s** . . . appear**ed** . . . want**ed** . . . need**ed**   **8.** I **intend/am intending** . . . when I **finish/ have finished**   **9.** rang . . . **was** doing . . . dri**ed** . . . answer**ed** . . . I heard . . . husband**'s** . . . I **was**   **10.** I **have been** . . . I **have** done . . . things . . . (have) **seen** . . . places   **11. had** already **hidden** itself   **12. was** writing . . . knock**ed**

◇ **WORKBOOK:** Practice 44. Have students take Practice Test(s).

☐ **EXERCISE 66, p. 67.** *Prepositions of time.*

TECHNIQUE: *Seatwork, fill-in-the-blanks, teacher-led oral.* ★

Because these prepositions are related to time, they are presented in this chapter on verb tenses. These prepositions are assumed to be review for the students. General guidelines you might want to point out:

> *in* + *the morning/the afternoon/the evening/(the) summer/(the) fall/(the) winter/(the) spring*
> *at* + *night/noon/midnight/"clock time"/present*
> *in* + *month/year*
> *on* + *day/date*

ANSWERS: **2.** in   **3.** in   **4.** at   **5.** at [also: *about/around*]   **6.** at [also: *about/around/ before/after*]   **7.** on   **8.** in   **9.** in [also: *before/after*]   **10.** on [also: *before/after*]   **11.** on   **12.** on [April Fool's Day is always on April 1. It is traditionally a day when people play tricks on each other for amusement.]   **13.** in   **14.** in   **15.** At   **16.** at   **17.** in   **18.** in

---

★ See the INTRODUCTION, pp. xiv, for suggestions for handling error analysis exercises and preposition exercises.

Chapter 2: MODAL AUXILIARIES AND SIMILAR EXPRESSIONS

ORDER OF CHAPTER	CHARTS	EXERCISES	WORKBOOK
Form of modals	2-1	Ex. 1	Pr. 1
Polite requests	2-2 → 2-5	Ex. 2 → 6	Pr. 2 → 6
Necessity, prohibition	2-6 → 2-7	Ex. 7 → 9	Pr. 7 → 8
Advisability	2-8 → 2-9	Ex. 10 → 15	Pr. 9 → 11
Expectations: *be supposed to, be to*	2-10	Ex. 16 → 18	Pr. 12 → 13
Cumulative review and practice		Ex. 19 → 20	
Suggestions	2-11 → 2-12	Ex. 21 → 23	Pr. 14 → 15
Degrees of certainty	2-13 → 2-16	Ex. 24 → 33	Pr. 16 → 20, 23
Progressive form of modals	2-17	Ex. 34	Pr. 21 → 22
Used to and *be used to*	2-18	Ex. 35 → 36	Pr. 24 → 25
Would	2-19 → 2-20	Ex. 37 → 39	Pr. 26 → 27
Can/could	2-21 → 2-22	Ex. 40 → 42	Pr. 28
Cumulative review and practice	2-23	Ex. 43 → 46	Pr. 29 → 33 Pr. Tests A & B

General Notes on Chapter 2

• OBJECTIVE: Modal auxiliaries are used in English to express opinions, give advice, and indicate politeness; they express a variety of attitudes. Mistakes with modal auxiliaries can, therefore, sometimes cause bad feelings or misunderstandings between speaker and listener. Students should become aware that sometimes a small change in a modal auxiliary can signal a large difference in attitudes and meanings.

• APPROACH: Students using this textbook are probably already familiar with the most common meanings of the modal auxiliaries. The focus at the beginning of this chapter is on the basic forms, and Exercise 1 calls attention to errors that should be avoided. The rest of the chapter takes a semantic approach, grouping together modals and other expressions that have similar meanings. Matters of pronunciation, spoken/written usages, and formal/informal registers are noted in the charts.

• TERMINOLOGY: The terms "modal auxiliary" and "modal" are both used. Most modal auxiliaries are single words (e.g., *must, should*). Many have synonyms consisting of two- or three-word phrases (e.g., *have to, be supposed to*). No technical term (such as "periphrastic modals") is used for these synonyms in this book, except to call them "similar expressions."

CHART 2-1: INTRODUCTION

• Point out that all the sentences in example (a) express present and/or future time. Students should understand that *could* and *would* express present/future time as used in this chart, but that, in some other situations, it is also possible to use *could* as the past form of *can* and *would* as the past form of *will* (in the sequence of tenses in noun clauses). Students are sometimes not aware that *shall* and *should* are separate modals, not present and past forms of one modal.

• The chart mentions that each modal auxiliary has more than one meaning or use. These are presented in charts and exercises throughout the chapter and summarized in Chart 2-23.

☐ **EXERCISE 1, p. 69.** *Form of modal auxiliaries.*

TECHNIQUE: *In-class discussion.*
    Ask students to find the error in each sentence and to say the correct form of the sentence. Explain that modal auxiliaries follow rules that affect the form of other verbs in the sentence. If they ask why modal auxiliaries are so different from other verbs, tell them that long centuries of use and change have resulted in these forms; they are traditional in English.

ANSWERS: **1.** She can see it. [no *to*]   **2.** [no *s* on modal auxiliary *can*]   **3.** [no *s* on main verb *see*]   **4.** She can see it. [Modals are immediately followed only by the simple form.]   **5.** [no *to*]   **6.** Can you see it? [no *do*; begin questions with the modal]   **7.** They can't go there. [no *do*; add negation after the modal]

◇ **WORKBOOK:** Practice 1.

CHARTS 2-2 and 2-3: POLITE REQUESTS

• Discuss how polite requests allow the speaker to show respect to the listener. A person who says "Give me your pencil" or "Pass the salt" may seem to be abrupt, aggressive, or unfriendly.

• Point out the levels of politeness and formality in these charts; e.g., a change from *may* to *can* usually signals a slight or subtle difference in the relationship between the people who are conversing.

• The word *please* is frequently used in conversation. This is another way to show respect and friendliness.

• Another typical response to a request, especially in informal American English, is "Okay."

☐ **EXERCISE 2, p. 70.** *Asking and answering polite questions.*

TECHNIQUE: *Oral (books closed).*
    When you set up each situation for two students to roleplay, add specific details. Set the scene for them. For example, #1: "Olga, you and Anna are having dinner at the Four Seasons Restaurant. You want the butter, but you can't reach it. It's on the table near Anna."
#2: "Frederico, your chemistry class has just ended, and you walk to the front of the lecture hall to talk to your teacher. You want to ask her a question. Yoko, you are the teacher."

POSSIBLE ANSWERS: **1.** A: Could/Would you pass the salt, please? B: Yes, of course. **2.** A: May I ask you something? **3.** (...), may/can I use your phone? **4.** Could you pick me up at the airport next Tuesday at 5? **5.** Can you meet me...? **6.** May I please leave class early today? **7.** Excuse me. May I come in? **8.** Could I see Dr. North later this afternoon? **9.** Would/Could you check the oil (please)? **10.** Excuse me. Could you please explain the formula on page 100? I don't quite understand it. **11.** Hello. May/Can I speak to Mary? **12.** (...), can I see your dictionary for a minute? **13.** Excuse me. Could/Would you please keep an eye on my luggage for a minute? **14.** (...), I have to go to a meeting tonight. Could you possibly tape the six o'clock news for me on your VCR? [VCR = video cassette recorder]

CHART 2-4: POLITE REQUESTS WITH *WOULD YOU MIND*

• An alternative way of asking permission is "Do you mind if I close the window?" Using *would* is a bit more formal or polite than using *do*.

• In casual conversation, the auxiliary and subject pronoun are often omitted and a present—not past—verb is used: "Mind if I sit here?"

• Another informal response is "No. Go ahead," or sometimes even a positive response: "Sure. Go ahead." Both mean "You have my permission to proceed."

☐ EXERCISE 3, p. 72. *Verb forms following* would you mind.

TECHNIQUE: *Fill-in-the-blanks, discussion.*

ANSWERS: **1.** ...if I left **2.** repeating **3.** mailing **4.** ...if I stayed **5.** explaining **6.** opening [if the other person opens the window]/if I opened **7.** if I asked **8.** if I smoked [Note: "I'd really rather you didn't" is a polite and indirect way of saying "I don't want you to smoke."] **9.** speaking **10.** changing [if the other person changes the channel]/if I changed

◇ WORKBOOK: Practices 2 and 3.

CHART 2-5: USING IMPERATIVE SENTENCES TO MAKE POLITE REQUESTS

• Assumption: Students are already familiar with imperatives. Here, the focus is on softening their effect and making them more polite when they are used to make a request.

• A review of tag questions may be useful. (See Appendix 1, Chart B-4, in the textbook.) Of course, a tag on an imperative always contains the pronoun *you*. Caution: Sometimes a tag on an imperative gives the meaning of impatience or mild anger. For this reason, students should be careful in using a tag question after an imperative.

☐ EXERCISE 4, p. 73. *Polite requests.*

TECHNIQUE: *Oral (books closed).*
    To make certain the students understand the difference between orders and polite requests, tell them that you are going to give an order or make a rude request that they are then to soften.

Say your cues a little rudely so that the students can clearly discern the difference between what you say and what they say. Point out that often simply adding *please* and changing one's tone of voice can make a big difference.

Say the imperative cue, then allow two or three students to give different forms of the polite requests. Occasionally, have the class imitate your tone of voice for a polite request. Keep the pace moving and lively.

NOTES ON POSSIBLE RESPONSES: In **2, 3,** and **5,** *may I please have* is the most polite request. Other forms may show some impatience or mild anger.

In **10,** note the parallel verbs, which should have the same form in each request: "Please close . . . and turn"/"Would you mind closing . . . and turning."

In **11,** a person typically might say, "Excuse me. Could I get through?" or "Pardon me. May I get through, please?" Point out that a person would never say, "Let me out of the elevator!" unless s/he were panicked or very, very rude. Questions such as "Would you please let me out of the elevator?" or "Would you mind letting me out of the elevator?" show some irritability. Use **11** to point out again how subtle the use of modals can be, and tell the students to keep a sharp ear open for how native speakers make polite requests.

◇ **WORKBOOK:** Practice 4.

☐ **EXERCISE 5, p. 73.** *Using polite requests.*

TECHNIQUE: *Oral (books closed).*

This works best as a teacher-led activity. Use names of class members instead of "your friend" or "a student." Set the scene by adding specific details to the cues. Keep the pace moving, but be sure everyone understands each situation and response. Some of the situations can also be acted out as dialogues between students.

POSSIBLE ANSWERS: **1.** through **15.** [Follow the examples in Exercise 4.]   **16.** Excuse me. Could you tell me the time?/Can you tell me what time it is?   **17.** Pardon me. Can you show me how to get to the bus station?/Could you tell me where the bus station is?   **18.** Hello. Could you tell me what time Flight 62 arrives, please?   **19.** Could you please tell me how much this sweater costs?   **20.** Excuse me. Can you show/tell me where the library is?/Could you direct me to the library?

☐ **EXERCISE 6, p. 74.** *Using polite requests.*

TECHNIQUE: *Oral/Written.*

Small groups can brainstorm on two or three items, trying to think of as many requests as possible. Two or more groups can work on the same items, then compare their requests.

ADDITIONAL ITEMS: in a bookstore, in a bank, at the post office, in a library, in the headmaster's/professor's office, at a doctor's/dentist's office.

EXPANSION ACTIVITY: Assign your students to write down any requests they hear—polite or not—during the coming week. Also suggest that they write down requests that they themselves make. At the end of the week, use the students' papers for discussion.

◇ **WORKBOOK:** Practices 5 and 6.

CHART 2-6: EXPRESSING NECESSITY: *MUST, HAVE TO,*
           HAVE GOT TO

- This chart contains information about pronunciation, formal/informal usage, spoken/written forms, and one past form. Students should note and discuss these points.

- Note especially that *must* is used primarily with a forceful meaning. *Have to* and *have got to* are much more frequently used.

- Encourage students to use conversational pronunciations. These are the most natural and frequent forms in spoken English. The phonetic representations of these pronunciations follow:

  have to = /hæftə/ OR /hæftu/   *has to* = /hæstə/ OR /hæstu/
  got to = /gadə/ OR /gɔtə/

- *Have got to* (necessity) is not the same as *have got* (possession). For example:

  "I've got to get some money." (I need money.)
  "I've got some money." (I have money.)

☐ EXERCISE 7, p. 75. *Pronouncing* have to *and* have got to.

TECHNIQUE: *Oral (books closed).*
     Ask item **1** of the whole class and let several students call out answers. Encourage them to pronounce *have to* as "haftu" or "hafta" and *got to* as "gotta." (One common mistake is to say "I've gotta to go," inserting an additional *to*.)
     Ask the remaining items of individual students, using classmates' names in the blank spaces.

POSSIBLE ANSWERS: **1.** I've/We've got to study tonight.   **2.** He/She has to go to the bookstore.   **3.** I've got to go home and clean my room.   **4.** He's/She's got to meet some friends at the library.   **5.** I really must write a letter to my aunt.   **6.** Yesterday I had to wash my hair.   **7.** Where do you have to go this evening? [In British English, an alternative is "Where have you to go?" But both British and American English more often use *do* in these questions.]

ADDITIONAL ITEMS requiring more imaginative answers:
  a. What colors do you have to mix to produce the color green?
     (yellow + blue = green; yellow + red = orange, etc.)
  b. How did the astronauts prepare for space travel?
     (They had to train physically for weightlessness, had to learn how to fly the spacecraft, had to learn how to operate computers, etc.)
  c. How can you become a successful language learner?
     (You must be willing to take risks; you have to practice and repeat often; you've got to learn from your mistakes, etc.)
  d. How can you become a good soccer player/musician/dancer, etc.?
     (You have to practice, have to get some equipment, etc.)
  e. What are the best ways to maintain good health?
     (You have to eat a balanced diet, have to get plenty of exercise, have to get enough sleep, etc.)

CHART 2-7: LACK OF NECESSITY AND PROHIBITION

- *Need not* (principally British) and *don't need to* are similar in meaning to *don't have to*; *dare not* (principally British) is similar in meaning to *must not*. Like *need not*, *dare not* is followed by the simple form of a verb: *I dare not **ask** him about it.*

□ **EXERCISE 8, p. 76.** Must not *vs.* do not have to.

TECHNIQUE: *Fill-in-the-blanks.*
Allow time for students to think about the meaning of each item. The context determines which answer is appropriate. Help students understand the situational context of each item, perhaps by means of roleplaying and discussion.

ANSWERS: **3.** don't have to (needn't/don't need to) **4.** doesn't have to (doesn't need to/need not [Note: no *-s* is added to the modal *need*.]) **5.** must not (dare not) **6.** don't have to (needn't/don't need to) **7.** doesn't have to (needn't/doesn't need to) [There may be some disagreements with the truth of this statement, but the grammar is correct!] **8.** must not **9.** don't have to (needn't) **10.** doesn't have to (needn't/doesn't need to) [This item refers to U.S. university rules. Every student chooses a major field of study, but it is not necessary for a first-year student (freshman) to decide.] **11.** don't have to (don't need to) [Bats are mammals that fly at night.] **12.** must not (dare not) **13.** must not (dare not) **14.** must not/dare not [if you feel strongly that tigers should be protected] OR don't have to (need not) [if you feel that we can decide either to protect tigers or to neglect them] **15.** don't have to (needn't)

□ **EXERCISE 9, p. 77.** Must not *vs.* do not have to.

TECHNIQUE: *Oral (books closed).*
Keep the pace lively, but allow a student to think of a reasonable answer. Then, additional possible answers can be offered by some other students. This could be done in small groups or as written work, but a teacher-led exercise may be preferable.

POSSIBLE ANSWERS: **1.** argue with their parents **2.** pay taxes **3.** exceed the speed limit **4.** renew their licenses every year **5.** come to school on holidays **6.** forget our homework **7. & 8.** [depend on using a familiar name] **9.** spill food on a customer **10.** cook the food, just serve it **11. & 12.** [depend on personal opinions]

◇ **WORKBOOK:** Practices 7 and 8.

CHART 2-8: ADVISABILITY	

• Advice or a suggestion is usually friendly. It is often given by one's supervisor, parent, or friend. It is not as forceful as necessity.

• Note the special meaning of *had better*. It is used in giving advice to a peer or a subordinate, but not to a superior.

□ **EXERCISE 10, p. 78.** *Using* should, ought to, *and* had better.

TECHNIQUE: *Oral.*
This could be led by you or done in pairs, followed by a brief class discussion.

POSSIBLE ANSWERS: **1.** I have a test tomorrow **2.** I have a test tomorrow [Items 1 and 2 convey the same meaning.] **3.** I'll fall behind **4.** I don't have time **5.** I won't have anything to wear tomorrow **6.** go swimming **7.** take an umbrella **8.** you don't, you'll have to pay a fine **9.** you have an early appointment tomorrow **10.** you'll be too tired to do well on the test tomorrow

□ **EXERCISE 11, p. 79:** *Giving advice.*

TECHNIQUE: *Oral (books closed).*

Keep the pace lively, but give students time to think of a reasonable response. Discuss some additional responses if students mention them.

POSSIBLE ANSWERS: **1.** You ought to look it up in a dictionary. **2.** You'd better eat some hot soup and get some rest. **3.** You should sit near the front. **4.** You'd better put on a sweater/jumper. **5.** You ought to stamp it on the ground a few times. **6.** You should phone home. **7.** You should discuss it with a legal advisor. **8.** You should tell him/her to sleep on his/her stomach. **9.** You'd better enroll in an English course. **10.** You should get more sleep. **11.** You'd better return it to the library right away. **12.** You'd better stop by the grocery store on your way home. **13.** You ought to go to the bank. **14.** You should clean it up tonight. **15.** You'd better get some gas/petrol. **16.** You should see a dentist. **17.** You'd better go home and go to bed. **18.** You should call a travel agent and check on the flight time. **19.** You'd better drink some cold water./You should blow into a paper bag. [Explore traditional remedies for hiccups with the class.]

□ **EXERCISE 12, p. 80.** *Meanings of modals.*

TECHNIQUE: *Oral.*

Lead a brief discussion of each pair of sentences so that students understand the contexts and meanings. Small groups of advanced learners could do this with some imagination.

ANSWERS [Sentences with the stronger meaning in each pair]: **1.** b. **2.** b. **3.** a. **4.** a. **5.** b. **6.** a.

◇ **WORKBOOK:** Practices 9 and 10.

□ **EXERCISE 13, p. 80.** *Using* should *and* must/have to.

TECHNIQUE: *Fill-in-the-blanks.*

Students can write in their answers, then discuss them in small groups or as a class. You should help resolve disagreements.

ANSWERS: **1.** must/has to **2.** should **3.** must/have to [*Must* is a bit more formal, as in a list of rules for students.] **4.** should **5.** must/have to [if it's a requirement] OR should [if it would help my general education] **6.** should **7.** must/have to **8.** should ["I think having goals is helpful."] OR must/has to ["In my opinion, it isn't possible to live a good life if one doesn't have certain goals."] **9.** must/has to **10.** should **11.** must/have to **12.** must/have to/will have to [*Have to* is preferable here because the situation is neither formal nor urgent.] **13.** should **14.** should **15.** must/have to [spoken with enthusiasm and emphasis]

EXPANSION ACTIVITY: In an advanced class, ask the students to go back over Ex. 13 and use either *ought to* or *had better* if possible. Note that *ought to* (but not *had better*) is always an appropriate synonym for *should*. *Had better* falls between *should* and *must/have to* in strength in items 3, 5, 7, 11, 12, 13. *Had better* is not possible in items 1 and 9 because no "bad result" can be inferred in those two sentences.

CHART 2-9: THE PAST FORM OF *SHOULD*

• Sometimes students confuse the past form of modals with the present perfect tense because the **form** of the main verb is the same (*have* + past participle). If students ask about "tense," tell them that "*have* + past participle" here doesn't carry the same meaning as the present perfect tense; it simply indicates past time.

• The information in Chart 2-12 (e), p. 87, says that the past form of *should* is used to give "hindsight advice." You may want to introduce that concept here: We use "should have done something" when we look at the past (i.e., we look at something in hindsight), decide that what was done in the past was a mistake, and agree that it would have been better if the opposite had been done.

• The short answer to a question is "Yes, I should've" (or British "Yes, I should've done"). Note the pronunciation of *should've*, which is exactly like *should* + *of*. In fact, some people mistakenly spell the contraction as if it were two words: "should of." Also, students should remember to pronounce *should* like *good*, with no sound for the letter *l*.

☐ **EXERCISE 14, p. 81.** *Using the past form of* should.

TECHNIQUE: *Oral.*
    You or a good student can read the situation aloud, then one student can give an opinion about it, using the past form of *should*. The class should discuss anything that is unclear.

POSSIBLE ANSWERS: [Spoken contracted forms are given here.]   **2.** You should've gone (to the meeting).   **3.** She should've gone to (see) the doctor.   **4.** I should've (invited him).
5. She shouldn't've sold it.   **6.** He should've read the contract before he signed it. / He shouldn't've signed it without reading it carefully.

☐ **EXERCISE 15, p. 82.** *Using the past form of* should.

TECHNIQUE: *Oral (books closed).*
    You could do three or four of the items with individual students answering and the whole class listening. The rest of the exercise can be done in pairs or small groups; one student reads the item and another responds. If less advanced students have difficulty, they can open their books.

POSSIBLE ANSWERS: [Spoken contracted forms are given here.]   **1.** I should've worn a coat.   **2.** I should've looked it up.   **3.** I should've written (to) him.   **4.** [The idiom *to be broke* means to be without money.] I shouldn't've spent all my money.   **5.** I shouldn't've opened the window.   **6.** I should've gone . . . .   **7.** I should've set . . . .   **8.** I should've gone . . . .   **9.** He should've married her.   **10.** He shouldn't've married her.   **11.** I should've had . . . .   **12.** I should've stopped . . . .   **13.** I shouldn't've gone . . . .   **14.** I should've gone outside/shouldn't've stayed inside . . . .   **15.** I should've bought (her) something else.
16. She should've told the truth.   **17.** I shouldn't've eaten so much food/so many hamburgers.   **18.** I should've returned the book sooner.   **19.** I shouldn't've lent/loaned my car to him/her.   **20.** She should've put her purse in a safe place./She shouldn't've fallen asleep.

◇ **WORKBOOK:** Practice 11.

CHART 2-10: EXPECTATIONS: *BE SUPPOSED TO* AND *BE TO*

• The important difference between expectations and necessity (Chart 2-6) is that necessity can sometimes originate within oneself. Expectations come from outside, from other people; therefore, *be supposed to* and *be to* are similar to passive verb phrases with no agent. "He is supposed to come" means "He is expected (by someone) to come."

• Similarly, advisability (Chart 2-8) can originate within oneself, as if one's conscience were speaking. But expectations come from other people.

• Another meaning of *be supposed to* is "it is generally believed." For example, "Sugar is supposed to be bad for your teeth." *Be to* cannot be used with this meaning. (If students ask "Why?," just tell them it's traditional in English.)

• The negative form of these modals inserts *not* after *be*: "I'm not supposed to . . . ," "You're not to . . . ," "He isn't/He's not supposed to . . . ," etc.

☐ **EXERCISE 16, p. 83.** *Be supposed to.*

TECHNIQUE: *Error analysis (oral).*

The most common errors: a) omitting *be* before *supposed to*, and b) omitting *-d* at the end of *supposed* because it is not clearly pronounced when *to* is the next word. Other errors involve subject-verb agreement and use of the auxiliary *do*.

ANSWERS: **1. is** supposed to **2.** suppose**d** to **3.** suppose**d** to **4. I'm** suppose**d** to **5.** you **are** not suppose**d** to [Vocabulary note: An "allowance" is a small sum of money that parents give their children every week or month for their own use.]

☐ **EXERCISE 17, p. 84.** *Using* be to *in stating a rule.*

TECHNIQUE: *Oral.*

These are common signs that are posted in the United States in public places such as buildings, buses, and streets. You might compare them with some visual signs such as those for NO SMOKING or NO PARKING and ask students to verbalize the rule of behavior that is represented by the symbol.

ANSWERS: **2.** You/We are to keep off/are not to walk on the grass. **3.** You are not to eat or drink here. **4.** You are to move to the rear of the bus. [Passengers are to fill the rear section of the bus first.] **5.** You are not to joke with the inspectors [especially about carrying weapons or bombs!]. **6.** You are not to use the elevator if the building is burning [because the electricity will probably be cut off]. You are to use the stairs.
7. You are not to litter [throw paper or food on the ground] this area. **8.** If your car moves slowly [perhaps on a hill], you are to move it to the right side of the roadway [so that faster vehicles can pass/overtake on the left]. [In Britain, these positions are opposite.]

☐ **EXERCISE 18, p. 84.** *Using* be to.

TECHNIQUE: *Oral (books closed).*

Set up each situation as clearly as possible, using the students' names. Get the students to imagine themselves in the given situation.

ANSWERS: [Answers depend on students' ideas.]

◇ **WORKBOOK:** Practice 12.

☐ **EXERCISE 19, p. 85.** *Review of modals.*

TECHNIQUE: *Oral.*

This exercise compares the modal auxiliaries from Charts 2-6, 2-8, and 2-10. Students may create a context for each item and decide who the speakers are. For example, items 1 to 4 involve people who are riding in an airplane or automobile; they might be father and son, flight attendant and passenger, two business partners, etc. Students decide which sentence is stronger, and they might also discuss its appropriateness for the context they have created. Some statements are too strong between people of equal status and would cause the listener to become angry.

ANSWERS [The more forceful statement in each pair]: **1.** a. **2.** a. **3.** a. [*Had better* is strong, but *must* allows no choice.] **4.** a. **5.** a. **6.** b. **7.** b. **8.** a. [*Had better* implies a warning.]

☐ **EXERCISE 20, p. 85.** *Making meaningful sentences with modal auxiliaries.*

TECHNIQUE: *Oral.*

This could be a written exercise, including stated reasons. Alternatively, it could be used for group work with students discussing their intended meanings.

ANSWERS: [Answers depend on students' ideas.]

◇ **WORKBOOK**: Practice 13.

CHART 2-11: MAKING SUGGESTIONS

• These three expressions are followed by the simple (i.e., base) form of the main verb. For example: "Let's *be* careful"; "Why don't you *be* more quiet?" (mildly angry); and "Shall I *be* your partner in this game?"

• *Shall* is used only with *I* or *we*. It is not appropriate to ask "Shall he," "Shall you," etc.

• These suggestions are similar to polite requests, but also may include both speaker and listener in the suggested activity.

• In informal British usage, "Don't let's" is a possible alternative form of "Let's not." "Don't let's" is also heard in American English but is generally considered nonstandard.

☐ **EXERCISE 21, p. 86.** *Making suggestions in a dialogue.*

> TECHNIQUE: *Oral.*
>   Give pairs of students 5 minutes or so to make up dialogues. Then have each pair present their conversation. Encourage imagination and drama. Insist on five to ten lines so that the students can build a recognizable context around their suggestions. Some students might want to write their dialogues. (Memory is short in a second language!) But you should then insist that they say them as naturally as possible, not read verbatim from their papers.
>   The given sentence can appear anywhere in the dialogue. It needn't be the first sentence. The sentence with "Why don't" should follow the given sentence.

◇ **WORKBOOK**: Practice 14.

CHART 2-12: MAKING SUGGESTIONS: *COULD*

• Make sure the students understand that *could* refers to present or future time here. Sometimes learners mistakenly think of *could* only as "the past tense of *can*," but *could* has many uses and meanings. (See p. 112 in the textbook for other uses.)

• *Could* is used to make suggestions when there are several good alternatives. It often occurs with *or*: e.g., "You could do this, or you could try that."

☐ **EXERCISE 22, p. 87.** *Understanding* should *and* could.

> TECHNIQUE: *Discussion, teacher-led.*
>   Students read the dialogues aloud, then paraphrase the *should/could* sentences. The purpose of this type of exercise is to give additional examples of the structure for students to discuss and explore.
>
> *POSSIBLE ANSWERS:* **1.** B: I advise him to see a doctor./My advice is to see a doctor.
> **2.** I'm making several suggestions.   **3.** I'm giving definite advice about how to save money.
> **4.** I'm listing several possibilities.   **5.** I'm giving hindsight advice.   **6.** I'm listing hindsight possibilities.

□ **EXERCISE 23, p. 88.** *Making suggestions.*

> TECHNIQUE: *Oral (books closed).*
> This could be done as group work, but it's very effective to have the students give you advice. They usually enjoy feeling like experts for a change!
> Elicit from the students two or three suggestions with *could*. Then elicit one response with *should*.
> This exercise benefits greatly from the use of names and places that are familiar to the students. Don't feel that you must read every item exactly as it appears in the textbook. You can create a fuller context, change the order of items, and use more natural phrases to make the exercise more meaningful to your students.

◇ **WORKBOOK:** Practice 15.

CHART 2-13: EXPRESSING DEGREES OF CERTAINTY: PRESENT TIME	

• The percentages are, of course, not exact. They show the relative strength of one's certainty.

• Call students' attention to the note about *maybe* and *may be*, as confusing the two is a common written error.

□ **EXERCISE 24, p. 89.** *Expressing certainty with* must.

> TECHNIQUE: *Oral (books closed).*

POSSIBLE ANSWERS: **1.** S/he must be tired.   **2.** S/he must have caught a cold.   **3.** S/he must be married.   **4.** S/he must be (feeling) cold/chilly. [Idiom note: "Goose bumps" or "goose flesh" refers to the small bumps that appear on your skin when you feel cold or afraid.] **5.** S/he must be hungry.   **6.** S/he must have an itch. / S/he must have a mosquito bite. **7.** S/he must be nervous.   **8.** S/he must still be thirsty.   **9.** S/he must be happy. **10.** S/he must be very sad.   **11.** The phone must be dead/out of order.   **12.** It must serve good food at reasonable prices.   **13.** The battery must be dead.   **14.** It must be a good film.   **15.** It must be about (two) o'clock.

□ **EXERCISE 25, p. 90.** *Expressing less certainty.*

> TECHNIQUE: *Oral (books closed).*
> Point out that the answers in this exercise express less certainty than the answers in Exercise 24.

□ **EXERCISE 26, p. 90.** *Expressing degrees of certainty.*

> TECHNIQUE: *Completion.*

ANSWERS: **2.** He must be rich.   **3.** He must be crazy. ["A nut" means, in slang, "a crazy/insane person."]   **4.** She could/may/might be at a meeting.   **5.** You must have the wrong number. [This is a telephone conversation.]   **6.** You must be very proud.   **7.** You must feel terrible.   **8.** ...it may/might/could fit Jimmy.   **9.** You must miss them very much. **10.** She must be about ten (years old).

◇ **WORKBOOK:** Practices 16 and 17.

CHART 2-14: DEGREES OF CERTAINTY: PRESENT TIME NEGATIVE

• The percentages are not exact; they show only relative certainty.

• Note that the percentages in this chart are not simply the opposites of those in Chart 2-13. *Could* indicates less than 50 percent certainty, but *couldn't* indicates 99 percent certainty. Tell your students they are right if they complain that language is not always a logical structure!

☐ EXERCISES 27 → 29, pp. 93–94.   *Understanding expressions of certainty.*

TECHNIQUE: *Completion and discussion of meaning, teacher-led oral.*
  In Ex. 27, compare *must not* with simple present verbs (*she must not study* vs. *she doesn't study*).
In Ex. 28, compare *can't/couldn't* with simple present verbs (*it couldn't be Mary* vs. *it isn't Mary*).
In Ex. 29, elicit from the students probable/possible reasons for the speakers' verb choices. The last item in Ex. 29 can be done in pairs, then performed and compared.

CHART 2-15: DEGREES OF CERTAINTY: PAST TIME

• Note the parallels between the **affirmative** expressions in this chart and in Chart 2-13.

• Then note the parallels between the **negative** expressions here and in Chart 2-14.

• Point out to students that modal auxiliaries are very useful in communicating opinions, emotions, politeness, and many other notions. Other languages may use very different kinds of expressions for these ideas, so English modals can be difficult to learn.

☐ EXERCISE 30, p. 95.   *Using past expressions of certainty.*

TECHNIQUE: *Oral (books closed).*
  Take an active role in this exercise, helping each dialogue develop in a fairly natural way:
  a. Say the first line to the class, using the name of a student instead of "Jack."
  b. Wait for several students to give some good guesses.
  c. Then read the "What if" question and wait for new responses.

☐ EXERCISE 31, p. 96.   *Degrees of certainty in the past.*

TECHNIQUE: *Teacher-led discussion of meaning.*
  Assign the roles of the speakers to students. Read the situation cue aloud, then ask the students to read their assigned sentences aloud. They should add information to clarify the meaning of the verb form they have used, or simply explain what they mean by their verb choice.
  Situation 2 might seem odd. It refers to a game called "Clue" that is often played in the United States. The players are given clues to a murder mystery, then they try to solve the mystery and identify the criminal. Note for students that the pronunciation of "Colonel" is the same as "kernel." Also in Situation 2, discuss the use of "you know" as a sentence tag. Students should be aware of its existence but cautioned about its overuse. Perhaps you could illustrate its potential for annoying overuse by telling the class a personal experience story and adding "you know" to each sentence you say. ("Yesterday I went downtown, you know. I had to go to the main post office, you know. My mother sent me a package, you know, but, you know, she didn't put on enough postage, you know. So I have to go pick it up, you know.")

Using forms of must *to express degree of certainty.*

TECHNIQUE: *Fill-in-the-blanks.*
Assign speaker roles and ask students to present the dialogues without looking at their texts.

ANSWERS: **2.** must not like [It is possible but not usual to contract *must not* when it expresses "degree of certainty"; the contraction *mustn't* more typically signals "prohibition."] **3.** must have (must've) been **4.** must be **5.** must have (must've) forgotten. **6.** must not **7.** must have (must've) left **8.** must be **9.** must have (must've) hurt **10.** must mean **11.** must have (must've) been **12.** must have (must've) misunderstood

◇ WORKBOOK: Practices 18 and 19.

CHART 2-16: DEGREES OF CERTAINTY: FUTURE TIME

• Of course, no one can be 100 percent sure about future events. But we can make promises with *will* and confident predictions (as in Chart 1-20) using *will*.

• This chart is titled "future time," but for convenience in section (b), the past forms *should have* and *ought to have* are included. Compare *should have* meaning "unfulfilled expectation" with *should have* in Charts 2-9 and 2-12 meaning "hindsight advice." The forms are identical, but the contexts change the meanings.

☐ EXERCISE 33, p. 98. *Using modals to express certainty.*

TECHNIQUE: *Fill-in-the-blanks.*
Discuss the fine line between *will* and *should/ought to* to express future certainty, as in item 2. (Learners may sometimes sound brasher or more assertive than they intend if they use *will* instead of other "softer" modals.)

ANSWERS: **3.** must [certainty at the present time] **4.** should/ought to OR will [depends on speaker's degree of certainty] **5.** should/ought to **6.** I'll [a promise, a high degree of future certainty] **7.** should/ought to **8.** will **9.** must **10.** She'll OR should/ought to **11.** should/ought to **12.** should/ought to OR will [possibly depending upon the skill and self-confidence of the cook!] **13.** should/ought to **14.** should/ought to **15.** must **16.** must

◇ WORKBOOK: Practice 20.

CHART 2-17: PROGRESSIVE FORMS OF MODALS

• You could elicit more examples. Tell the students: "(. . .) is at home/in the next classroom/in the school office/at the park right now." Then ask them to describe (. . .)'s possible activities at the present moment.

Use the same situations but in a past context to elicit past progressive modals: what (. . .) could/may/ might have been doing.

• Every progressive form must contain both a form of *be* and a verb + *ing*.

• Point out similarities and differences with other progressive verb forms in Chapter 1:

  Chart 1-8: Present Progressive (*is sleeping* vs. *might be sleeping*)
  Chart 1-13: Past Progressive (*was sleeping* vs. *might have been sleeping*)

TECHNIQUE: *Fill-in-the-blanks.*
Call students' attention to the situations, reminding them that the progressive is necessary for actions that are in progress "right now" or were in progress at a specific point in the past.

ANSWERS: **3.** must be burning **4.** might/could/may be talking [in both sentences] **5.** must be playing **6.** might/may/could be staying [in both sentences] **7.** should/ought to be studying [advisability] **8.** must be kidding [an idiom meaning "I can't believe what I just heard. I think you are joking." "Hitchhike" means to ask drivers to give you a ride; traditionally, you ask by pointing your thumb in the direction you want to travel.] **9.** may/might/could have been kidding **10.** must have been kidding [more certainty]

◇ WORKBOOK: Practices 21, 22, and 23.

CHART 2-18: USING *USED TO* AND *BE USED TO*

• Point out that these two phrases look similar but have very different meanings.

• When *be* occurs, *used to* means "be accustomed to."

• The word *to* in *used to* is part of an infinitive phrase, so it must be followed by the simple form of a verb: *used to go, used to be,* etc. However, the word *to* in *be used to* is a preposition, so it must be followed by a noun, pronoun, or gerund: *be used to the weather, be used to it, be used to living,* etc.

• Special note about *be accustomed to*: In American English *to* is a preposition, but in British English *to* may be considered to be part of an infinitive phrase. So, in British English it is possible to say "be accustomed to live in a cold climate."

• Negative forms of *used to*: [These sentences are more often spoken than written.]

   I didn't use to like fish, but I do now.
   I used to not like fish, but now I do./I used not to like fish, but now I do.
   I usedn't to like fish, but now I do. (British English)

• Question form:

   Did you use to play tennis? (Pronunciation is /yus/.)

• The simple verb *use* means "employ as a tool" and is pronounced /yuz/. Compare these statements:

   I use /yuz/ a pen to write in my notebook.
   I am used /yust/ to using /yuzɪŋ/ a pen.
   I used /yust/ to use /yuz/ a pencil, but now I use /yuz/ a pen.
   Yesterday I used /yuzd/ a pencil because I lost my pen.

□ EXERCISE 35, p. 102. *Used to* vs. *be used to.*

TECHNIQUE: *Fill-in-the-blanks.*

ANSWERS: **3.** am **4.** Ø **5.** Ø **6.** are **7.** is **8.** Ø **9.** Ø **10.** Ø **11.** is **12.** are . . . am

□ EXERCISE 36, p. 102. *Using* used to, be used to, get used to.

TECHNIQUE: *Oral (books closed); teacher-led or small groups.*
Some of these items could also be written as homework.

ANSWERS: [Depend on students' ideas.]

◇ WORKBOOK: Practices 24 and 25.

```
┌─────────────────────────────────────────────────────────────┐
│ CHART 2-19:  USING WOULD TO EXPRESS A REPEATED                │
│              ACTION IN THE PAST                               │
├─────────────────────────────────────────────────────────────┤
```

• Compared to *used to*, habitual *would* is somewhat more formal. *Would* is often preferred in writing, whereas *used to* may be preferred in speech.

• Note the important limitation on *would*: it cannot express a situation, only an action.

• This use of *would* is unusual in British English.

☐ EXERCISE 37, p. 104.   Would *vs.* used to.

TECHNIQUE: *Fill-in-the-blanks.*

ANSWERS: **2.** would give   **3.** used to be [a situation]   **4.** used to be . . . would start
5. used to be . . . would get . . . would spend . . . would find . . . would gather   **6.** would ask . . .
would never let   **7.** would make . . . would put   **8.** would take   **9.** would wake . . . would
hike . . . would see   **10.** would be sitting [in progress at that moment] . . . would always smile and
say . . . would stand . . . clear [Note that the modal is usually not repeated in a parallel structure
after *and*.] ["Clear her throat" means to make a vocal sound in the throat, usually spelled
"Ahem."]

◇ WORKBOOK: Practice 26.

```
┌─────────────────────────────────────────────────────────────┐
│ CHART 2-20:  EXPRESSING PREFERENCE: WOULD RATHER              │
├─────────────────────────────────────────────────────────────┤
```

• In a question, either the word *or* or the word *than* can follow *would rather*:

   Would you rather eat fruit or candy?
   Would you rather eat fruit than candy?

• In a negative question, only the word *than* is possible for a preference:

   Wouldn't you rather eat fruit than candy?

☐ EXERCISE 38, p. 106.   *Practicing* would rather *to express preferences.*

TECHNIQUE: *Oral completion.*
      Encourage students to use contractions in their spoken answers. The contraction *'d* is often
difficult to hear and may be difficult to pronounce for some learners. Sometimes students omit it
because they don't hear it.

☐ EXERCISE 39, p. 106.   *Using* would rather.

TECHNIQUE: *Oral (books closed).*
      [Answers depend on students' preferences.]
      EXPANSION: Try a round-robin sequence like this:
            Teacher to A: *What would you rather do than go to class?*
            Student A: *I'd rather go bowling than go to class.*

Teacher to B: *What would you rather do than go bowling?*
Student B: *I'd rather play chess than go bowling.*
Teacher to C: *What would you rather do than play chess?*
etc.

◇ **WORKBOOK:** Practice 27.

CHART 2-21: USING *CAN* AND *BE ABLE TO*

• An additional common use of *can* is with stative verbs of sense perceptions [see Chart 1-9 (4), p. 13] that are not used in progressive tenses. For example:

I can smell bread baking in the oven right now. ("I'm smelling bread" is incorrect.)
I can't hear (right now) the lecture. ("I am not hearing" and "I don't hear" are incorrect.)

• Pronunciation notes:

Can't has two acceptable pronunciations. Most Americans say /kænt/. But along the northern Atlantic coast, the pronunciation is similar to the British /kant/.

Can also has two pronunciations. Before a verb, it is usually /kən/. In a short answer ("Yes, I can."), it is /kæn/.

In typical intonation, *can't* is stressed and *can* is unstressed.

☐ **EXERCISE 40, p. 107.** *Pronunciation of* can *and* can't.

TECHNIQUE: You should read the sentences aloud, choosing *can* or *can't* at random. Then ask the students to tell you what you said.

☐ **EXERCISE 41, p. 108.** *Using* can *and other modals.*

TECHNIQUE: *Teacher-led discussion or group work.*

ANSWERS: [Answers depend on students' ideas; some possibilities are listed below.]
  1. physical abilities: *can walk, talk, lift my pen*; negative: *can't fly*
  2. acquired abilities: *can write, read, play tennis*; negative: *can't speak Swahili*
  3. [depend on students' ideas]
  4. a. *can walk, can ride my bike, can take a bus.* [possible because certain conditions exist]
     b. *may walk, may ride my bike, may take a bus.* [less than 50 percent certainty]
  5. [both give permission, but a. = informal situation; b. = formal situation]
  6. [depend on students' ideas]
  7. a. *may* expresses idea of "maybe" [less than 50 percent certainty]
     b. *can* expresses idea that "certain conditions exist, so I can choose to do it if I want to"
     c. *will* expresses a prediction or plan
  8. [possibly assign to pairs for dialogue construction]

CHART 2-22: PAST ABILITY: *COULD*

• The focus of this chart is the common mistake noted in (c).

• An additional alternative in (d) is *succeed in*: "They succeeded in reaching the top yesterday."

☐ **EXERCISE 42, p. 109.** *Using* could *for past ability.*

TECHNIQUE: *Oral, discussion; teacher-led.*

This exercise can be confusing.* Focus the students' attention on two points: (1) NOT using *could* to express a single past event that occurred at one particular time in the past; and (2) using *could* to express ability in the affirmative ONLY when it expresses the idea of "used to be able to."

ANSWERS: **4.** could watch [used to be able to] **5.** could type [used to be able to]
8. could catch [used to be able to] **10.** could convince [used to be able to] (All other items contain a single past event, no *could*.)

◇ **WORKBOOK:** Practice 28.

CHART 2-23: SUMMARY CHART OF MODALS AND SIMILAR EXPRESSIONS

• By the time the students reach this chart, they should be familiar with its contents. It summarizes for them what they have been learning in the past 42 pages of the text.

☐ **EXERCISE 43, p. 112.** *Differences between modal auxiliaries.*

TECHNIQUE: *Discussion of meaning.*

Ask leading questions to elicit student interpretations of meaning. In addition to a review of grammar, this kind of exercise provides the students with the opportunity to develop their oral skills by explaining something they already know and understand. It challenges them to express their understandings in spoken English. Encourage them to invent possible contexts as a way of explaining differences in meaning.

In some items there is no difference in meaning; in other items there are distinct differences in meaning. In still other items, there might be a subtle difference in politeness or in forcefulness. All of the sentences in this exercise are grammatically correct.

ANSWERS:
1. a and b = a little more polite/formal than c; c = might be spoken to a friend/family member
2. a and b = advisability   c = expected to   d = no choice
3. a = advisability   b = stronger than a; implies a bad result   c = stronger than a or b
4. a = prohibition   b = lack of necessity
5. a = 100 percent   b = 90 percent
6. a, b, c = the same   d = 95 percent
7. a = a guess, 50-50   b and c = 99 percent certain
8. a = maybe he went home, 50-50   b = 95 percent certain   c = a fact, necessity
9. a = advisability   b and c = essentially the same, no choice
10. a = suggesting one possibility   b = giving definite advice
11. a, b = necessity   c = advisability   d = expected   e = possible bad result
f = preference
12. a = "hindsight advice"   b = "hindsight possibility"
13. a and b = same, repeated action in past

---

*The modal *could* can be confusing. It has many uses, most of which are close in meaning. For example, compare the following:
    I could run fast if I wanted to. [present/future contrary-to-fact conditional]
    I could run fast when I was young. [past ability]
    I could run or I could walk. [50-50 possibility, present/future]
    You could run to improve your physical condition. [present/future suggestion]
Don't be surprised if the students have difficulty with it!

☐ **EXERCISES 44 & 45, pp. 114–117.** *Using modal auxiliaries appropriately.*

TECHNIQUE: *Fill-in-the-blanks.*

The students have to think of only one possible answer, not all of the possibilities. In the following section, the most likely answers are given first and others are in parentheses.

EX. 44 ANSWERS:

1. had better shut (should/ought to/have to/must shut)
2. could/would you hand (can/will you hand)
3. had to pay...should have returned
4. don't/won't have to go
5. May/Could I make (Can I make)
6. had better take (should/ought to take)
7. can already say (is already able to say)
8. mustn't tell (shouldn't/had better not/can't tell)
9. Could/Would you please repeat (Would you mind repeating)
10. must/have to attend
11. could run (was able to/would run)...can't run
12. had to wait
13. could go
14. would rather go
15. must not have seen
16. can cook
17. had better clean (should/ought to/must/have to clean)
18. can't/couldn't be...may/might/could belong (must belong)
19. would do (used to do)
20. should/ought to/had better/have to/must learn...can be

EX. 45 ANSWERS:

1. should/ought to/had better get (has to/must get)
2. can't keep...had better go (should/ought to/have to go)
3. cannot go (must not go)
4. shouldn't have laughed
5. Could/Can/Would you cash
6. shouldn't stick (oughtn't [to] stick) [Idiom: "stick one's nose in other people's business" means to meddle, to become involved where one is not wanted.]
7. can't live...have to/must find (had better find)
8. May/Can/Could I speak...can't come...May (/Can/Could) I take
9. have to go/have got to go
10. should/ought to take (could take)...can get
11. had to study...should have come
12. don't have to make (shouldn't make)
13. had better answer (should/ought to/have to answer)...might/could/may be
14. must have passed
15. should have been/was supposed to be
16. could/might/may be
17. must have been daydreaming
18. was able to wake (managed to wake) [*Awaken* can also be used instead of *wake*.]
19. would rather have stayed home and watched/should have stayed home and watched
20. could/might/may have been...should have asked (could have asked)

◇ **WORKBOOK:** Practices 29, 30, 31, 32, and 33.

☐ **EXERCISE 46, p. 118.** *Recognizing errors with modals.*

TECHNIQUE: *Error analysis.*

ANSWERS:
1. If you have a car, you **can travel** around the United States. (OR If you **had** a car, you **could travel** . . . .)
2. During class the students **must sit** quietly. When the students have questions, they **must raise** their hands. [no **to**]
3. When you send for the brochure, you should **include** a self-addressed, stamped envelope. OR When you **sent** for the brochure, you **should have included** a . . . .
4. A film director must **have** control over every aspect of a movie.
5. When I was a child, I **could go** to the roof of my house and **see** all the other houses and streets.
6. While I was working in the fields, my son would **bring** me oranges or candy.
7. I **broke** my leg in a soccer game three months ago. [one time in the past]
8. **Would/Could/Can** you please help me with this? [**May** is used with **I/we**.]
9. Many students would rather **study** [no **to**] on their own than **go** to classes.
10. We **are** supposed to bring our books to class every day.

◇ **WORKBOOK:** Have students take Practice Test A and/or B.

☐ **EXERCISES 47 & 48, pp. 118–119.** *Using prepositions and phrasal verbs.*

TECHNIQUE: *Seatwork, fill-in-the-blanks, teacher-led oral.*

EX. 47 ANSWERS: **2.** of **3.** out/off **4.** up **5.** at **6.** from [so they couldn't find it]
7. with **8.** in [arrive **in** a country or city] **9.** at [arrive **at** a specific building]
10. from **11.** for **12.** of **13.** at/with **14.** with **15.** to

EX. 48 ANSWERS: **2.** away/out **3.** out/off **4.** up **5.** off [A "raincheck" is a ticket that admits you to the theater another time without additional payment.] **6.** up **7.** out [from a library; "I.D." is an abbreviation for i̲dentification card.] **8.** about **9.** up
10. back . . . out of

Chapter 3: THE PASSIVE

ORDER OF CHAPTER	CHARTS	EXERCISES	WORKBOOK
Forming the passive	3-1	Ex. 1 → 3	Pr. 1 → 6
Using the passive and "*by* phrase"	3-2	Ex. 4 → 5	Pr. 7 → 8
Indirect objects as passive subjects	3-3	Ex. 6	Pr. 9
Cumulative review and practice		Ex. 7 → 10	Pr. 10 → 13
Passive form of modals	3-4	Ex. 11 → 12	Pr. 14 → 16
Cumulative review and practice		Ex. 13	
Stative passive	3-5	Ex. 14 → 16	Pr. 17 → 21
The passive with *get*	3-6	Ex. 17 → 19	Pr. 22 → 23
Cumulative review and practice		Ex. 20	
Participial adjectives	3-7	Ex. 21 → 24	Pr. 24 → 26
Cumulative review and practice		Ex. 25 → 26	Pr. 27 → 29 Pr. Tests A & B

General Notes on Chapter 3

• OBJECTIVE: In speaking and writing, about one sentence in eight uses the passive structure. In scientific, academic, and informative reporting, usage increases to about one passive in every three sentences. The passive allows one to focus on actions and the receivers of actions, but it does not require identification of the actor because often it is not important or necessary to know who did something. Therefore, the passive is a useful structure for learners to understand and use. However, they should be encouraged to continue using active sentences for direct, forceful, or persuasive purposes when the agent/actor is known.

• APPROACH: Students are given plenty of practice in forming and using passive sentences throughout the chapter. Special attention is given to passive modals, the verb *get* as a passivizer, and the often confusing participial adjectives (*interesting* vs. *interested*). With the charts and exercises, students learn to use various tenses with the passive and to decide whether to use the passive or active form.

• TERMINOLOGY: It is assumed that students understand the grammatical terms "subject," "object," and "(in)transitive verb." The term "*by* phrase" is used for the prepositional phrase that includes the agent of the verb's action.

CHART 3-1: FORMING THE PASSIVE

• Students must understand the difference between transitive and intransitive verbs; refer them to Appendix 1, Chart A-1. Some other languages use transitivity in very different ways, leading students to make mistakes in English (INCORRECT: "The accident was happened" or "My shoe was fallen off").

• In reviewing the tense forms listed at the bottom of the chart, you might have students change some of the statements into questions or negatives. This focuses their attention on the required use of the auxiliary *be* in every passive sentence.

☐ EXERCISE 1, p. 121. *Forms of* be *in the passive.*

TECHNIQUE: *Transformation, seatwork.* [See the INTRODUCTION to this *Guide* for information about classroom techniques.]

ANSWERS: **2.** is being   **3.** has been   **4.** was   **5.** was being   **6.** had been   **7.** will be **8.** is going to be   **9.** will have been

EXPANSION ACTIVITY: Before or after Exercise 1, you might want to demonstrate the passive in all the tenses. Ask a student to assist you, then include his or her actions in your sentences. For example: (*"John" touches your book, then takes his hand from it.*)

TEACHER: John touched the book.
STUDENTS: The book was touched by John.
(*You touch the book with your hand and do not take your hand from it.*)
TEACHER: I am touching the book.
STUDENTS: The book is being touched by you.
(*Continue with sentences like the following:*)
(*simple present*) Mr. Lee touches the book during class each day.
(*simple past*) When we started this lesson, Baiwong touched the book.
(*present perfect*) Ruth hasn't touched the book yet.
(*past progressive*) A few minutes ago, John was touching the book.
(*past perfect*) Before I touched the book, John had touched it.
(*future*) Kevin will probably touch the book next.
(*future*) Pierre is going to touch the book when I ask him to.
(*future perfect*) Soon Maria will have touched the book.

◇ WORKBOOK: Practices 1 and 2.

☐ EXERCISE 2, p. 121. *Changing active to passive.*

ASSUMPTIONS: Students can form negatives and questions.

TECHNIQUE: *Transformation, seatwork followed by discussion.*
   This exercise may be done individually or in small groups. In an advanced class where this is review only, a "student-teacher" could lead the exercise.
   Every sentence in this exercise should include a "*by* phrase" in the passive form. Focus attention on the <u>forms</u> at this point in the chapter. Check the students' pronunciation of *-ed* endings.

ANSWERS:
   2. Ann will be invited to the party by Bill.
   3. That report is being prepared by Alex.
   4. Customers are served by waitresses and waiters.
   5. The lesson is going to be explained by the teacher.
   6. A new idea has been suggested by Shirley.

7. The farmer's wagon was being pulled by two horses.
8. The book had been returned (by Kathy) to the library (by Kathy). [Either position is acceptable.]
9. By..., the announcement will have been made by the president.
10. That note wasn't written by me. It was written by John.
11. That pie wasn't made by Alice. Was it made by Mrs. French?
12. Is that course taught by Prof. Jackson? I know (that) it isn't taught by Prof. Adams.
13. Those papers haven't been signed (yet) by Mrs. Andrews (yet). [Either position is acceptable.] Have they been signed by Mr. Andrews?
14. Is your house being painted by Mr. Brown?
15. I won't be fooled by his tricks.

◇ WORKBOOK: Practice 3.

☐ EXERCISE 3, p. 122. *Transitive and intransitive verbs.*

   TECHNIQUE: *Oral, transformation, with teacher-led discussion.*
   The items include intransitive verbs that are often used incorrectly in a passive form by learners (INCORRECT: "My cat was died"; "I am agree with you").

   ANSWERS:
   3. no change [Compare *died* (intransitive verb) and *is dead* (*be* + adjective).] [Items 3, 4, 7, 9, 11, 12, 13, 15 cannot be passive because they contain intransitive verbs.]
   5. That theory was developed by....
   6. The cup was dropped by Timmy.
   8. I was interviewed by....
   10. ...was destroyed by....
   14. ..., the chalkboard is always erased by....

◇ WORKBOOK: Practices 4, 5, 6.

CHART 3-2: USING THE PASSIVE

• Point out that a combination of factors may determine when the "*by* phrase" is omitted. It is not used:

   —when it can easily be assumed who, in general, performs such an action. (*Rice is grown "by farmers." Arithmetic is taught in elementary school "by teachers."*) In such cases, the "*by* phrase" is implied.
   —when the speaker doesn't know who performed the action. (*The house was built in 1890 "by some unknown people who engaged in house building." My shoes were made in Italy "by some unknown shoemakers."*)
   —when the focus is on the action and it is not important to know who performed the action. (*This olive oil was imported from Spain "by people in a company that imports olive oil."* It's not important to know who those people are. The focus is solely on the origin of the olive oil.)

   COMPARE: The active is usually used when the actor is specifically known. (*Mr. Lee grows rice on his farm. Ms. Hill teaches arithmetic in elementary school. My grandfather built our house. The Acme Trading Company imports olive oil from Spain.*)

• The "*by* phrase" is included (in other words, the passive is used even when there is an acceptable active equivalent with a known agent) when the speaker wants to focus attention on the **receiver** of the action (e.g., "this rug" vs. "that rug") rather than on the actor. To illustrate this common use of the passive, as in (f), you might ask two students to draw a simple picture or write a word on the chalkboard. Then you identify the distinction between the two drawings or words by pointing and saying, "This one was drawn/written by (...). That one was drawn/written by (...)."

□ **EXERCISE 4, p. 123.** *Understanding the use of the passive.*

TECHNIQUE: *Discussion of meaning, teacher-led.*
     You could ask the students some leading questions about the sentences, such as: *Why is the passive used here instead of the active? Who is the actor or agent? Change the sentence to its active form; what's the difference in meaning or forcefulness?*
     ADDITIONAL SUGGESTION: For homework, ask the students to find examples of passive sentences and copy them out to bring to class the next day. Tell them to look in a newspaper, an encyclopedia, a textbook, etc. (This shows them that the passive occurs frequently in many contexts.) At the beginning of the next class, some of the students could write on the chalkboard the sentences they found. Or they could hand in their sentences, which you could then duplicate for further class discussion.

POSSIBLE ANSWERS:
1. We don't know who made the sweater, and it is not important to know. The equivalent active sentence is "Someone (in England) made my sweater (in England)." The passive is preferred here because the actor is unknown and unimportant.
2. The implied "*by* phrase" is "by people who build highways." The passive expresses all the necessary information without the "*by* phrase."
3. "by language teachers," no additional important information
4. It's obvious that the symphony was performed "by the symphony orchestra," not by a high school band or by a guitar player. If the symphony had been performed by any agent other than the obvious one, either the active would be used or the "*by* phrase" would be included.
5. "by television stations"
6. The "*by* phrases" give necessary details. The active forms of these sentences are equally useful. The difference is that the passive focuses attention on two compositions rather than on their authors. Information about the authors is given to identify or distinguish between the two compositions.
7. The "*by* phrase" is used because it contains the important information of "hundreds." The active sentence is equally viable, but the passive focuses attention on the monument.
8. "by people" is uninformative
9. Note that there are four passives here. No "*by* phrases" are necessary. Point out how useful the passive can be when the speaker's/writer's purpose is to give information about the receivers of actions without knowing who performed those actions.
10. The "*by* phrase" is necessary because the agent is known. The active equivalent could be used, but the passive focuses attention on "paper" rather than on "the Chinese." [Items 9 and 10 are related. Even though the active could easily be used in 10, point out that the use of the passive allows a parallel contrast between "parchment" and "paper."]

□ **EXERCISE 5, p. 124.** *Using the passive.*

TECHNIQUE: *Oral; teacher-led or group work.*
     This exercise allows students to apply the rules they have learned so far about the passive: using the correct tense with *be*, omitting or including a "*by* phrase," not using an intransitive verb in the passive, observing singular/plural agreement between subject and verb.

ANSWERS:
3. This antique table was made in 1734.
4. (no change)
5. My purse was stolen.
6. The coffee was being made when . . . . [The active sentence is perhaps more direct and preferable.]
7. That book has been translated . . . .
8. That picture was drawn by Jim's daughter. This picture was drawn by my son.

9. The applicants will be judged on . . . .
10. (no change)
11. Is that course being taught by Professor Rivers this semester?
12. When was the radio invented?
13. The mail had already been delivered by the time I . . . .
14. When are the results . . . going to be announced? [Note the plural verb.]
15. After the concert was over, the rock music star was mobbed (outside the theater) by hundreds of fans (outside the theater).
16. . . . because I was told that . . . .
17. The new hospital is going to be built next year. The new elementary school has already been built. [The active sentences with impersonal *they* are acceptable in casual conversation.]
18. If a film is exposed to light while it is being developed, the negatives will be ruined. [The passive makes the sentence more formal and the speaker/writer more distant from the listener/reader.]

◇ WORKBOOK: Practices 7 and 8.

CHART 3-3: INDIRECT OBJECTS AS PASSIVE SUBJECTS

• Students may or may not already be familiar with direct vs. indirect objects.

☐ EXERCISE 6, p. 125. *Using indirect objects as passive subjects.*

TECHNIQUE: *Oral, transformation, teacher-led.*
   You should focus the students' attention on indirect objects. The principal purpose in using the passive in these sentences would be to focus attention on the person (**I.O.**), not on the "thing" (**D.O.**).

ANSWERS: 2. Peggy has been awarded . . . by Indiana University.   3. Fred was paid . . . . [no "*by* phrase"]   4. Maria has been offered . . . by a local . . . .   5. You will be sent a bill . . . . [no "*by* phrase"]   6. The starving people will be given . . . .[no "*by* phrase"]

◇ WORKBOOK: Practice 9.

☐ EXERCISE 7, p. 125. *Changing active to passive.*

TECHNIQUE: *Oral (books closed).*
   This should be a fast-paced exercise. You may want to add specific details to make the items relevant to your students' lives.

ANSWERS: 1. I was invited . . . .[Note the change from question's "you" to answer's "I."]
2. . . . book was written . . . .   3. (include the "*by* phrase")   4. Rice is grown . . . .   5. The letter is being typed by . . . .   6. The game is being televised.   7. Reading is taught in . . . .
8. (. . .) has been offered a good job.   9. I was told to . . . .   10. That book was published in 1985.   11. (. . .) has been sent an . . . .   12. That hat was made in Mexico.   13. Dinner will be served at six.   14. . . .is going to be served.   15. The news will be announced . . . .
16. The exam will be given next week.   17. The bill has been paid.   18. A mistake has been made.   19. The plants have been watered. [Note the plural verb.]   20. A test is being given (by the teacher) in . . . .   21. I am being asked (by the teacher) to . . . .

□ **EXERCISE 8, p. 126.** *Using the passive in conversation.*

TECHNIQUE: *Oral (books closed); chain dialogue.*

You may not want to use every item in this exercise; just choose those that are apt to be most interesting to your students.

Each item will involve you and two students. Student A changes your cue to a passive sentence. Then you turn to Student B and ask a conversational question (from the second column) about the information in Student A's passive sentence. Student B then answers that question with a statement.

As the students speak, you should observe their pronunciation of *-ed* endings. Often students tend to omit the endings or to add unnecessary vowel sounds.

ANSWERS: **1.** A: My pen was stolen. B: It was stolen. **2.** A: Spanish is spoken in many countries. B: Yes. It's spoken in many countries. **3.** A: Soccer is played in many countries. B: (etc.) **4.** That book was written by Mark Twain. **5.** I went to a movie last night, but I was bored. **6.** My letter was returned. **7.** The bank was robbed. **8.** The bank robber was caught (by the police). **9.** The bank robber was sent to jail (by a judge). **10.** Each international student is required to have a visa. **11.** This school was established in 1900. **12.** There's a party tomorrow night, and I've been invited (to go). OR I've been invited (to go) to a party tomorrow night. **13.** I was confused. **14.** Gold was discovered in California in 1848. **15.** A village was attacked by terrorists. OR He/She/The teacher read in the newspaper about a village that was attacked by terrorists. **16.** Candles were used for light in the seventeenth century. **17.** The hijacked plane was flown to another country. **18.** When I had car trouble, I was helped by a passing motorist. **19.** The coffee had already been made by the time I got up this morning. **20.** The chair had already been sold by the time I returned to the store.

□ **EXERCISE 9, p. 127.** *Using verb tenses with the passive.*

TECHNIQUE: *Controlled completion.*

This exercise can be done as written seatwork and then discussed, or it can be done orally. It works equally well with small groups and as a class exercise.

ANSWERS: **2.** is surrounded **3.** is spelled/spelt **4.** is going to/will be built **5.** was/has been divided **6.** is worn **7.** was/had been caused **8.** was ordered **9.** was/had been killed **10.** was reported **11.** was surprised **12.** was offered **13.** were frightened **14.** was confused **15.** is expected

□ **EXERCISE 10, p. 128.** *Using active and passive appropriately.*

TECHNIQUE: *Fill-in-the-blanks.*

ANSWERS: **1.** is produced **2.** will probably be won/is probably going to be won **3.** saw ... was interviewed **4.** are controlled ... are determined **5.** blew ... didn't want ... (had) cost **6.** is being treated **7.** was caught ... was being chased ... jumped ... kept [A "purse-snatcher" is a thief who steals a woman's purse.] **8.** is exposed ... affects ["Frostbite" is the formation of small ice crystals under the skin. In serious cases, it can result in severe damage to the skin.] [Point out that "affect" is a verb; "effect" is a noun.] **9.** appeared ... have been named and described [*Have been* is usually not repeated after *and*.] ... are (being) discovered **10.** has been poisoned ["First aid" is immediate medical treatment.] **11.** is supported ["It" refers to the school.] **12.** was informed ... was told ["Age discrimination" is a legal term similar to racial or sex discrimination. It refers to a situation in which someone is treated unfairly because of his/her age.] **13.** were sent **14.** was discovered ... called ... was translated ... had been built ... do not exist

◇ **WORKBOOK:** Practices 10, 11, 12, 13.

CHART 3-4: THE PASSIVE FORM OF MODALS

- ASSUMPTION: Students are familiar with the meanings of modal auxiliaries (Chapter 2).

- Students should note that there is no difference between singular and plural forms of the passive modals (modal + *be* . . . ; modal + *have been* . . .). Remind them that a modal is always followed immediately by the simple form of a verb. Similar expressions, such as *have to* and *be supposed to*, must agree in number with the subject.

- You might add examples relevant to your students' lives. Have them change passive sentences to active. Examples:

   This room has to be cleaned. → *Someone has to clean this room.*
   Olga should be told about tomorrow's test. → *Someone should tell Olga about* . . . .

☐ **EXERCISE 11, p. 130.** *Using active or passive with modals.*

TECHNIQUE: *Fill-in-the-blanks.*
Compare similar items so that students can see the differences in pairs of sentences where one is passive and the other is active. Encourage discussion of confusing items.

ANSWERS: **4.** must be kept   **5.** must keep   **6.** couldn't be opened   **7.** couldn't open
8. may be offered   **9.** may offer   **10.** may already have been offered   **11.** may already have offered   **12.** ought to be divided   **13.** ought to have been divided   **14.** have to be returned   **15.** has to return   **16.** had better be finished   **17.** had better finish   **18.** is supposed to be sent   **19.** should have been sent   **20.** must've been surprised

☐ **EXERCISE 12, p. 133.** *Using various modals with the passive.*

TECHNIQUE: *Fill-in-the-blanks.*
Encourage more than one answer to some of the items. Students usually enjoy experimenting with various combinations. In the following, the most likely answers are given first, and others are in parentheses.

ANSWERS:
   2. must be married [By custom, a wedding ring is worn on the next-to-last finger of the left hand.]
   3. have to/must be written (are to be written)
   4. must've been left
   5. should/ought to/has to be postponed (had better/must be postponed)
   6. shouldn't be given (must not be/can't be given)
   7. ought to/should be encouraged (must be encouraged)
   8. may/could/might/will be misunderstood
   9. can't be explained [A "UFO" is an Unidentified Flying Object, which some people believe comes from advanced civilizations on distant planets.]
   10. must've been embarrassed
   11. has to be pushed (must be pushed)
   12. should/ought to have been built
   13. must/should be saved (have to be/ought to be saved)
   14. must/has to be done (ought to be/should be done)
   15. ought to/should [advisability] /must/has to [necessity] /will [prediction] be elected (may/might/could [possibility] be elected) [Point out how the meaning significantly changes according to choice of modal.]

◇ **WORKBOOK:** Practices 14, 15, 16.

☐ **EXERCISE 13, p. 134.** *Creating sentences with the passive.*

TECHNIQUE: *Open completion.*

Encourage students to create more than one sentence for each item. Because there are many items, you may wish to divide the students into groups, each with four or five items. Then each group can present their answers to the rest of the class, and discussion of alternatives may follow. This exercise may also be teacher-led with students' books closed.

ANSWERS: [Depend on the students' creativity.]

CHART 3-5: STATIVE PASSIVE

• The stative passive is frequently used in both spoken and written English.

• You may want to demonstrate the relationship between "regular passive" and "stative passive" by using things in your classroom. Examples:

[Close a book.] *I just closed the book.*
                The book was closed by me. [describes an action]
                Now the book is closed. [describes an existing state]

[Have a student (Ali) break a piece of chalk.]

                Ali broke the chalk.
                The chalk was broken by Ali.
                Now the chalk is broken.

☐ **EXERCISE 14, p. 135.** *Forming the stative passive.*

TECHNIQUE: *Fill-in-the-blanks.*

ANSWERS: **2.** was closed [describes an existing state in the past.] **3.** is made   **4.** is (not) shut   **5.** are bent . . . are folded   **6.** is finished [Contrast with the past active: "Class finished at 10 o'clock."]   **7.** are turned   **8.** is not crowded   **9.** is stuck ["To stick" = to be unable to move, as if glued.]   **10.** was stuck   **11.** is made . . . is swept . . . are washed   **12.** is set . . . are done . . . are lighted/lit   **13.** It's gone!   **14.** is torn   **15.** is hidden

☐ **EXERCISE 15, p. 136.** *Using the stative passive.*

TECHNIQUE: *Controlled completion.*

ANSWERS: **2.** is . . . crowded   **3.** is scheduled   **4.** I'm exhausted.   **5.** I'm confused. **6.** are turned off   **7.** is insured   **8.** It's stuck.   **9.** are divorced   **10.** It's gone. **11.** are . . . qualified   **12.** am married   **13.** is spoiled/spoilt   **14.** is blocked   **15.** is located   **16.** was born   **17.** is . . . plugged in   **18.** are . . . done ["done" = "ready"]

◇ **WORKBOOK:** Practices 17 and 18.

☐ **EXERCISE 16, p. 138.** *Using prepositions with the stative passive.*

TECHNIQUE: *Fill-in-the-blanks.*
You may wish to ask students to spell some of the verbs aloud to review the spelling rules in Chart 1-6, p. 9. [See Appendix 2 for a list of verbs with prepositions.]

ANSWERS: **2.** is composed of   **3.** am accustomed to   **4.** is terrified of   **5.** is finished with   **6.** am opposed to   **7.** is covered with   **8.** am satisfied with   **9.** is married to **10.** is divorced from   **11.** am . . . acquainted with   **12.** am tired of   **13.** Are . . . related to

14. is dedicated to   **15.** is disappointed in/with   **16.** is scared of ["Scared of his own shadow" is an idiom describing someone who is very timid or shy.]   **17.** is committed to **18.** are devoted to   **19.** is dressed in   **20.** are done with

ADDITIONAL SUGGESTION: After the exercise is completed, ask the students to close their books. Quickly go through the whole exercise again orally by starting the sentence yourself, pausing for the students to supply a preposition, then finishing the sentence yourself. Use the same sentences in the book or make up your own. Example:

      TEACHER: *Ali is interested* . . . .[pause]
      STUDENTS: *in*
      TEACHER: *in ancient history (rock music/classical art, etc.).*

◇ **WORKBOOK:** Practices 19, 20, 21.

CHART 3-6: THE PASSIVE WITH *GET*

• *Get* has a meaning similar to *become*; in other words, it signals a changing situation or an altered state. To discuss this meaning of *get*, you might ask students to make up their own sentences with *get* + adjective, using a few of the adjectives in the list in the chart's footnote.

☐ **EXERCISE 17, p. 139.**   *Using the passive with* get.

    TECHNIQUE: *Controlled completion.*
      Students can have fun if they read their answers rather dramatically, accompanied by gestures, as if performing in a theater.

    ANSWERS: **2.** I'm getting sleepy.   **3.** It's getting late.   **4.** got wet   **5.** It's getting hot **6.** get nervous   **7.** It's getting dark   **8.** got light   **9.** I'm getting full.   **10.** It's getting better.   **11.** Get busy. ["Shake a leg" = "get moving" = "step on it." All are idioms meaning to move or work faster, to hurry up.]   **12.** Get well [Point out that *well* is an adjective in this sentence and that a "get-well card" is sent only to someone who is ill.]

☐ **EXERCISE 18, p. 140.**   *Forming the passive with* get.

    TECHNIQUE: *Fill-in-the-blanks.*
      This is also a verb tense review exercise.

    ANSWERS: **2.** got hurt   **3.** got lost   **4.** get dressed   **5.** did . . . get married   **6.** get accustomed   **7.** am getting worried   **8.** get upset   **9.** got confused   **10.** get done **11.** got depressed   **12.** Did . . . get invited   **13.** got bored   **14.** get packed   **15.** get paid   **16.** got hired   **17.** got fired   **18.** didn't get finished   **19.** got disgusted   **20.** got engaged . . . got married . . . got divorced . . . got remarried

◇ **WORKBOOK:** Practices 22 and 23.

☐ **EXERCISE 19, p. 142.**   *Creating sentences with the passive and* get.

    TECHNIQUE: *Oral (books closed), open completion.*

    ANSWERS: [Depend on students' creativity.]

□ **EXERCISE 20, p. 142.** *Review of verb tenses, active and passive.*

> TECHNIQUE: *Fill-in-the-blanks.*
>
> *ANSWERS:*
> 1. is usually/usually gets delivered
> 2. were working . . . occurred . . . was/got hurt
> 3. was not admitted (didn't get admitted) . . . had already begun
> 4. is spent [An amount of money is singular grammatically, even though the noun ends in *-s*. See Chart 5-15.]
> 5. was/got held up ["hold up" = delay] . . . took
> 6. had already been offered
> 7. will be used (is going to be used)
> 8. have been studying . . . is getting
> 9. is being organized
> 10. will never be forgotten (is never going to be forgotten)
> 11. arrive . . . will be met . . . will be wearing [at that moment] . . . is [an existing state] . . . has . . . will be standing
> 12. was . . . happened . . . flunked ["Flunk" (slang) = fail a test or a course in school.] . . . dropped . . . was walking . . . fell . . . was stolen ["You should have stayed in bed" is a common expression meaning "If you had not gotten out of bed this morning, you could have avoided all these problems."]

CHART 3-7: PARTICIPIAL ADJECTIVES

• The active meaning of the present participle (the *-ing* form of a verb) is also observed in the progressive. [See Chapter 1.]

• The passive meaning of the past participle (the *-ed* or irregular "third" form of a verb) is also observed in the passive, especially the stative passive.

□ **EXERCISE 21, p. 144.** *Comparing adjectival present and past participles.*

> TECHNIQUE: *Transformation, discussion of meaning.*
>
> Encourage students to raise questions and discuss meanings during this exercise. You may want to explain that the present participle has an active ("giving" or "causing") meaning, but the past participle has a passive ("taking" or "receiving") meaning.
>
> *ANSWERS:* **3.** exciting **4.** excited **5.** surprising **6.** surprised **7.** frightened **8.** frightening **9.** exhausting **10.** exhausted

□ **EXERCISE 22, p. 144.** *Using participial adjectives.*

> TECHNIQUE: *Oral (books closed), transformation.*
>
> *ANSWERS:* **1.** amazing . . . amazed **2.** depressing . . . depressed **3.** tired . . . tiring **4.** boring . . . bored **5.** interested . . . interesting [etc.]

◇ **WORKBOOK:** Practice 24.

□ **EXERCISE 23, p. 145.** *Using participial adjectives.*

> TECHNIQUE: *Fill-in-the-blanks.*
>
> Check on the spelling of the participles, especially "*y*" vs. "*i*" and doubling of consonants.
>
> *ANSWERS:* **2.** satisfying **3.** terrifying **4.** terrified **5.** embarrassing **6.** broken

52 □ *CHAPTER 3, The Passive*

7. damaging   **8.** damaged   **9.** crowded. ["Elbowed" means to push people aside with one's elbow or arm.]   **10.** enduring [In this sense, "endure" means to last or continue for a long time.]   **11.** deserted   **12.** locked   **13.** lasting   **14.** injured   **15.** frozen

☐ **EXERCISE 24, p. 146.**   *Using participial adjectives.*

TECHNIQUE: *Fill-in-the-blanks.*

ANSWERS: **2.** annoying   **3.** given . . . following   **4.** challenging   **5.** expected
6. growing . . . balanced   **7.** sleeping [This saying means: "Don't change anything and cause problems."]   **8.** spoiled/spoilt [A child who is accustomed to receiving immediately everything he/she wants is said to be "spoiled," in other words unpleasant, like rotten food.]   **9.** leading
10. wasted   **11.** thrilling ["Hair-raising" means so frightening that it causes one's hair to stand up on one's neck or head.]   **12.** flying   **13.** abandoned [A "tow truck" is a service vehicle that pulls broken-down cars.]   **14.** thinking   **15.** required   **16.** bustling ["bustling" = busy, somewhat noisy, crowded]

◇ **WORKBOOK:** Practices 25 and 26.

☐ **EXERCISE 25, p. 147.**   *Correct usage of the passive, tenses, spelling, etc.*

TECHNIQUE: *Error analysis.*

ANSWERS: **1.** interest**ed**   **2.** people [no -*s*] . . . have you [no *been*] invited   **3.** everything **was quiet** . . . walk**ed** . . . **got** undress**ed** . . . **went**   **4.** had already [no *been*] eaten   **5.** confus**ed**
6. frighten**ed**   **7.** we **were** very . . . [possibly *those*—in the past, therefore distant; *these* is also acceptable] . . . we **ran** . . . scar**ed** . . . **see**   **8.** axe **fell** . . . began . . . **did** not

◇ **WORKBOOK:** Practices 27, 28, 29.

☐ **EXERCISE 26, p. 148.**   *Using tenses, active, passive, etc., in writing.*

TECHNIQUE: *Written homework.*
Tell the class how long you expect their compositions to be. Discuss possible methods of organization: for example, an introductory paragraph followed by several paragraphs containing a chronological summary of the person's life, leading to a conclusion about that person's life.
Sometimes students tend to overuse the passive for a while after they have been concentrating on it in class. Remind them that most sentences are active. Most of the sentences in this exercise will be active, but the passive will also occur (*was born, was married, is interested in, has always been committed to,* etc.).

◇ **WORKBOOK:** Have students take Practice Test A and/or B.

☐ **EXERCISE 27, p. 148.**   *Phrasal verbs.*

TECHNIQUE: *Seatwork, fill-in-the-blanks, teacher-led oral.*
[See Appendix 2 for a list of common two-word and three-word verbs.]

ANSWERS: **1.** in   **2.** on . . . off   **3.** back   **4.** in/by [*Over* is also possible.]   **5.** out
6. out   **7.** up   **8.** up . . . away   **9.** out [Note: One "fills *out*" a large item such as an application form, but "fills *in*" a small space such as a blank in an exercise. Also: "fill *up*" (British) = "fill *in*" (American).] . . . back   **10.** up ["catch up with him" (American) = "catch him up" (British)]   **11.** on   **12.** out

Chapter 4: GERUNDS AND INFINITIVES

ORDER OF CHAPTER	CHARTS	EXERCISES	WORKBOOK
Form of gerunds	4-1		
Gerunds as the objects of prepositions	4-2	Ex. 1 → 4	Pr. 1 → 2
Verbs followed by gerunds	4-3 → 4-4	Ex. 5 → 7	Pr. 3
Cumulative review and practice		Ex. 8	
Verbs followed by infinitives	4-5	Ex. 9 → 11	Pr. 4 → 6
Verbs followed by infinitives or gerunds	4-6	Ex. 12	Pr. 7
Cumulative review and practice		Ex. 13 → 15	Pr. 8
Reference lists of verbs	4-7 → 4-8	Ex. 16 → 17	Pr. 9 → 13
Gerunds as subjects	4-9	Ex. 18	Pr. 14
It + infinitive	4-9	Ex. 19 → 21	Pr. 15
Infinitive of purpose	4-10	Ex. 22 → 23	Pr. 16
Infinitives with adjectives, *too, enough*	4-11 → 4-12	Ex. 24 → 27	Pr. 17 → 18
Passive gerunds and infinitives	4-13 → 4-14	Ex. 28 → 30	Pr. 19 → 22
Gerunds with possessive modifiers	4-15	Ex. 31	Pr. 23
Cumulative review and practice		Ex. 32	Pr. 24 → 25
Special verbs and expressions	4-16 → 4-19	Ex. 33 → 37	Pr. 26 → 30
Cumulative review and practice		Ex. 38 → 41	Pr. 31 → 35 Pr. Tests A & B

General Notes on Chapter 4

• OBJECTIVE: Gerunds and infinitives are common features of both spoken and written English (as the following underlines demonstrate). A person who tries to speak English without using gerunds and infinitives will produce very unnatural-sounding sentences. Learning to understand and use these structures fluently is important for students.

• APPROACH: The chapter begins with gerunds and their functions, then introduces infinitives, then special groups of verbs followed by either a gerund or an infinitive. Next, other uses of gerunds and infinitives are presented, and then uses of the simple form are introduced. Throughout, the emphasis is on becoming comfortable with these structures through practice, not memorization. The cumulative exercises include review of various verb tenses and the passive, which were introduced in earlier chapters.

• TERMINOLOGY: Like many traditional terms in grammar, "gerund" and "infinitive" were borrowed from analyses of the Latin language; they do not fit the description of the English language equally as well. In this text, the combination "to + simple form of a verb" is called an **infinitive** (*to be, to fly*). The **"simple" form of a verb** is the base form with no indication of tense or number (*be, fly*). A **gerund** is a "verb + *ing*" that functions like a noun (*being, flying*).

CHART 4-1: GERUNDS: INTRODUCTION

• Students should learn that "gerund" is the name of a <u>form</u> based on a verb. A gerund may have the <u>function</u> of subject or object in a sentence.

• In Chapter 1, students learned that some verbs (such as *know, need, want*) usually have no progressive form, and they may hesitate to use the -*ing* form of these verbs. Point out that these verbs can be used as gerunds:

    INCORRECT: *I am knowing John.* [progressive form is not appropriate]
    CORRECT: *Knowing John is a pleasure.* [gerund as subject]
    CORRECT: *I insist on knowing the truth.* [gerund as object of a preposition]

• Because a gerund is based on a verb form, it can have an object and be modified by adverbial phrases.
    I play games. = vb + obj → *Playing games is fun.* = gerund + obj
    We play in the park. = vb + prep. phr. → *Playing in the park is fun.* = gerund + prep. phr.
    → *Playing games in the park is fun.* = gerund + obj + prep. phr

• You may wish to introduce the term "gerund phrase." A gerund with its associated object or modifier is called a "gerund phrase." In the above examples, *playing games, playing in the park,* and *playing games in the park* are gerund phrases.

CHART 4-2: USING GERUNDS AS THE OBJECTS OF PREPOSITIONS

• A gerund can immediately follow a preposition, but an infinitive cannot.

• The exception that proves the rule: in one idiom, a preposition is followed by an infinitive, not by a gerund: *be about,* meaning "ready for immediate action." For example: *I am <u>about to open</u> my book.*

☐ **EXERCISE 1, p. 151.***   *Gerunds after prepositions.*

After students work out a few of the answers, you might divide the class in half and do this exercise orally and rather quickly. As a variation, you read aloud from the book, pause for one group to say the preposition, signal the other group to say the gerund, then finish the sentence yourself. For example:

---

*The types of exercises in this chapter are similar to those in the preceding three chapters. See the INTRODUCTION, pp. ix–xvii, for suggestions about techniques for using exercises.

TEACHER: *Alice isn't interested . . . .[pause]*
GROUP A: *in*
GROUP B: *looking*
TEACHER: *in looking for a new job.*

Group B's answer will always be a gerund, thus underscoring the main point of Chart 4-2.

Appendix 2 contains a list of prepositional combinations with verbs and adjectives. The students can refer to it if they wish.

ANSWERS: **2.** about leaving   **3.** of doing   **4.** for being   **5.** to having [possible in British English: *to have*]   **6.** from completing   **7.** about having   **8.** of studying   **9.** for helping **10.** (up)on knowing   **11.** by drawing [*By* + gerund = **how** something is done; see Exercise 4.] **12.** of living   **13.** for not going   **14.** in searching   **15.** for making   **16.** for not wanting **17.** for washing and drying [Point out parallel structure.]   **18.** to going   **19.** from speaking **20.** to going   **21.** of clarifying   **22.** of stealing   **23.** of taking . . . (of) keeping [parallel structure]   **24.** to wearing   **25.** to eating . . . (to) sleeping [parallel structure]

□ **EXERCISE 2, p. 152.** *Using gerunds after prepositions.*

You may wish to point out that short answers ("Yes, she did.") are more natural in response to conversational questions. However, in this exercise the students should respond with complete sentences in order to practice using gerunds.

ANSWERS:
 1. Yes, I had a good excuse for being late . . /No, I didn't have . . . .
 2. Yes, I'm (really) looking forward to visiting them./No, I'm not looking . . . .
 3. Yes, I thanked him/her for picking it up./No, I didn't thank . . . .
 4. No, I'm not accustomed to living . . . /Yes, I'm accustomed to living . . . .
 5. Yes, I'm excited about going . . . /No, I'm not excited about going . . . .
 6. Yes, I apologized . . . ./No, I didn't apologize for interrupting her . . . .
 7. Yes, all of them participated in doing . . . /No, some of them did not participate in doing the pantomimes.
 8. No, I don't know . . . /Yes, I know who is responsible for breaking . . . .
 9. No, I'm not used to having . . . /Yes, I'm used to having my biggest meal . . . .
 10. The hot/cold weather prevents me from (. . .)ing . . . .
 11. No, s/he doesn't complain . . . /Yes, s/he complains about having to do a lot of homework.
 12. No, I don't blame him/her for staying home in bed. [A negative answer is expected.]
 13. S/He [past tense verb] instead of studying.
 14. In addition to studying grammar last night, I [past tense verb].

□ **EXERCISE 3, p. 153.** *Using gerund phrases after prepositions.*

This can be done as individual homework or small group seatwork. Then some sentences can be written on the chalkboard and discussed. Alternatively, students can simply call out their completions.

ANSWERS: **2.** . . . for lending me (her dictionary).   **3.** . . . about going to . . . .   **4.** . . . to living (in . . .)   **5.** . . . about having (a headache).   **6.** . . . for not wanting (another roommate).   **7.** . . . for being (late).   **8.** . . . about missing (my bus).   **9.** . . . in finding out about . . . .   **10.** about going . . . .   **11.** . . . for being . . . .   **12.** . . . to driving (fast). **13.** . . . from going . . . .   **14.** . . . for taking care of . . . ?

◇ **WORKBOOK:** Practices 1 and 2.

EXERCISE 4, p. 154. *Using* by *+ a gerund.*

You can read the beginning of a sentence and have one or two students finish it by calling out their completions. Discuss any problems.

POSSIBLE ANSWERS: [Depend on students' ideas.]

CHART 4-3: COMMON VERBS FOLLOWED BY GERUNDS

• This chart and the next exercises present just a few of the verbs that are followed by gerunds. Students may want to memorize the list, but a more effective way to learn them is to practice them both orally and in writing.

EXERCISE 5, p. 155. *Using gerunds after certain verbs.*

Encourage the students to use various tenses and to include interesting information in their sentences.

ANSWERS: [Depend on students' creativity.]

EXERCISE 6, p. 155. *Using gerunds.*

POSSIBLE ANSWERS: **2.** Opening/closing/shutting **3.** raining/snowing **4.** running/going **5.** going for/taking **6.** studying/working **7.** having/giving/hosting, etc. **8.** laughing/giggling **9.** crashing into/colliding with/hitting/running into **10.** going/travel(l)ing **11.** doing/starting **12.** making **13.** going/flying **14.** taking/riding **15.** being

---

CHART 4-4: *GO* + GERUND

• Some grammarians disagree about the nature of these *-ing* words: are they gerunds or participles? For your students, terminology is much less important than idiomatic use. We will call these structures gerunds.

• Definitions of some vocabulary items in the chart:

birdwatching = a hobby for people who enjoy identifying birds in natural habitats
bowling = an indoor sport in which a heavy ball is rolled toward 9 or 10 wooden pins to knock them down
camping = living in a tent or trailer for fun; "getting back to nature"
canoeing = floating on a river or lake in a small, simple boat called a canoe (pronounced /kə-**nu**/)
hiking = athletic walking in the mountains or countryside (possibly while carrying equipment in a pack on one's back = *to go backpacking*)
jogging = running somewhat slowly for exercise
sailing = floating on a lake or sea in a boat that has a sail or perhaps a motor for power
sightseeing = touring; traveling to see famous or beautiful places
sledding = in winter, going down a snowy hill using a sled, which is a wooden seat on metal bars that can slide quickly over the snow
tobogganing = similar to sledding; a toboggan is a long, flat wooden structure for several people to sit on while going down a snowy hill
window shopping = looking into shop windows, but perhaps not intending to buy anything

• Depending upon their cultural attitudes, students may enjoy learning the expression *go skinny dipping* (to go swimming without a bathing suit).

□ **EXERCISE 7, p. 156.** *Verbs & gerunds.*

This can be used for pair or group work as an alternative to teacher-led oral. All of the sentences require the use of gerunds.

ANSWERS: [Depend on students' ideas.] Note that items 8, 10, 12, 14, and 18 have two gerunds together; e.g., **8.** . . . talk(ed) about *going swimming* . . . .

◇ **WORKBOOK:** Practice 3.

```
┌─────────────────────────────────────────────────────────────┐
│ CHART 4-5: COMMON VERBS FOLLOWED BY INFINITIVES              │
├─────────────────────────────────────────────────────────────┤
```

• The passive examples (f) and (g) assume that students are familiar with the basic forms in Chapter 3. If they aren't, you may need to explain them, because the passive is used in Exercises 8 through 11.

• The alternative structures in the notes below this chart are important for the following exercise. You should call the students' attention to these sentences.

◇ **WORKBOOK:** Practice 4.

□ **EXERCISE 8, p. 157.** *Verbs followed by infinitives or gerunds.*

POSSIBLE ANSWERS: **3.** to find/look for/get **4.** to do/hand in **5.** playing/watching **6.** to lend/loan **7.** to come **8.** to finish ["ASAP" is spoken as individual letters, not as a word. It is not often used outside an office context.] **9.** to get/buy **10.** to be . . . talking **11.** getting . . . to wait **12.** to use **13.** to write **14.** not to touch **15.** being/living, etc. **16.** to be **17.** (not) to know **18.** to write **19.** to own/keep/have **20.** to take **21.** to mail/open/hold, etc. **22.** to mail/open **23.** to find **24.** to find **25.** finding **26.** finding **27.** to take **28.** taking

□ **EXERCISE 9, p. 159.** *Verbs + infinitives to report speech.*

The answers are in the form of reported (or indirect) speech. The cues are in quoted (or direct) speech. Chapter 7 contains charts 7-6 and 7-7 on quoted and reported speech, but students probably don't need that lesson in order to complete this exercise. Students can understand that verb + infinitive is a way of reporting what someone has said. You may wish to point out the equivalency between modals/imperatives in quoted speech and verb + infinitive in reported speech. Or you may wish not to discuss the concept of quoted vs. reported speech at all.

Show the students how item 1 was produced. Give them time to write their answers. Then review all their answers orally, with each student reading one answer aloud. Discussion can follow each item that causes difficulty.

ANSWERS: **2.** The secretary asked me to give this note to Sue./I was asked to give this note to Sue. **3.** My advisor advised me to take Biology 109. [This rather awkward sentence includes both "advisor" and "advised."]/I was advised to take Biology 109. [This sentence avoids the awkwardness.] **4.** When . . . , the judge ordered me to pay . . . /. . . , I was ordered to pay . . . . **5.** During . . . , the teacher warned Greg to keep his eyes on his own paper./. . . Greg was warned to keep his . . . . **6.** During . . . , the teacher warned Greg not to look at his neighbor's paper./. . . , Greg was warned not to look . . . . **7.** At . . . , the head of the department reminded the faculty to turn in their . . . /. . . , the faculty were (OR was) reminded to turn in their . . . . **8.** Mr. Lee told the children to be quiet./The children were told to be quiet. **9.** The hijacker forced the pilot to land the plane./The pilot was forced to . . . . [A hijacker is someone who takes control of a plane, train, bus, etc. by force.] **10.** When . . . , my parents allowed me to stay up late .../..., I was allowed to stay up late.... **11.** The teacher encouraged the students to speak slowly and clearly./The students were encouraged to speak slowly and clearly. **12.** The teacher always expects the students to come to class on time./The students are always expected to come...

☐ **EXERCISE 10, p. 161.** *Using verbs followed by infinitives.*

You may want to allow students to work in small groups. Then, an individual can read the cue aloud rather dramatically, and two other students can read the reported forms. No ''*by* -phrase'' should be included in the answers.

ANSWERS:

   2. The general ordered the soldiers to surround.../The soldiers were ordered to surround....
   3. Nancy asked me to open the window./I was asked to....
   4. Bob reminded me to take my book.../I was reminded to....
   5. Paul encouraged/advised me to take singing lessons./I was advised to take....
   6. Mrs. Anderson warned the children not to play with matches./The children were warned not to....
   7. The Dean of Admissions permitted me to register for school late./I was permitted to register....
   8. The law requires every driver to have a.../Every driver is required to have a....
   9. My friend advised me to get.../I was advised to get....
   10. The robber forced me to give him all of my money./I was forced to give (the robber) all of my money (to the robber). [either position]
   11. Before..., the teacher advised/told/warned/reminded the students to work quickly. [The choice of verb gives information about *how* the teacher spoke to the students.]/Before..., the students were... to work quickly.
   12. My boss asked/advised/ordered/reminded/told me to come.../I was... to come.... [Again, the verb contains important information about *how* the boss spoke.]

◇ **WORKBOOK:** Practices 5 and 6.

☐ **EXERCISE 11, p. 161.** *Verbs followed by infinitives, active/passive.*

This exercise follows the same pattern as Exercises 9 and 10. Students should now be able to use their own ideas to create appropriate sentences.

ANSWERS: [Depend on students' ideas.]

CHART 4-6: COMMON VERBS FOLLOWED BY EITHER INFINITIVES OR GERUNDS

• The complex history of the English language—elements from German, French, Norse, etc.—has produced the parallel forms in Group A. Learners should be confident that using the infinitive or gerund with these verbs causes no real change in meaning.

• Native speakers of English do not always agree on the use of the forms in Group A. Some differences exist among speakers in various geographical regions.

• The differences with Group B verbs are great, and students need practice in order to understand and use them appropriately. Using an infinitive instead of a gerund with one of these verbs causes a significant change in meaning.

☐ **EXERCISES 12 & 13, pp. 163–165.**   *Choosing between gerunds and infinitives.*

The answers to these two exercises will probably raise many questions that need to be discussed briefly. Therefore, it is best to do the two orally with the whole class, although you might have students work in small groups on Exercise 13.

EX. 12 ANSWERS: **2.** to leave/leaving   **3.** to lecture/lecturing   **4.** to swim/swimming   **5.** to see/seeing [*Living* is a present participle (adjective) that modifies the gerund (noun) *being*; a living being is a human or an animal.]   **6.** to move/moving...to race/racing...to move...to race [Choose the infinitive after a progressive verb.]   **7.** driving...taking   **8.** to drive... (to) take [Some people might also use gerunds.]   **9.** to turn   **10.** being   **11.** to give   **12.** playing   **13.** doing   **14.** to do   **15.** to do   **16.** carrying [It is traditional for a husband to carry his new wife through the doorway (over the threshold) of their first home.]   **17.** watching   **18.** to do   **19.** to inform   **20.** not listening   **21.** to explain   **22.** holding...feeding... burping [to burp = (to cause) to belch or to expel air from the stomach through the mouth]... changing.

EX. 13 ANSWERS: **2.** cleaning   **3.** to take   **4.** to leave   **5.** to talk/talking   **6.** waiting... doing   **7.** to stay...paint [*To* is usually not repeated after *and*.]   **8.** quitting...opening   **9.** to take   **10.** looking...to answer   **11.** postponing   **12.** watching...listening   **13.** to read/reading   **14.** to go camping [''To go to camp'' includes the <u>noun</u> *camp* after the preposition *to*—not an infinitive.]   **15.** singing   **16.** to take...to pay   **17.** to stand   **18.** not to wait

◇ **WORKBOOK:** Practice 7.

☐ **EXERCISE 14, p. 166.**   *Using infinitives and gerunds after verbs.*

This is a good opportunity to review verb tenses, singular-plural agreement, and modals as well as infinitives and gerunds. You may want to follow the oral exercise with an assignment for the students to write 10 or 15 of their best sentences for homework. Or you could turn the exercise into a quiz, with the students writing sentences from your spoken cues.

ANSWERS: [Depend on students' creativity.]

☐ **EXERCISE 15, p. 166.**   *Using infinitives and gerunds after verbs.*

This is a review of Chapter 4 to this point.

ANSWERS: **1.** talking   **2.** to play...not to make   **3.** to look after   **4.** paying   **5.** to chase/chasing   **6.** going...to go   **7.** going skiing   **8.** not to smoke   **9.** not to know/not knowing   **10.** whistling...to concentrate   **11.** to quit...(to) look for   **12.** to turn off [*Turning off* would give a quite different meaning and would be unlikely in this situation; possibly one might say, ''Think carefully. Do you remember turning off the stove? We don't want our house to burn down!'' Also: *stove* = *cooker* in British English.]   **13.** to renew   **14.** not to wait   **15.** not to play   **16.** to call   **17.** to throw away...(to) buy [The second *to* is usually omitted in parallel structure.]   **18.** dropping out of...hitchhiking...trying to find   **19.** to tell...to call...going swimming   **20.** to ask...to tell...to remember to bring

◇ **WORKBOOK:** Practice 8.

• These lists are for students to refer to, not to memorize. The following exercises and the workbook provide a lot of practice, but learners don't have to learn the lists by heart.

• Ask for and answer any questions about vocabulary.

• You could create an oral (books closed) exercise using these charts. Select some of the sentences at random and ask students to put the verbs in their proper gerund or infinitive forms. For example:

TEACHER (choosing #7 from Section A in Chart 4-8): "I don't care" [pause] "see that show."
STUDENT: "I don't care to see that show."
TEACHER: (Perhaps repeat the correct answer. Then choose another item, such as #5 from Chart 4-7): "He avoided" [pause] "answer my question."
STUDENT: "He avoided answering my/your question."
etc.

□ EXERCISE 16, p. 170.   *Choosing between gerunds and infinitives.*

This is a mechanical exercise so that students can focus on choosing the gerund or the infinitive after certain verbs. The whole class can answer together. As suggested in the book, you could then repeat the exercise, with individual students using their own words to complete each sentence.

ANSWERS:

1. to do it	11. to do it	21. to do it	31. doing it
2. doing it	12. to do it	22. doing it?	32. to do it
3. to do it	13. to do it	23. doing it?	33. to do it
4. to do it	14. doing it	24. to do it	34. to do it
5. to do it	15. to do it	25. doing it	35. doing it
6. doing it	16. to do it	26. doing it	36. to do it
7. doing it	17. to do it	27. to do it	37. to do it
8. to do it	18. to do it	28. doing it	38. doing it
9. doing it	19. doing it	29. to do it?	39. doing it
10. doing it	20. to do it	30. doing it	40. doing it

□ EXERCISE 17, p. 170.   *Using gerunds and infinitives.*

If they did Exercise 16 well, students should be able to complete most of these sentences without looking at the reference charts. However, they may have trouble remembering some items, so you might allow them to look at the charts or to discuss those problems briefly with each other.

ANSWERS:

1. to race	7. to know	13. worrying	19. to have
2. to bring	8. being	14. to play	20. being
3. pronouncing	9. telling	15. telling	21. hearing
4. to eat	10. to be	16. taking	22. promising to visit
5. to hang up	11. to do	17. to buy	23. hoping . . . praying
6. to pull	12. to return . . .	18. to change	24. to persuade . . . to
	(to) finish		stay . . . (to) finish

◇ WORKBOOK: Practices 9, 10, 11, 12, 13.

```
┌──────────────────────────────────────────────────────────────────────┐
│   CHART 4-9:  USING GERUNDS AS SUBJECTS:  USING IT +                    │
│               INFINITIVE                                                │
├──────────────────────────────────────────────────────────────────────┘
```

• You may need to point out that a gerund subject is singular and requires a singular form of the verb: *Playing games is fun.*

• The emphasis in Chart 4-9 and Exercises 18 to 21 is on the **it** + *infinitive* structure, a frequent pattern in both speech and writing.

• Of course, **it** + *gerund* is also possible, and some students may produce some examples. Also, an infinitive can be the subject of a sentence. Commend students if they use these correctly, but return their attention to the more common **it** + *infinitive* and *gerund as subject* patterns in this lesson.

☐ **EXERCISE 18, p. 172.** *Gerunds as subjects.*

After giving the example, ask students to complete the same sentence with other gerund phrases. Ask for several different responses for each item so that students have a chance to think of meaningful sentences in this pattern. Encourage them to use a whole phrase (e.g., ''climbing to the top of a mountain''), not just the gerund.

ANSWERS: [Depend on students' creativity.]

☐ **EXERCISE 19, p. 172.** *Gerund vs. it + infinitive.*

Students can work in pairs, or one student in class can read the item and another respond. This is a mechanical exercise, allowing students to focus on the forms. They should understand that both forms of a sentence have the same meaning.

ANSWERS: **3.** It is important to vote . . . .   **4.** Meeting the king and queen was exciting. **5.** It would be interesting to hear . . . .   **6.** Seeing Joan awake . . . is unusual.   **7.** If you know how, floating in water for a long time is easy.   **8.** It takes time and patience to master . . . . **9.** It will take us ten hours to drive to Atlanta.   **10.** Diving into the sea from a high cliff takes courage.

☐ **EXERCISE 20, p. 173.** *Using gerunds and infinitives.*

Students must listen carefully to each other in this exercise. Student A's answer is used by Student B. As with Exercise 18, you could ask for several different responses to each item for additional practice.

ANSWERS: [Depend on students' creativity.]

☐ **EXERCISE 21, p. 173.** *Using for (someone) + infinitive.*

This exercise has two purposes. One is to teach the correct **location** of the ''*for (someone)*'' phrase between the adjective and the infinitive. (For example, it is incorrect in English to say *It is important to go for me./It for me is important to go./It is for me important to go.*)
    The other purpose is to demonstrate the **meaning** and **use** of the ''*for (someone)*'' phrase. It limits the meaning of a general statement. For example, item 3 (''It's easy to speak Spanish.'') is not true for most people, so it's necessary to limit that statement to some person or group (''It's easy for Venezuelans to speak Spanish.'').

POSSIBLE ANSWERS: **3.** It's easy for Carlos to speak Spanish.   **4.** It's important for us to learn English so that we can read scientific books.   **5.** It's unusual for Jerry to be late for dinner because he's always hungry.   **6.** It's essential for you to get a visa if you plan to visit the Soviet Union on your trip next summer. Etc.

◇ **WORKBOOK:** Practices 14 and 15.

> **CHART 4-10: INFINITIVE OF PURPOSE:** *IN ORDER TO*
>
> • Additional examples for the footnote:
>
>   (general) *An encyclopedia is used for locating facts and information.*
>   (specific) *I used the encyclopedia to locate facts about India.*
>
>   (general) *Knives are used for cutting or slicing.*
>   (specific) *My brother used a knife to cut his birthday cake.*

☐ **EXERCISE 22, p. 174.** *Typical errors with infinitives of purpose.*

Allow students some time to find errors in the sentences, then lead the class in a discussion of their corrections.

ANSWERS: **1.** Helen borrowed my dictionary *(in order) to* look up . . . .   **2.** I went to the library *(in order) to* study last night.   **3.** The teacher opened the window *(in order) to* get some fresh air in the room.   **4.** I came to this school *(in order) to* learn English.   **5.** I need to get a part-time job *(in order) to* earn . . . .

☐ **EXERCISE 23, p. 174.** *Using infinitives and prepositions of purpose.*

This exercise contrasts the infinitive of purpose (*in order to*) with a prepositional phrase of purpose (*for* + noun). Encourage students to give more than one completion for each item.

POSSIBLE ANSWERS: **3.** . . . to buy some soap.   **4.** . . . for some soap.   **5.** . . . to have my blood pressure checked.   **6.** . . . for a checkup.   **7.** . . . to keep in shape.   **8.** . . . for health and fitness.   **9.** . . . to get some gas(oline)/petrol.   **10.** . . . for gas(oline)/petrol.

ADDITIONAL PRACTICE: Here is an Oral (books closed) exercise from the first edition of the textbook. It enables you to give additional communicative practice using the students' names and couching the cue in familiar situations. For example:
    CUE: (. . .) went to the library. He/She wanted to study.
    TEACHER: *Ali is a good student. He studies every night. Last night he went to the library. He wanted to study grammar. Why did Ali go to the library?* (Ask one student or all.)
    STUDENT(S): *He went to the library (in order) to study grammar.*
  1. (. . .) picked up the phone. She wanted to call her husband./He wanted to call his wife.
    TEACHER: *Yesterday Tania was at home. Dinner was ready, but her husband still wasn't home. He was at his office. She decided to call him. Why did Tania pick up the phone?* [**Answer:** . . . to call her husband and ask why he wasn't home.]
  2. Before class, (. . .) walked to the front of the room. He/She wanted to ask me a question.
  3. (. . .) took out his/her dictionary. He/She wanted to look up a word.
  4. (. . .) wants to improve his/her English. He/She reads a lot of books and magazines.
  5. (. . .) wanted to pay his/her bill at the restaurant. He/She took out his/her wallet.
  6. (. . .) turned off the lights. He/She wanted to save energy.
  7. (. . .) turned on the stove/cooker. He/She wanted to heat some water for tea.

◇ **WORKBOOK:** Practice 16.

CHART 4-11: ADJECTIVES FOLLOWED BY INFINITIVES

• This list is not complete; however, many of the most frequently used adjectives are included here.

• Many of these adjectives can be followed by other structures. For example:
I was *happy about going* to the circus. (preposition + gerund)
I was *happy watching* the clouds float by. (present participle)
It is not necessary to mention these structures to the learners at this point. Their focus should remain on *adjective + infinitive*.

☐ **EXERCISE 24, p. 175.** *Adjectives followed by infinitives.*

EXPECTED ANSWERS: **3.** to be **4.** to die/to surrender/to fight **5.** to go **6.** to stay...read [*To* is usually not repeated after *and.*] **7.** to help **8.** to study/to learn **9.** to slip/to fall **10.** to walk **11.** to walk/to drive/to go/to stay/to be **12.** to be **13.** to see **14.** to hear/to learn/to read

☐ **EXERCISE 25, p. 176.** *Using infinitives after adjectives.*

This exercise can be done as a dialogue between you and the students or as student-student pair work. If the contexts seem unreal or inappropriate for your situation, you may want to substitute other items. No exercise in this book can be perfect for every circumstance, so you should consider changing some items to suit your needs.

ANSWERS: [Depend on students' ideas.]

◇ **WORKBOOK:** Practice 17.

CHART 4-12: USING INFINITIVES WITH *TOO* AND *ENOUGH*

• Learners of English often fail to understand that the word *too* before an adjective has a negative meaning.

• The word order with *enough* is important to practice: it comes <u>after</u> an adjective or adverb but usually <u>before</u> a noun. Note the difference in structure and meaning:

(a) We don't have **enough big envelopes.** = We have an insufficient number; *enough* modifies the noun *envelopes.*
(b) We don't have **big enough envelopes.** = Our envelopes are too small; *enough* modifies the adjective *big.*

☐ **EXERCISE 26, p. 177.** *Using too with infinitives.*

Students must understand what a "negative result" is. In item 1, for example, the speaker obviously wants to buy a ring. But, because the ring is *too* expensive, the result is negative: he/she is <u>not able</u> to buy the ring.

POSSIBLE ANSWERS: **3.** I can't get to class on time. It's too late for me to.... **4.** We can't go swimming. It's too cold for us to.... **5.** I don't want to study it. It's too...for me.... **6.** I can't watch TV now. I'm too busy to.... **7.** He shouldn't play football. He's too young to.... **8.** They can't climb the cliff. It's too steep for them to.... **10.** I can go to the meeting. I'm not too tired to.... **11.** I can lift/carry it.... **12.** I can watch TV now....

◇ **WORKBOOK:** Practice 18.

☐ **EXERCISE 27, p. 178.** *Using* enough *and* too *with infinitives.*

Because the students' books are closed, you may need to repeat a cue or add some brief contextual information to help them understand the cue. This exercise intends to touch upon typical student misunderstandings in the use of *too* instead of *very* (e.g., INCORRECT: *My country is too beautiful.*).

POSSIBLE ANSWERS:

1. A child is too young to read a long novel, but an adult is old enough to appreciate good literature. [Have the students come up with various ideas, then compare "too young" with "very young" in item #2.]
2. She's very young. [Also: She's old enough/not too young to begin walking and talking.]
3. very [Note: In the negative, *too* and *very* can express the same idea: "It wasn't too good/It wasn't very good." = "I didn't like it much." But here the cue says it was a good dinner.]
4. very ["It's *too* difficult" = "It's impossible to learn," which is not true. Perhaps give your students a pep talk and praise their progress.]
5. very [Ask your students if something can be "too clean."]
6. very OR too [depending on student's idea, with *too* implying negative result]
7. [demonstrate *enough* and *too*]
8. very
9. very [The highest mountain in the world is Mt. Everest: 5.5 miles, 8.9 kilometers above sea level; approximately 29,000 feet or 8,800 meters.]
10. [Discuss placement of *enough*: when it follows a noun, it may seem somewhat formal or literary. In everyday English, it usually comes in front of a noun.]

CHART 4-13: PAST AND PASSIVE FORMS OF INFINITIVES AND GERUNDS

• Chapter 3 presents the passive. You may wish to review the notions of "passive verb" and "*by*-phrase" with your students.

• Students may want to consult the reference lists of verbs followed by infinitives or gerunds, pp. 168–169.

• The following chart might be helpful for your students when you explain that an infinitive or gerund can be either simple or past, and that these forms can be either passive or active.

		SIMPLE	PAST
ACTIVE	inf:	to see	to have seen
	ger:	seeing	having seen
PASSIVE	inf:	to be seen	to have been seen
	ger:	being seen	having been seen

◇ **WORKBOOK:** Practices 19 and 20.

☐ **EXERCISE 28, p. 179.** *Passive & past forms of infinitives & gerunds.*

This exercise requires students to think about tenses, verbs that require infinitives or gerunds, and relationships in time. Allow plenty of time for them to prepare their answer to an item, then discuss any misunderstanding.

As the footnote on page 179 explains, sometimes a simple gerund can be used with a past tense main verb even though the gerund's action occurred earlier in time. This shows that the English language is changing—not everyone always uses these forms in the same way. But both forms are still in common use, so students need to learn their normal functions.

ANSWERS: 4. being hit ["barely" = almost unable]   5. to be told [by us]   6. having written   7. having been asked [Note: Something that has a base (a building, a candle) is usually said to "burn down." Other things "burn up."]   8. to have been given   9. being told 10. to be loved . . . needed [*To be* is usually not repeated in the parallel structure.] 11. watching   12. not having written [*sooner* = earlier, before now]

☐ EXERCISE 29, p. 180.   *Passive & past forms of infinitives & gerunds.*

ANSWERS: 1. being photographed   2. to have escaped   3. to have had   4. having gone 5. meeting/having met   6. to be sent   7. to be told   8. to have recovered . . . to be 9. having had   10. having   11. not having been told . . . to be informed

◇ WORKBOOK: Practices 21 and 22.

CHART 4-14: USING GERUNDS OR PASSIVE INFINITIVES FOLLOWING *NEED*

• British English can also use *want* in (c) and (d), but American English can use only *need* in those cases. For example: *The fence wants painting.*

☐ EXERCISE 30, p. 181.   *Using gerunds or passive infinitives following* need.

ANSWERS: 1. to fix . . . fixing/to be fixed   2. to be cleaned/cleaning . . . to clean 3. changing/to be changed   4. to be ironed/ironing   5. to be repaired/repair(ing) [The noun *repair* could be used instead of the gerund *repairing*.]   6. to take . . . to be straightened/ straightening   7. to be picked/picking   8. washing/to be washed

---

CHART 4-15: USING A POSSESSIVE TO MODIFY A GERUND

• This is another example of change in the English language. Formal usage keeps the traditional possessive form of the noun or pronoun before a gerund. Less formal usage permits the objective form.

☐ EXERCISE 31, p. 182.   *Using a possessive to modify a gerund.*

This could be done in small groups, but it's probably more beneficial for the whole class to discuss the difference between formal and informal usage.

ANSWERS: 3. We greatly appreciate your having taken/your taking the time to help us. **4. formal:** The boy resented our talking . . . .   **informal:** . . . us talking . . . .   **5.** Their running away/Their having run away . . . shocked everyone.   **6. formal:** I don't understand your not wanting to do it. **informal:** . . . you not wanting . . . .   **7. formal:** Sally complained about Ann's borrowing/having borrowed her clothes . . . .   **informal:** . . . Ann borrowing her clothes . . . . **8. formal:** We should take advantage of Helen's being here . . . .   **informal:** . . . of Helen being here . . . .

◇ WORKBOOK: Practice 23.

□ **EXERCISE 32, p. 182.** *Review of Charts 4-1 through 4-15.*

This exercise is quite long, so you might want to lead the class through it quickly. It takes about 10 minutes if the students are prepared.

ANSWERS: **1.** to be asked   **2.** drinking [possible in British English: *to drink*]   **3.** washing
4. (in order) to relax   **5.** to answer   **6.** telling   **7.** beating ["beat your head against a brick wall" = try to do something that is impossible]   **8.** not being able   **9.** to be awarded
10. to accept   **11.** getting . . . (in order) to help   **12.** to travel . . . (to) leave   **13.** Helping
14. to be liked . . . (to be) trusted   **15.** wondering   **16.** to have been chosen   **17.** Living
18. doing . . . to interrupt   **19.** to take/to have taken   **20.** (in order) to let   **21.** to cooperate   **22.** to turn   **23.** hearing/having heard   **24.** leaving/having left . . .   going/ (having) gone . . . (in order) to study   **25.** asking/having asked   **26.** driving . . . to drive
27. (in order) to get   **28.** not being/not having been

◇ **WORKBOOK:** Practices 24 and 25.

CHART 4-16: USING VERBS OF PERCEPTION

- "Verbs of perception" refer to four of the five senses: sight, hearing, touch, smell (but not taste).

- Additional examples:
  (e) The cat **watched** the bird **fly** away. (The bird disappeared.)
  (f) The cat hungrily **watched** the bird **flying** above its head. (The bird continued to fly near the cat.)

- The "simple form" of a verb is the form that is usually listed in a dictionary, the form with no tense or endings. SIMPLE VERB: *go, accept*   SIMPLE INFINITIVE: *to go, to accept*

□ **EXERCISE 33, p. 185.** *Understanding verbs of perception.*

Students can have fun demonstrating some of the situations in the entries, as if performing in a theater. Other students can describe the situation. For example, Carlos acts out being in an earthquake. Another student reports: "Carlos could feel the ground shake/shaking."

ANSWERS: **2.** shake/shaking   **3.** ring/ringing   **4.** sing/singing   **5.** come/coming
6. knock/knocking   **7.** look at/looking at   **8.** take off/taking off . . . land/landing [Use the same form for both verbs.]   **11.** walking [in progress at this moment]   **12.** walk . . . open . . . get in [Each step in the process was completed, not continuing.]   **13.** walking [in progress as I watched]   **14.** calling [in progress at this moment]   **15.** call [He said my name one time, not over and over.]   **16.** singing . . . laughing [continuing]   **17.** burning [in progress at this moment]   **18.** land [a single action, not continuing or repeated]

◇ **WORKBOOK:** Practices 26 and 27.

CHART 4-17: USING THE SIMPLE FORM AFTER *LET* AND
HELP

- The American English preference is (c), the simple form of a verb rather than an infinitive after *help*. The British English preference is (d), the infinitive after *help*.

The purpose is to accustom the students to using simple forms after *let* and *help*. If additional practice is needed, you and the students can think of new sentences. The *Workbook* also has more items in Practices 28 and 29.

ANSWERS: [Depend on students' creativity.]

CHART 4-18: USING CAUSATIVE VERBS: *MAKE, HAVE, GET*

• A "causative" verb carries the meaning that something/someone produces (causes) a result. This may be a difficult concept in some cultures, and languages express the notion of causation in very different ways. Therefore, you may need to discuss causation with your students.

• The method of causation is expressed by choosing one of the three verbs: *make* = use force; *have* = request or order; *get* = use persuasion or perhaps trickery.

□ EXERCISE 35, p. 187.   *Understanding causative verbs.*

Each response should perhaps be discussed so that students understand (1) the verb form and (2) the meaning of the causative verb.

ANSWERS: **3.** write   **4.** wash   **5.** to clean   **6.** cashed [passive: by whom?]   **7.** to go
8. shortened [passive: by whom?]   **9.** redo [redo = do again, pronounced /riy-**du**/]
10. filled   **11.** to lend   **12.** removed   **13.** cry [*Peeling*, a gerund, is the subject, so the verb *makes* ends in -s.]   **14.** to do   **15.** take   **16.** cleaned [by whom?]

□ EXERCISE 36, p. 188.   *Using causative verbs.*

ANSWERS: [Depend on students' ideas.]

◇ **WORKBOOK:** Practices 28 and 29.

**CHART 4-19: SPECIAL EXPRESSIONS FOLLOWED BY THE
                     -ING FORM OF A VERB**

• In (c) through (g), you might substitute other expressions of time, money, and place that are more familiar to your students. For example:

    (c) Jose *spends **five hours a day** studying* English.
    (d) Yoko *wasted **fifty yen** riding* the bus.

The students can probably think of other good examples, too.

• Additional examples for (h) and (i):

    (h) When Tom got home, he **found** his wife **crying** over a broken vase.
         Looking for my glasses, I **found** them **sitting** on my nose.
    (i) During the exam, the teacher **caught** a student **cheating.**
         Judy **caught** her sister **wearing** her favorite jeans.

□ **EXERCISE 37, p. 189.** *Special expressions followed by -ing verbs.*

> ANSWERS: **2.** understanding **3.** doing **4.** waiting **5.** taking **6.** going/driving/riding/traveling, etc. **7.** listening **8.** going **9.** getting **10.** making **11.** watching **12.** eating **13.** A: doing/getting.... B: [Depends on students' ideas.] **14.** through **16.** [Depend on students' creativity.]

◇ **WORKBOOK:** Practice 30.

□ **EXERCISES 38 & 39, pp. 190–194.** *General review of Chapter 4.*

There are plenty of items in these exercises for additional practice of all the material in Chapter 4. You might do a few with the whole class, then let them do the rest in small groups. After enough time, discuss only those items which caused difficulty. Again, see the INTRODUCTION, pp. xv–xvi, for various ways of using fill-in-the-blanks exercises.

EX. 38 ANSWERS: **1.** looking **2.** make **3.** watching...swim/swimming **4.** to pay **5.** to ignore **6.** studying **7.** feel **8.** draw **9.** laugh **10.** convincing **11.** open **12.** trickling/trickle **13.** filled [passive] **14.** telling **15.** being elected **16.** lying [Check the spelling.] **17.** (to) move **18.** play...joining **19.** drink [This is a folk saying. It means that you cannot always persuade a person to do what is reasonable.] **20.** play **21.** to be...(to) listen **22.** thinking **23.** taken **24.** to be told [by you] **25.** have...join **26.** being...being **27.** understanding **28.** tear ["tear my hair out" = feel frustration or anger] **29.** doing **30.** drive

EX. 39 ANSWERS:

1. take
2. translate
3. to say...understand
4. to begin
5. to be done [by someone]
6. to discover
7. put
8. feel...to be intimidated
9. failing
10. twiddling ["twiddling your thumbs" = doing nothing]
11. (in order) to let...run
12. make
13. talking
14. being
15. going
16. being/to be forced to leave...(in order) to study...having
17. to have...to know
18. Looking...realize...to be
19. sipping...eating
20. being
21. staying...getting
22. to force...to use...to feel...(to) share
23. sleeping
24. having...adjusting
25. to be admitted
26. to get...cut...trimmed

◇ **WORKBOOK:** Practices 31, 32, 33, 34, 35.

□ **EXERCISE 40, p. 194.** *Review of Chapter 4.*

> ANSWERS:
> 1. My parents made me [no *to*] promise to write them once a week.
> 2. I don't mind *having* a roommate.
> 3. Most students want *to* return home as soon as possible.
> 4. When I went [no *to*] shopping last Saturday, I saw a man [no *to*] drive his car....
> 5. I asked my roommate to let me [no *to*] use his shoe polish.
> 6. It is very interesting to learn about another country. OR Learning/To learn about another country is very interesting.
> 7. I don't enjoy *playing* card games.
> 8. I heard a car door *open and close/opening and closing* [*Open and close* = once; *opening and closing* = repeatedly. Both words should be in parallel form.]

9. I had my friend [no *to*] lend me his car.
10. I tried very hard ***not to*** make any mistakes.
11. It is ***very*** beautiful.
12. The music director tapped his baton ***(in order) to begin*** the rehearsal.
13. Some people prefer ***saving their*** money to ***spending*** it./Some people prefer ***to save their*** money ***(rather) than (to) spend*** it.
14. The task of ***finding*** a person . . . .
15. All of us needed to ***go*** to the cashier's window.
16. I am looking forward to ***going swimming*** in the ocean.
17. When ***you're/you are*** planting a garden, it's important to ***know*** about soils.
18. My mother always ***makes*** me [no *to be*] slow down if she ***thinks*** I am driving ***too*** fast.
19. One of our fights ended up with ***me/my*** having to ***be*** sent to the hospital ***for*** stitches/***(in order) to get*** stitches.

◇ **WORKBOOK:** Have students take Practice Test A and/or B.

☐ **EXERCISE 41, p. 195.** *Written composition.*

Students should be able to produce several informal paragraphs on a topic. After they finish, they or a partner might underline all the gerunds and infinitives.

All of the topics require use of more than one verb tense. Topic 1 is basically about the past but might also include the present perfect. Topic 2 combines the present and the past. Topic 3 requires the present and either present perfect or past.

It is not necessary for students to answer each question directly. These questions are designed to produce ideas or to recall memories which the students can write about.

☐ **EXERCISE 42, p. 195.** *Using phrasal verbs.*

(See Appendix 2 for lists of phrasal verbs.)

ANSWERS: **1.** up   **2.** in . . . over   **3.** up   **4.** after   **5.** up   **6.** out   **7.** up   **8.** down   **9.** up   **10.** out

Chapter 5: SINGULAR AND PLURAL

ORDER OF CHAPTER	CHARTS	EXERCISES	WORKBOOK
Singular and plural (final -s/-es)	5-1	Ex. 1 → 6	Pr. 1
Irregular plural nouns	5-2	Ex. 7	Pr. 2 → 3
Possessive nouns	5-3	Ex. 8	Pr. 4
Using apostrophes			Pr. 5 → 6
Nouns as modifiers	5-4	Ex. 9	Pr. 7 → 9
Count and noncount nouns	5-5 → 5-7	Ex. 10 → 12	Pr. 10 → 14
Expressions of quantity	5-8 → 5-11	Ex. 13 → 20	Pr. 15 → 22
Subject-verb agreement	5-12 → 5-15	Ex. 21 → 25	
Cumulative review and practice		Ex. 26 → 28	Pr. 23 → 24
Pronouns	5-16 → 5-20	Ex. 29 → 33	Pr. 25 → 27
Cumulative review and practice			Pr. 28
Forms of *other*	5-21	Ex. 34 → 36	Pr. 29 → 31
Cumulative review and practice		Ex. 37	Pr. 32 → 34 Pr. Tests A&B

General Notes on Chapter 5

• OBJECTIVES: Students can review and gain control of such important features of English grammar as the singular/plural and count/noncount distinctions, possessive forms, some expressions of quantity, and the use of pronouns.

• APPROACH: This chapter begins with a review of some rules for spelling and pronouncing the final -s suffix. Then irregular plural forms and possessive forms of nouns are quickly reviewed. The main sections deal with the problem of number: count/noncount, quantities, and singular/plural agreement between subject and verb. The last sections focus on personal pronouns and forms of *other*.

• TERMINOLOGY: Some grammar books and dictionaries refer to **noncount** nouns as ''mass'' or ''uncountable'' nouns. The term **expression of quantity** is used for any quantifier (e.g., *many, much, a lot of, few*), determiner (e.g., *no, each, every, some, any*), or predeterminer (e.g., *all, both*) that expresses amount or size.

□ **EXERCISE 1, p. 197.** *Singular and plural.*

This is a pre-test or preview. Give the students a couple of minutes to add *-s/-es*, then discuss. Possible points of discussion:

- grammatical explanations for final *-s/-es*

- pronunciation of *-s/-es*: /s/, /z/, and /əz/*

- variations in spelling: *-s* vs. *-es; -ys* vs. *-ies*

- basic grammar terminology: noun, verb, adjective, singular, plural

- the basic structure of the simple sentence: subjects, verbs, and complements

- count vs. noncount nouns

- expressions of quantity: *every, nine, many, a lot of*

- *A* vs. *the* vs. *Ø*. (The symbol *Ø* is used here to mean ''no article is needed.'' See Appendix 1, Unit D, ''Articles.'')

Use the chalkboard so that everyone can focus on the word that requires *-s/-es*. Also discuss why other words do NOT have an *-s/-es* ending.

The students are assumed to be familiar with the above-mentioned points, so they can provide much of the information. You may wish to tell them that you know this exercise is ''too easy'' but that, for the average learner, problems with singular/plural persist through many years of English study and use—hence, this review of basics.

ANSWERS: **2. works** /s/ [a simple present tense verb with a third person singular subject, *Tom*] (Note: *every* is a ''singular word'' followed by a singular, never plural, noun; therefore, *day* does not take a final *-s* here.) **3. consists** /s/ [a present tense verb; subject, *system*] . . . **planets** /s/ [plural count noun] **4. rotates** /s/ [verb; subject, *earth*] **5. animals** /z/ [plural noun] (*water* = noncount noun, so has no final *-s*) **6. needs** /z/ [verb; subject, *dog*] **7. students** /s/ . . . **tests** /s/ [plural nouns] **8. sunsets** /s/ [plural noun] (An adjective, *beautiful*, does not take a final *-s*.) **9. contains** /z/ [verb; subject, *library*] . . . **books** /s/ [plural noun] **10. Encyclopedias** /z/ . . . **things** /z/ [plural nouns] (*information* = noncount noun) **11. Butterflies** /z/ [plural noun] (*-y* is changed to *-i*. Also: an adjective, *beautiful*, does not take a final *-s*.) **12. watches** /əz/ [verb; subject, *Martha*] (*-es* is added, not just *-s*, and pronunciation adds a syllable.) **13. changes** /əz/ [verb; subject, *Alex*] (Only *-s* is added, but the pronunciation adds a syllable.)

EXPANSION ACTIVITY (for use now or later in the unit): Using copies of any paragraph(s) you choose, have the students circle and discuss every word that ends in *-s*. (Some words, of course, are simply spelled with a final *-s*, e.g., *bus*.)

CHART 5-1: FINAL *-S/-ES*

- Most of your students are probably well aware of the elementary grammar in this chart but they may still frequently omit final *-s/-es*. The text seeks to reinforce student awareness of *-s/-es* by a review of rules and an emphasis on oral production. Encourage the clear pronunciation of *-s/-es* in your students' speaking throughout the term.

---

*For pronunciation symbols, see p. xxi in the INTRODUCTION to this *Guide*.

☐ **EXERCISE 2, p. 198.** *Adding -s or -es.*

ANSWERS: **1.** passengers /z/ **2.** taxes /əz/ **3.** talks /s/ **4.** blushes /əz/ **5.** discovers /z/ **6.** develops /s/ **7.** seasons /z/ **8.** flashes /əz/ **9.** halls /z/ **10.** touches /əz/ **11.** sketches /əz/ **12.** presses /əz/ **13.** methods /z/ **14.** mixes /əz/ **15.** tries /z/ **16.** trays /z/ **17.** ferries /z/ **18.** guys /z/ **19.** enemies /z/ **20.** pries /z/ **21.** prays /z/

◇ **WORKBOOK:** Practice 1.

☐ **EXERCISE 3, p. 199.** *Pronunciation of final -s/-es.*

See p. xxi of this *Teacher's Guide* for information about voiced and voiceless sounds. Words you can use if you want to practice *th* + final *-s* follow:

voiceless /θ s/: *moths, months, tenths;*
voiced /ðz/: *soothes, smoothes, clothes;*
voiceless vs. voiced: *baths* vs. *bathes, breaths* vs. *breathes.*

EXPANSION ACTIVITY: After the three groups of words have been practiced, you may want to try a game in which you spell a word aloud and then a student must pronounce it correctly—with special attention to the *-s/-es* pronunciation.

☐ **EXERCISE 4, p. 200.** *Pronunciation of final -s/-es.*

Students could work in pairs and correct each other's pronunciation.* They could note pronunciation in their books using the symbols /s/, /z/, and /əz/. Another possibility is to have each student make three cards with the symbols /s/, /z/, and /əz/. When a student says a word with a final *-s/-es*, someone (the speaker, another student, you, the rest of the class, or everyone) holds up the card that represents the sound being said.

PRONUNCIATION NOTES: **1.** encourages /jəz/ . . . students /nts/ **2.** chickens /nz/ . . . ducks /ks/ . . . turkeys /iz/ . . . eggs /gz/ **3.** possesses /səz/ . . . qualities /iz/ **4.** wages /jəz/ . . . taxes /ksəz/ **5.** serves /vz/ . . . sandwiches /čəz/ . . . itches /čəz/ OR /čɪz/ **6.** coughs /fs/ . . . sneezes /zəz/ . . . wheezes /zəz/ **7.** shapes /ps/ . . . sizes /zəz/ **8.** scratches /čəz/ OR /čɪz/ . . . itches /čəz/ OR /čɪz/ **9.** practices /səz/ . . . sentences /səz/ **10.** shirts /ts/, shoes /uz/ . . . socks /ks/ . . . dresses /səz/ . . . slacks /ks/ . . . blouses /səz/ OR /zəz/ . . . earrings /ŋz/ . . . necklaces /ləsəz/

EXPANSION ACTIVITY: Have the students make a chart (or you make it and hand it out) with the following headings: **/s/ /z/ /əz/.** Divide the class into teams, groups, or pairs. Have a student say a word that ends in *-s/-es.* (You can supply the words or let the students make up their own. Instruct them to use plural nouns or singular verbs. Or take three cards with the symbols on them, show one card privately to a student, and have that student say a word with that ending.)

---

*See the INTRODUCTION to this *Teacher's Guide* (pp. ix–xviii) for suggestions for classroom techniques that can be used with the various types of exercises.

Everyone writes down the word under the symbol for correct pronunciation. For example, the first student says "windows." Student 2 says "reaches." Student 3 says "students," Student 4 says "passes," etc.

	/s/	/z/	/əz/
1.		*windows*	
2.			*reaches*
3.	*students*		
4.			*passes*
5.	*etc.*		

☐ EXERCISE 5, p. 200.   *Pronunciation.*

See the INTRODUCTION in this *Teacher's Guide* for techniques for using Oral (books closed) exercises. This exercise could be led by the teacher giving the cue or be used for group or pair work, with the students monitoring each other's pronunciation.
[A note on sentence stress: In these sentences, the loudest (stressed) words are the **second** word and the **last** word.]

ANSWERS: **1.** A stamp collector collects /kts/ stamps /ps/.   **2.** An animal trainer trains /nz/ animals /lz/.   **3.** . . . robs /bz/ banks /ŋks/.   **4.** . . . catches /čəz/ dogs /gz/.
5. . . . publishes /šəz/ books /ks/.   **6.** . . . collects /kts/ taxes /ksəz/.   **7.** . . . takes /ks/ tickets /ts/.   **8.** . . . extinguishes /šəz/ fires /rz/. [A fire extinguisher is a metal bottle that contains a special liquid to spray on a small fire.]   **9.** . . . reads /dz/ minds /ndz/. [This term is used humorously when someone seems to know what another is thinking without being told.]
10. . . . fights /ts/ bulls /lz/. [It is traditional to write *bullfighter* and *storyteller* (item 12) as one word.]   **11.** . . . earns /rnz/ wages /jəz/   **12.** . . . tells /lz/ stories /riz/.

☐ EXERCISE 6, p. 200.   *Final -s/-es.*

The students should have fun trying to make generalizations about the given nouns. Provide additional vocabulary for the completions as needed. Keep calling attention to final *-s/-es*.

As an alternative format, you could give plural cues, e.g., *birds* instead of *bird*. Or you could vary singular and plural cues so that the students have to listen carefully for final *-s/-es* sounds. If you say *bird*, the sentence has to begin with "A bird . . . ." If you say *birds*, the sentence must begin with "Birds . . . ."

POSSIBLE ANSWERS: **1.** A baby cries/coos/crawls.   **2.** A telephone rings/wakes someone up.
3. A star shines/twinkles/falls.   **4.** A dog barks/growls/runs.   **5.** A duck quacks (pronounced /kwæks/)/waddles/swims.   **6.** A ball bounces/flies through the air.   **7.** A heart beats/pounds/pumps blood/swells with pride/fills with love/breaks with sadness.   **8.** A river flows/floods.
9. A cat meows/purrs/sleeps/pounces/stalks its prey.   **10.** A door opens/closes/slams.
11. A clock ticks/keeps time/tells the time/runs down.   **12.** An airplane flies/takes off/lands/crashes.   **13.** A doctor heals the sick/works in a hospital/prescribes medicine.   **14.** A teacher

instructs/teaches/marks papers/helps students.   **15.** A psychologist (pronounced /saikaləjıst/) studies the mind/analyzes behavior.

EXPANSION ACTIVITY: Add other nouns for vocabulary discussion and further practice with *-s/-es*. For example, students often find it interesting and entertaining to find out what sounds animals make in English: a duck quacks, a cow moos, a snake hisses, a horse whinnies or neighs, a chicken clucks, a rooster (American)/cock (British) crows "cockadoodledoo," a goose honks, a pig oinks, a mule or donkey brays, etc. You could also include nouns about professions (an architect, a welder, a day care worker, a banker, etc.); machines or devices (a computer, a camera, a toaster, a bulldozer, etc.); and things in nature (a planet, a volcano, a tree, etc.).

CHART 5-2: IRREGULAR PLURAL NOUNS

• In (c) it can be pointed out that final *-o* is followed by *-s*, not *-es*, when the noun is a shortened form (e.g., *auto-automobile, memo-memorandum*) and when the *-o* is preceded by another vowel. Students should be encouraged to consult their dictionaries when in doubt, just as native speakers have to do.

• The list in the chart is not inclusive. Others that could be mentioned: *buffaloes/buffalos, haloes/halos, grottoes/grottos; ghettos, kangaroos; waifs, oafs, serfs, sheriffs, tariffs; one offspring/two offspring, one moose/two moose, one shrimp/two shrimp* [possible in British English: *two shrimps*]; *fungus-fungi, vita-vitae, radius-radii, alumna-alumnae, alumus-alumni.*

• If students ask why some nouns are irregular, you might explain that throughout its history, the English language has had close contact with other European languages. It has been influenced by German, Danish, Latin, Greek, and French, especially; a few forms from those languages occur in some English words today. In addition, some irregular forms come from Middle and Old English.

☐ **EXERCISE 7, p. 201.** *Spelling of plural nouns.*

Students could write their answers on the chalkboard for everyone to check.
ANSWERS: **3.** mice   **4.** monkeys   **5.** industries   **6.** women   **7.** foxes   **8.** geese
9. sheep   **10.** series   **11.** beliefs [The ***v*** *believe* is always spelled with a "*v*": *believes*.]
12. leaves   **13.** selves [usually in words like *ourselves, yourselves, themselves*]   **14.** echoes
[pronounced /ɛkowz/]   **15.** photos   **16.** analyses [pronounced /ənæləsi:z/]   **17.** hypotheses
[pronounced /haipaθəsi:z/]   **18.** curricula [also possible: *curriculums*]   **19.** phenomena
20. stimuli [pronounced either /stımyul**ai**/ or /stımyuli:/]

EXPANSION ACTIVITY: A traditional classroom game is a "spelling bee." Students all stand. The teacher says a word to one student. The student repeats the word, then must spell it correctly, letter by letter, from memory. If the spelling is incorrect, the student must sit down. The next student who is standing must then spell the same word. If the spelling is correct, he or she remains standing, and the teacher says a new word to the next student. The game continues in this way until only one student, the "champion speller," is standing. (If your class is large, you may want to ask for only a few volunteers to play the game. The others can "bet" on who the winner will be.)

In a spelling bee with plural endings, the teacher can say the word and the student can spell it with the appropriate ending. Some possible words for a bee: *custom, disease, skyscraper, appearance, hospital, career, calendar, label, succeed, surround, describe, mask, ladder, mirror, ghost, ticket, passenger, occasion* (or consult a list of frequently misspelled words);* *wish, ash, splash, crash,*

---

*Avoid words whose American and British spellings differ, such as *color/colour, airplane/aeroplane, program/programme, analyze/analyse, defense/defence.* (See p. xx in the INTRODUCTION for differences in spelling between American and British English.)

leash, push; pass, boss, kiss, cuss, mess, embarrass, lose, choose, choice; itch, pitch, patch, fetch, ditch; fix, hoax, six, wax, hex, fox; decay, fairy, balcony, diary, dairy, destroy, berry, penalty, mystery, enemy, holiday, category; and any of the words in Chart 5-2.

◇ **WORKBOOK:** Practices 2 and 3.

CHART 5-3: POSSESSIVE NOUNS

• Another way to explain the possessive form is to say that (in writing) a noun always adds *'s*: *boy's*, *men's*. However, in the case of a noun that already ends in *s*, we take away the second *s* and leave the apostrophe.

  boy + *'s* = *boy's* (singular, possessive)
  men + *'s* = *men's* (irregular plural, possessive)
  boys + *'s* = *boys's* (plural, possessive)—but take away the second *s*: **boys'**

□ **EXERCISE 8, p. 202.** *Possessive forms of nouns.*

ANSWERS: **2.** boy's   **3.** boys'   **4.** children's   **5.** child's   **6.** baby's   **7.** babies'   **8.** wives'   **9.** wife's   **10.** Sally's   **11.** Phyllis'/Phyllis's [pronounced/fɪlɪsəz/]   **12.** boss' [pronounced/bɔsəz/   **13.** bosses' [also pronounced /bɔsəz/]   **14.** woman's   **15.** women's   **16.** sister's   **17.** sisters'   **18.** yesterday's   **19.** today's   **20.** month's

◇ **WORKBOOK:** Practices 4, 5, and 6.

CHART 5-4: USING NOUNS AS MODIFIERS

• Some grammar books use the term "noun adjunct" for a noun that modifies a following noun.

□ **EXERCISE 9, p. 203.** *Using nouns as modifiers.*

When you read or listen to the students' answers, pay special attention to two common problems: (1) the modifying noun must be singular in form, and (2) the article *a/an* is required for singular count nouns. It is useful to have students write their answers on the chalkboard.

ANSWERS: **2.** It is a ***student*** handbook.   **3.** They have a ***ten-month-old*** baby.   **4.** We took a ***three-day*** trip.   **5.** She is a ***child*** psychologist.   **6.** I wrote a ***fifty-dollar*** check.   **7.** It is a ***three-credit*** course.   **8.** It is a ***nine-room*** house.   **9.** It is ***dog*** food. [no article because *food* is a noncount noun—see the next chart] [Possible point of comparison: *dog food* vs. *that dog's food*.]   **10.** It is a ***guest*** room.   **11.** She asked us to write a ***five-page*** paper.   **12.** I have a ***ten-year-old*** sister and a ***twelve-year-old*** brother.

◇ WORKBOOK: Practices 7, 8, 9.

CHART 5-5: COUNT AND NONCOUNT NOUNS

- Some noncount nouns, like *furniture*, are called ''mass nouns'' in other grammar books.

- This count/noncount distinction is one of the most difficult points for students to control.

- The following are some common student mistakes:

INCORRECT	CORRECT COUNT FORM	CORRECT NONCOUNT FORM
many homeworks	many assignments	a lot of homework
some slangs	some slang expressions	some slang
many vocabularies	many vocabulary words/items	a large vocabulary

---

☐ **EXERCISE 10, p. 204.** *Recognizing count and noncount nouns.*

The purpose of this exercise is to help the students understand the two charts that follow (5-6 and 5-7). As you go through the exercise, discuss the ideas presented in Chart 5-6. In items 1 through 5, point out that a noncount noun refers to a ''whole'' that is made up of different parts. For example, in item 1, *furniture* is the ''whole'' and *chairs, tables, desks* are the ''different parts.'' In item 6, point out that food terms representing fluids (*tea*), solids (*meat*), semi-solids (*butter*), and particles (*rice*) are often noncount (and also that language is not always consistent or logical: *e.g.*, *fruit* is usually noncount while *vegetables* is count). In 7 and 8, compare noncount and count usages of the same word, *iron*; the meanings are different. In 8 through 10, communicate the idea of ''abstractions'' (things you can't touch or hold because they have no physical form). In 11, point out that the first *baseball* is an ''abstract whole'' and the second *baseball* (a count noun) is a concrete thing. In 12, point out that many weather/natural phenomena terms are noncount. In 13, compare *black hair* (noncount ''whole'') and *black hairs* (concrete count noun).

You might give each student two cards (or the students can use their own paper). On one is a large letter ''C,'' and on the other is ''NC.'' As you read each sentence aloud, pause after each noun while the students hold up the piece that identifies the noun as ''C'' or ''NC.'' In this way, you can quickly see if any students are incorrectly identifying any nouns, and the students can have a little fun.

ANSWERS: **2.** pennies (C), nickels (C), and dimes (C) . . . money (NC) **3.** jewelry (NC) . . . our rings (C), six bracelets (C), and a necklace (C). **4.** beautiful mountains (C), fields (C), and lakes (C) . . . beautiful scenery (NC) **5.** food (NC) . . . a sandwich (C) and an apple (C) **6.** meat (NC), rice (NC), bread (NC), butter (NC), cheese (NC), fruit (NC), vegetables (C), and tea (NC) **7.** Gold (NC) and iron (NC) **8.** an iron (C) **9.** happiness (NC), health (NC), and luck (NC) **10.** chemistry (NC), history (NC), and English (NC) **11.** . . . baseball (NC) is called . . . you need a baseball (C) **12.** rain (NC), thunder (NC), fog (NC), sleet (NC) [*sleet:* rain with drops of partly frozen water], and snow (NC) . . . weather (NC). **13.** black hair (NC) and brown eyes (C)

• The concept of a noncount noun is covered in 5-6, followed by a list of common examples in 5-7.

• If it helps your students to understand, use the term "mass" to explain the idea of "a whole."

• Some of the nouns in 5-7 also have count uses. A noun is count or noncount depending on how it is used and the speaker's intended meaning. No noun is inherently count or noncount. The words listed in 5-7 are usually or always used as noncount nouns, but you may wish to discuss some of those with dual uses: *glass* (a material) vs. *a glass* (a container for drinking); *tea* (a drink) vs. *teas* (kinds of tea); *pepper* (a spice) vs. *a pepper* (a vegetable); *bridge* (a card game) vs. *a bridge* (a span across a river); *time* (an abstract concept) vs. *times* (occurrences).

☐ EXERCISE 11, p. 206. *Using count and noncount nouns.*

ANSWERS: **3.** I enjoy music.   **4.** . . . visit other cities   **5.** . . . has heavy traffic
6. . . . take trips. . . travel(l)ing   **7.** . . . full of garbage   **8.** . . . full of junk   **9.** . . . a lot of
stuff   **10.** . . . heard thunder   **11.** . . . called screwdrivers   **12.** . . . some hardware
13. . . . a lot of homework   **14.** . . . a lot of luggage   **15.** . . . found this information
16. I got advice   **17.** . . . with the progress

◇ WORKBOOK: Practices 10, 11, 12, and 13.

☐ EXERCISE 12, p. 208. *Identifying count and noncount nouns.*

A student can read an answer aloud to the class, but he or she should say the complete sentence, not only the nouns. The answers must be spoken loudly and clearly so everyone can hear.

ANSWERS: **3.** tree**s**, bush**es**, grass (no change), dirt (no change), and flower**s**   **4.** advice (no change) . . . suggestion**s**   **5.** word**s** . . . vocabulary (no change)   **6.** two glass**es** . . . water (no change)   **7.** Window**s** . . . glass (no change)   **8.** glass**es** . . . eyesight (no change)   **9.** time (no change) . . . homework (no change) . . . assignment**s**   **10.** three time**s** . . . a lot of time (no change)   **11.** typewriter**s**, copier**s**, telephone**s**, and stapler**s** . . . equipment (no change)
12. air (no change) . . . smoke, dust, and carbon monoxide (no changes) . . . substance**s** . . . air pollution (no change)   **13.** literature (no change) . . . novel**s**, poetry (no change), and essay**s** . . . poet**s** . . . poem**s**   **14.** machine**s** . . . a modern factory (no change) . . . Modern facto**ries** . . . machinery (no change)   **15.** star**s** . . . grain**s** . . . sand (no change)

◇ WORKBOOK: Practice 14.

☐ EXERCISE 13, p. 209. *Pretest on expressions of quantity.*

Give the class a couple of minutes to do the exercise, then review the correct answers. Introduce the term "expressions of quantity." Point out that *letters* is a count noun and *mail* is noncount.

ANSWERS: **1.** Draw a line through i, k, m.   **2.** Draw a line through a, b, c, d, h, j, l.

CHART 5-8: EXPRESSIONS OF QUANTITY

• *A lot of* and *lots of* have the same meaning. Both are somewhat informal, with *lots of* being the more informal.

• See Appendix 1, Unit C, for *not any* vs. *no*.

☐ EXERCISE 14, p. 210. *Expressions of quantity.*

ANSWERS: **1.** Draw lines through e, h, j. **2.** Draw lines through a, b, f, g, i. **3.** Draw lines through f, h. **4.** Draw lines through a, b, e, g.

◇ WORKBOOK: Practices 15 and 16.

☐ EXERCISE 15, p. 211. *Using* many *and* much.

This can be a rapid exercise with two-word answers, or a more thorough review with whole-sentence answers (have the students use *much* only in questions or negative sentences). Pay special attention to pronunciation of *-s/-es*.

ANSWERS: **1.** much furniture **2.** many desks **3.** many branches **4.** much equipment **5.** much machinery **6.** many machines **7.** many women **8.** many pieces **9.** many mice **10.** much advice **11.** many sheep **12.** much homework **13.** many prizes **14.** many geese **15.** much music **16.** much progress **17.** many races **18.** much knowledge **19.** many marriages **20.** much information **21.** much luck **22.** many hypotheses **23.** much mail **24.** many offices **25.** much slang **26.** many roofs **27.** many phenomena **28.** many human beings **29.** many shelves **30.** many teeth

CHART 5-9: USING *A FEW* AND *FEW*; *A LITTLE* AND *LITTLE*

• Sometimes students think there must be a difference in quantity between *a few* and *few*. They ask, ''How many is 'a few' and how many is 'few'?'' But the real difference is in the speaker's **opinion**: *a few* reflects a positive opinion of the quantity, and *few* reflects a negative or diminishing opinion, even if the quantity is the same in both cases.

• The following chart may be helpful for students.

COUNT	NONCOUNT
few = not many	*little = not much*
a few = some	*a little = some*

☐ EXERCISE 16, p. 212. *Using* a few, (very) few, a little, *and* little.

ANSWERS: **3.** a little salt **4.** very little salt **5.** (very) few students **6.** a little music **7.** (very) few friends **8.** a few letters **9.** (very) little mail **10.** a few days . . . a few days **11.** (very) little traffic **12.** a few months **13.** a little advice **14.** (very) few clothes **15.** a few more minutes **16.** a little more time **17.** A few days **18.** a little rain [The saying means that all people have unhappiness in their lives at some point.] **19.** a few nuts **20.** a little honey . . . a little milk **21.** (very) little patience **22.** (very) few problems

---

CHART 5-10: USING *OF* IN EXPRESSIONS OF QUANTITY

- This chart assumes familiarity with another dimension of English nouns: specificity.

- A common point of confusion is the difference between *most* and *the most*. (See the note at the bottom of page 215.)

- A common mistake is the use of "almost of": *almost of the (students)*. Mention the two correct possibilities: *most of the (students)* OR *almost all of the (students)*.

☐ **EXERCISE 17, p. 214.** *Using* of *in expressions of quantity.*

Pairs of sentences in this exercise look similar. Be sure students understand the important differences.

ANSWERS: **3.** Ø . . . Ø   **4.** of   **5.** Ø   **6.** of   **7.** Ø   **8.** of   **9.** Ø   **10.** of   **11.** Ø   **12.** of   **13.** of   **14.** of ["Junk mail" consists of advertisements, magazine contests, solicitations for money, etc.]   **15.** Ø   **16.** of   **17.** Ø . . . of   **18.** Ø   **19.** of   **20.** Ø

◇ **WORKBOOK:** Practice 18.

☐ **EXERCISE 18, p. 215.** *Using* of *in expressions of quantity.*

The concept of an optional *of* here may be confusing. You may need to explain the directions more clearly. Students need to know that both *all of the children* and *all the children* are correct, but that *all of children* is not correct. With an advanced class, you might mention that *half* has the same pattern: *half (of) the children*.

ANSWERS: **3.** (of)   **4.** Ø   **5.** Ø   **6.** (of)   **7.** (of)   **8.** (of)   **9.** Ø . . . Ø   **10.** Ø . . . Ø

◇ **WORKBOOK:** Practices 19 and 20.

CHART 5-11: SINGULAR EXPRESSIONS OF QUANTITY

- Learners frequently make mistakes when using *one of*—typically, the use of a singular rather than plural noun (e.g., INCORRECT: *One of the **book** on the table is . . . .*) or the use of a plural rather than singular verb (e.g., INCORRECT: *One of the books on the table **are** . . . .*).

- Have the students make up sentences beginning with *one of*. You could supply the nouns if necessary (and perhaps a pre- or postnominal modifier typical to this pattern). For example:

    TEACHER: *book (on the floor)*
    STUDENT: *One of books on the floor is mine.*

    TEACHER: *(your) book*
    STUDENT: *One of my books is orange and blue.*

Suggestions for nouns to use: *drawer (in your desk), (your) fingernail, woman (in this class), (Maria's) friend, article (in today's paper), (the most important) thing (in life), (the biggest) problem (you have ever had), (the worst) experience (you have ever had)*, etc.

☐ **EXERCISE 19, p. 216.** *Noun forms with expressions of quantity.*

This should be an oral exercise with discussion of similarities and differences between the sentences.

ANSWERS: **2.** . . . one of the girl*s* **3.** . . . each child **4.** Each of the child*ren*
5. . . . every member **6.** Every one of the member*s*

☐ **EXERCISE 20, p. 217.** *Singular expressions of quantity.*

ANSWERS: **2.** (no errors) **3.** one of the *countries* **4.** (no errors) **5.** (no errors)
6. Every *piece of* furniture/*All (of) the* furniture/*The* furniture **7.** One of the *machines*/*A piece of* equipment / *Some* of the equipment **8.** each of the *women*/each woman **9.** One of my favorite *places* **10.** (no errors) **11.** every *language*/all (of) the languages **12.** each of the *errors*/each error

◇ **WORKBOOK:** Practices 21 and 22.

☐ **EXERCISE 21, p. 217.** *Pretest on subject-verb agreement.*

Students should complete this exercise before studying the next section of this chapter. It contains the subject-verb agreement rules in Charts 5-12 through 5-15. You can give an overview of these charts when you discuss the answers to this exercise. Advanced classes that have little trouble with Exercise 21 can review the material on pages 218–225 quickly. Students who have difficulty identifying subjects and verbs should be referred to Appendix 1, Chart A-1, and the Appendix section in *Workbook A.*

ANSWERS: **1.** gets **2.** were **3.** are **4.** is **5.** is **6.** are **7.** is **8.** are
9. is **10.** is **11.** are **12.** Each . . . has **13.** has **14.** were [very formal: *was*]
15. is **16.** speak **17.** are **18.** is **19.** is **20.** is **21.** is **22.** like **23.** are
24. Japanese [language] is **25.** The Japanese [people] have **26.** are **27.** is

---

CHART 5-12: BASIC SUBJECT-VERB AGREEMENT

- English has very few inflections, but speakers of English are very sensitive to their correct use. Society's opinion of the people who neglect the correct use of *-s/-es, -ed, -ing*, etc., may be that they are perhaps poorly educated or lazy. Such judgments may influence decisions about employment, friendships, and other social relationships.

- The grammatical term "third person" refers to this pattern:
  SINGULAR: *I* = the person who is speaking, the "first person"
       you = the person who is being spoken to, the "second person"
       he/she/it OR **a singular or noncount noun** = the person or thing that is being discussed, the "third person"
  PLURAL: *we* = the speaker and included persons, the "first person plural" form
       you = all persons who are being spoken to or included in the audience, the "second person plural" form
       they OR **a plural noun** = people or things that are being discussed, the "third person plural" form

---

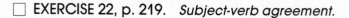

☐ EXERCISE 22, p. 219. *Subject-verb agreement.*

Students must be able to identify the grammatical subject, then select the correct form of the verb. The **grammatical** subject may not be the **logical** subject. Subjects with *every* and *each* (e.g., "every man, woman, and child") may seem to be plural because the expression can logically be understood to refer to many people, but the grammatical concept of *every* and *each* is singular. Naturally, this is a difficult point for learners.

ANSWERS: **1.** extent . . . astounds   **2.** subjects . . . are listed   **3.** Massachusetts **and** Connecticut are located   **4.** spider . . . has caused   **5.** oranges . . . **and** green lettuce are   **6.** The professor **and** the student agree   **7.** **every** professor and student . . . approves   **8.** **Each** girl and boy . . . has to do   **9.** Making . . . is   **10.** Getting . . . is   **11.** bag . . . was   **12.** do . . . parents live [Refer students to Appendix 1, Unit B, for information on subjects and verbs in questions.]   **13.** were Susan **and** Alex   **14.** Is having [gerund subject]

CHART 5-13: SUBJECT-VERB AGREEMENT USING EXPRESSIONS OF QUANTITY

• Charts 5-10 and 5-11 introduced expressions of quantity with singular and plural nouns. The focus in this chart is the agreement with verb forms.

• In addition to **none of** [examples (j) and (k)], **neither of** and **either of** + *plural count noun* can be followed by either a singular or plural verb, with the singular verb generally preferred in very formal English: *Neither of the boys is/are here.* (Chart 8-2 covers agreement when the subject includes paired (correlative) conjunctions: *Neither the boy nor the girl is . . . . Neither the boy nor the girls are . . . . Neither Tom nor I am* [formal] OR **are** [preferred informally] . . . .)

☐ EXERCISE 23, p. 220. *Subject-verb agreement with expressions of quantity.*

ANSWERS: **1.** fruit . . . is   **2.** apples . . . are   **3.** students . . . are   **4.** money belongs   **5.** students . . . are   **6.** clothing [noncount] . . . is   **7.** One . . . is   **8.** Each . . . has   **9.** Each . . . has   **10.** Everyone . . . is   **11.** animals . . . are [*formal:* none . . . is] . . . them are   **12.** students are   **13.** The number . . . is   **14.** one . . . is   **15.** Do . . . children [plural noun]   **16.** Does . . . homework [noncount noun]   **17.** were . . . students   **18.** was one   **19.** percentage . . . is   **20.** people [plural noun] . . . are   **21.** Do . . . you

---

CHART 5-14: SUBJECT-VERB AGREEMENT USING *THERE + BE*

• Very informally (many would say nonstandardly), many native speakers use a singular verb even if the noun that follows is plural: *There's some good programs on TV tonight.*

☐ EXERCISE 24, p. 221. *Subject-verb agreement using* there + be.

ANSWERS: **1.** aren't . . . letters   **2.** isn't . . . mail   **3.** are . . . problems   **4.** is a fly [A *flyswatter* is a square plastic or metal net with a long handle. It is used to "swat" (hit) insects and kill them.]   **5.** are . . . kinds   **6.** kinds . . . are [There are approximately 8,600 kinds of birds in the world.]   **7.** isn't . . . a hospital   **8.** is . . . pen   **9.** are [informal: *is*] . . . pen **and** . . . notebook   **10.** are [very informal: *is*] . . . pens **and** notebooks

CHART 5-15: SUBJECT-VERB AGREEMENT: SOME IRREGULARITIES

• The footnote about the word *people* may need further explanation. This word has two meanings, each requiring a different grammatical interpretation.

(a) the *people* of Great Britain = the British [plural]
(b) They are *one people.* = one nation [singular]

(a) the *people* of Canada = the Canadians [plural]
(b) They are *one people.* = one nation [singular]

(a) *Most people* in Great Britain and Canada *speak* English. [plural]
(b) *The peoples* of Great Britain and Canada *are* loyal to the Queen. [the peoples = 2 nations]

• Additional examples for (o): the Indochinese, the Lebanese, the Nepalese, the Sudanese.

☐ **EXERCISE 25, p. 222.** *Some irregularities in subject-verb agreement.*

ANSWERS: **1.** The United States (*it*) has **2.** news (*it*) . . . is **3.** Massachusetts (*it*) . . . is **4.** Physics (*it*) seeks **5.** Statistics (*it*) is **6.** The statistics (*they*) . . . are **7.** Fifty minutes (*It*) is **8.** Twenty dollars (*It*) is **9.** Many people (*They*) . . . do **10.** police (*they*) are **11.** The English (*They*) are **12.** English (*It*) is **13.** Many Japanese (*They*) commute **14.** Portuguese (*It*) is . . . isn't **15.** The poor (*They*) are **16.** effect (*it*) . . . depends . . . Most people (*They*) are . . . there have been instances

☐ **EXERCISE 26, p. 223.** *Review of subject-verb agreement.*

This can be a fast drill; you say the cue, and students respond with only *is* or *are*. Or students could work in pairs/small groups. In addition to oral practice, students could be asked to write out complete sentences.

ANSWERS: **1.** is **2.** are **3.** are **4.** is **5.** is **6.** are **7.** is **8.** is **9.** is **10.** is [the language] **11.** are [the people/they] **12.** is **13.** is **14.** are **15.** is **16.** is **17.** are **18.** is **19.** is **20.** are [clothes are/clothing is] **21.** is **22.** is **23.** are **24.** is **25.** is **26.** are **27.** are **28.** is **29.** are **30.** is **31.** are **32.** are **33.** is **34.** are **35.** is

☐ **EXERCISE 27, p. 224.** *Verb forms in subject-verb agreement.*

ANSWERS: **3.** One . . . keeps **4.** Sensitivity . . . makes **5.** Each . . . was **6.** license is **7.** Does . . . uncle **8.** Do . . . students **9.** bird [one bird] . . . is **10.** bird **and** . . . bird [two birds] are **11.** rates . . . are **12.** Are January **and** February **13.** land . . . is **14.** center . . . is **15.** Two hours . . . provides [a specific amount of time] **16.** article . . . oversimplifies **17.** car . . . is **18. A** number of people . . . plan **19.** news . . . concerns **20.** town . . . is **21. The** number . . . is **22.** information . . . appears **23.** there are . . . accidents **24.** news is [a famous saying that means: "When you hear no news, probably everything is peaceful; that is good. If there were trouble, we would hear about it."] **25. Every** member . . . speaks

◇ **WORKBOOK:** Practices 23 and 24.

☐ EXERCISE 28, p. 225.   *Using subject-verb agreement.*

POSSIBLE ANSWERS: **1.** All of the rooms in . . . are/have, etc.   **2.** In my country, there is + *singular noun*/are + *plural noun*   **3.** A lot of *singular noun* + is/*plural noun* + are   **4.** people . . . are/have, etc.   **5.** The number . . . is   **6.** A number . . . are/have, etc.   **7.** Each of . . . is/has, etc.   **8.** The United States is/has, etc.   **9.** The English language is/has, etc.   **10.** The English [people] are/have, etc.   **11.** English [the language] is/has, etc.   **12.** One of my . . . is/has, etc.   **13.** Most of the food . . . is/has/tastes, etc.   **14.** Most of my classmates are/have, etc.   **15.** Linguistics is, etc.   **16.** Linguists are/study, etc.

CHARTS 5-16 and 5-17: PERSONAL PRONOUNS: AGREEMENT

• Today women in English-speaking countries are active in almost every field that has traditionally been open to men only. The English language traditionally used only the male pronouns when speaking of people in general, e.g. "A doctor treats *his* patients kindly." Language reflects social change; today women have more equal representation in language usage, just as they do in society in general. Now English speakers try to use *he or she, she or he, s/he, his or her,* etc. The easiest way to avoid the problem of pronoun agreement is to use a plural rather than singular generic noun so that *they/them/their* (which are neither masculine nor feminine) may be used, e.g. "Doctors treat *their* patients kindly."

• In everyday spoken language, the majority of English speakers today use a plural pronoun to refer to an indefinite pronoun in order to avoid a feminine–masculine pronoun problem. Twenty years ago, it would have been unthinkable for an educated speaker to use *their* to refer to *someone*. Today it seems to have become the norm rather than the exception. However, singular personal pronouns are still expected in formal writing. Discuss with your class guidelines for feminine/masculine and singular/plural pronoun usage.

☐ EXERCISE 29, p. 226.   *Agreement of personal pronouns with nouns and indefinite pronouns.*

Students could discuss the various possibilities in small groups, but the principal purpose of the exercise is to provide material for discussion of the usage problems in 5-16 and 5-17. Students will want your advice.

ANSWERS: **2.** S/He; He or She; He   **3.** he; he or she; s/he does . . . his or her; his; her or his   **4.** s/he; he or she; he is   **5.** *informal:* they want OR *formal:* s/he; he or she; he wants; she wants   **6.** *informal:* their OR *formal:* his; her   **7.** *informal:* their OR *formal:* his; his or her   **8.** *informal:* they . . . their OR *formal:* he or she . . . his or her; he . . . his   **9.** it is [*possible:* he or she is]   **10.** She . . . She . . . she

---

CHART 5-18: PERSONAL PRONOUNS: AGREEMENT WITH
COLLECTIVE NOUNS

• The speaker's view of the collective unit determines the grammatical usage of the words in this chart. The English language is somewhat flexible on this point. If the speaker wants to emphasize unity or wholeness, the collective noun will be singular, and this number will influence both the pronoun and the verb. On the other hand, if the speaker wants to emphasize the individuals within the group, the collective noun will be considered plural (but it will not add *-s/-es*).

☐ **EXERCISE 30, p. 228.** *Agreement of personal pronouns with collective nouns.*

Through discussion of their mistakes and questions, help students develop an understanding of the difference between singular and plural uses of collective nouns. In general, the singular usage is impersonal or statistical, while the plural usage emphasizes the people involved.

ANSWERS: **2.** it consists [a statistical unit, not a group of real people]   **3.** they [the people on the team]   **4.** It doesn't   **5.** they   **6.** It was   **7.** They   **8.** It [a unit]   **9.** their [Individuals contributed money for the gift.]   **10.** It consists [an impersonal unit]   **11.** their [a couple = two people]   **12.** They are . . . their . . . them [class = the individuals in the group]   **13.** It is [class = an organized unit of people taught together]

◇ **WORKBOOK:** Practice 25.

CHART 5-19: USING REFLEXIVE PRONOUNS

• In very informal (some would say nonstandard) English, the reflexive pronouns are sometimes substituted for the object forms, perhaps because some people are unsure about using those forms correctly, especially after prepositions. Students may hear and wonder about this usage.

QUESTIONABLE USAGE: She gave the gift to Bob and *myself*.
PREFERRED USAGE: (a) She gave the gift to Bob and *me*.
                    (b) *I* gave a gift to *myself*.

☐ **EXERCISE 31, p. 229.** *Using reflexive pronouns.*

ANSWERS: **2.** by herself [= alone]   **3.** I myself [emphatic]   **4.** with ourselves [This is not the same as "to be honest with each other," which looks outward. "To be honest with oneself" looks inward.]   **5.** by themselves [= alone]   **6.** yourself [= emphatic]   **7.** yourselves [= alone, independently]   **8.** himself . . . for himself

◇ **WORKBOOK:** Practice 26.

☐ **EXERCISE 32, p. 230.** *Using reflexive pronouns.*

ANSWERS: **2.** enjoy himself [The verb *enjoy* requires an object; the omission of an object after *enjoy* is a common student error.]   **3.** proud of yourselves   **4.** pat yourself [When we congratulate someone, we often give them a light pat on the back with an open hand. But, if no one congratulates us, we may want to figuratively "pat ourselves on the back."]   **5.** killed himself   **6.** entertained themselves ["playing school" = playing a game in which children pretend to be teachers, students, principal (AmE), headmaster (BrE), etc.]   **7.** introduced myself   **8.** angry at himself   **9.** feeling sorry for yourself   **10.** promised herself   **11.** talking to yourself   **12.** laugh at ourselves [This is not the same as "to laugh at each other," which might be impolite.]

CHART 5-20: USING *YOU* AND *ONE* AS IMPERSONAL PRONOUNS

• Point out that when a speaker is using impersonal *you*, the "you" does not refer specifically to the listener. For example:

  A: *What are some of the customs in (your country) about touching another person?*
  B: *Well,* **you** *shouldn't touch someone else's head.*

Speaker B means "people in general should not do this." She is not giving personal instructions to the listener; the "you" does not refer to Speaker A.

☐ EXERCISE 33, p. 231.   *Understanding impersonal pronouns.*

Each item, like the example, has several acceptable answers. The students' task is to use pronouns **consistently** within an item. Verbs must also agree with their singular or plural subjects. The errors that need to be corrected for consistency are in italics:

2. *One* can't know what *he* can do until *you* try. [Change all pronouns to *one* OR *you* OR *a person . . . he . . . he tries.*]

3. It is important for *a person* to listen to *your* conscience. [*a person . . . his or her* OR *people . . . their consciences* OR *you . . . your*]

4. *You* can get to the airport . . . . *People* can catch the airport bus . . . .

5. Self-esteem is important to *one's* mental health. It is important for *you* to like *yourself*. [*Your . . . you . . . yourself* OR *one's . . . one . . . oneself/himself* OR *a person's . . . a person . . . herself/himself*]

6. It is important for *one* to take care of *their* health. For example, *you* should not smoke . . . . *One* should also be careful to get . . . . *People* can't be at *their* best if *one* **is** tired all the time. *We* also **need** to eat a wide variety of food to make sure *you* **get** all the nutrients *your* body needs. [The **verbs** must agree with their subjects.]

◇ WORKBOOK: Practices 27 and 28.

CHART 5-21: FORMS OF *OTHER*

• The phrase "every other" can have two meanings, depending on context and vocal emphasis:

  "*Every* other" = alternate (e.g., "I receive that magazine *every* other month.")
  "Every *other*" = all others (e.g., "George is the only student who missed the test; every *other* student took it last Friday.")

• Point out that *another* is a combination of the article "an" with "other," so "the" never precedes *another*. "The" and "a/an" are never used together. (A common mistake is, for example, "I bought *the another* book.")

☐ EXERCISES 34 & 35, pp. 232–234.   *Using forms of* other.

Do Exercise 34 as seatwork followed by discussion. Then, for additional practice, have the class do Exercise 35 more independently, perhaps in pairs or small groups, or as homework.

EX. 34 ANSWERS: 2. **Another** is . . . **Another** one . . . **Another** finger . . . **the other** finger
3. **The other** is [Throughout the unit on *other*, use your fingers and hands as discussed in items 2 and 3 to illustrate the meanings of *another, others, the other*, etc.]   4. **The others** can't   5. **The**

other people   **6.** any *others*   **7.** *other* books   **8.** *another* (means)   **9.** *Others* are
10. *the other (one)* is   **11.** *other* newspapers   **12.** *others* prefer   **13.** *each other/one another*
. . . *each other/one another* . . . *each other/one another* [in actual usage, there is no difference
between *each other* and *one another*.]   **14.** in *another* two years   **15.** *another* five minutes

EX. 35 ANSWERS: **1.** Another . . . Others . . . other   **2.** The other   **3.** Another . . .other
4. Another (one) . . . The other (one) . . . The other (one)   **5.** other   **6.** the others
7. others . . . others . . . other   **8.** the other   **9.** the others   **10.** another   **11.** each
other/one another   **12.** another   **13.** another   **14.** another   **15.** another

◇ **WORKBOOK:** Practices 29 and 30.

☐ **EXERCISE 36, p. 234.** *Using forms of* other.

    ANSWERS: [Depend on students' creativity.]

◇ **WORKBOOK:** Practice 31.

☐ **EXERCISE 37, p. 235.** *Cumulative review of number and agreement.*

    See the INTRODUCTION to this *Guide* (p. xiv) for suggestions on using error analysis
exercises. As another variation, you might divide the class into competing groups. Set a time
limit (about 5 minutes for advanced classes, 8 or 10 for intermediate students). The group that has
identified and corrected the most errors is declared the winner. (Deduct one point for each error
they overlook, for each correct word that they mistakenly identify as an error, and for each error
that they correct in an unacceptable way.) You may decide how to reward the winners—perhaps
by allowing their leader to be the "teacher" for Exercise 38.

    ANSWERS: **1.** That book *contains . . . kinds* of *stories* and *articles.*   **2.** There *are* a lot of
differences OR There is a lot of *difference* between . . . .   **3.** Ø English is . . . *languages* in the
world. ["The English language" is also correct, but using the word *language(s)* twice creates a
repetitious sentence.]   **4.** . . . in every possible *way.*   **5.** . . . to *do* all of my *homework/
assignments.*   **6.** . . . one of the best *armies*   **7.** There *is a lot of* equipment OR There are
many *kinds of/pieces of* equipment . . . .   **8.** All of the *guests* enjoyed *themselves* . . . .
9. I have a *five-year-old* daughter and a *three-year-old* son.   **10.** I am not accustomed to Ø cold
weather.   **11.** Each/Every *state* in the country *has* . . . .   **12.** Most of *the* people in my
apartment building *are* . . . .   **13.** A political leader . . . *himself/herself* OR Political *leaders* . . .
themselves   **14.** In my opinion, Ø foreign *students* should live in a dormitory because they . . . .
Also, if *they* live in a dormitory, *their* food is provided for *them.*   **15.** . . . apply for Ø another
one.   **16.** . . . all of the *other* students . . . .

◇ **WORKBOOK:** Practices 32, 33, and 34. Practice Tests A and B.

☐ **EXERCISE 38, p. 236.** *Prepositions.*

    At the end of every chapter, there are some exercises for prepositions and phrasal verbs. The
purpose is to introduce or review a few items at a time. There are no helpful rules for most
preposition combinations, so students need to practice them frequently to gain familiarity.
    To be sure that your students understand what a preposition is, you may wish to do Exercise 1
in Appendix A (page A2) with them. Appendix 2 (pp. A24–A28) lists common preposition
combinations that are used in the exercises.

    ANSWERS: **1.** believe *in*   **2.** engaged *to* [= promised to get married to]   **3.** substituted *for*
4. distinguish . . . *from*   **5.** forgive . . . *for*   **6.** rely *(up)on*   **7.** protect . . . *from*   **8.** excels
in [*excel* is pronounced /ɛksɛl/ and means "to be excellent or superior in performance"]

9. contributed . . . *to*   10. succeed *in*   11. fond *of*   12. rescued . . . *from*   13. care *for* [= like the taste of]   14. care *about* [= feel responsible for, worry about]   15. jealous *of*

☐ **EXERCISE 39, p. 236.**   *Phrasal verbs.*

Pairs of students should read these dialogues aloud. Everyone should be able to hear the answers clearly, and the "performers" should use some dramatic expression in their voices, as if in a theater.

ANSWERS: **1.** pass these papers out/around   **2.** to check into the hotel . . . and check out   **3.** get along   **4.** drop you off   **5.** looking after [= taking care of, feeding, etc.]   **6.** turn in [= go to bed]   **7.** take your sweater off   **8.** look it up   **9.** Pick out [= select, choose]   **10.** get over it [= become well again]

Chapter 6: ADJECTIVE CLAUSES

ORDER OF CHAPTER	CHARTS	EXERCISES	WORKBOOK
Adjective clauses: Introduction	6-1		
Using *who, who(m), which, that, whose*	6-2 → 6-4	Ex. 1 → 6	Pr. 1 → 8
Using *where, when*	6-5 → 6-6	Ex. 7 → 8	Pr. 9
Cumulative review and practice		Ex. 9 → 18	Pr. 10 → 11
Using adjective clauses to modify pronouns	6-7	Ex. 19	
Punctuation of adjective clauses	6-8	Ex. 20 → 22	Pr. 12 → 15
Special adjective clauses	6-9 → 6-11	Ex. 23 → 27	Pr. 16 → 18
Cumulative review and practice			Pr. 19
Reduction of adjective clauses to phrases	6-12 → 6-13	Ex. 28 → 31	Pr. 20 → 23
Cumulative review and practice		Ex. 32	Pr. 24 → 29 Pr. Tests A&B

General Notes on Chapter 6

• OBJECTIVE: Learners understand their need to express more complex relationships between ideas than is possible in simple sentences alone. Even with a limited vocabulary, those who can employ dependent and independent clauses can greatly increase their communicative competence in the new language. Adjective clauses are productive because they allow expansion of the information contained in noun phrases.

• APPROACH: For learners, the most important feature of an adjective clause is the words that link it to a sentence. The chapter thus begins with exercises on such linking words and their position in the clause. All possible patterns of restrictive adjective clauses using subject pronouns, object pronouns, or *whose* are presented first. Then *where* and *when* are added, followed by a series of summary oral exercises that contain all of these patterns. The use of commas in punctuating restrictive and nonrestrictive clauses is explained next, and then some less frequent uses of adjective clauses. Finally, the reduction of adjective clauses to phrases is practiced.

• TERMINOLOGY: A **clause** is defined as a structure containing a subject and verb. Clauses can be either **independent/main** (like a simple, self-standing sentence) or **dependent/subordinate** (not meaningful by themselves). A **phrase** is defined as a multiword structure that does not contain a subject-verb combination. There are many kinds of phrases.

The term **relative pronoun** is not used in the text. Relative pronouns (e.g., *who, whom, which*) are called ''subject pronouns'' and ''object pronouns'' to emphasize their connection with personal pronouns (e.g., *she, them, it*) in both meaning and grammatical function.

The terms **restrictive** and **nonrestrictive** are footnoted but otherwise not used. Restrictive/essential/identifying clauses are called "clauses that don't need commas," and nonrestrictive/nonessential/nonidentifying clauses are called "clauses that need commas."

Some teachers report that before beginning this chapter, they find it useful to introduce the traditional terms **simple, complex,** and **compound** to discuss sentence types. These terms are not used in the text but certainly could be introduced by the teacher.

CHART 6-1: ADJECTIVE CLAUSES: INTRODUCTION

• In literature and academic publications, writers often construct very complicated sentences with multiple clauses. This has the effect of highlighting some information while putting other details in the background. Students need not try to produce such exceedingly complex sentences, but they should understand the concept of subordination: that a dependent clause is subordinate in structure as well as in meaning to the independent clause. For intermediate students, the immediate task is to learn to control an independent clause with only one dependent clause correctly attached to it. This can be quite challenging. For advanced students, the task is to review the basic forms of adjective clauses so that they can correct possible problems in their own usage. All learners need to gain experience and fluency in this fundamental structure.

• By way of an overview, perhaps mention to the class that they will be studying three kinds of dependent clauses: adjective clauses (Chapter 6), noun clauses (Chapter 7), and adverb clauses (Chapters 8 and 9). Or you might prefer to wait until Chapter 8 to pull together an overview of complex sentence structures in English.

CHART 6-2: USING SUBJECT PRONOUNS: *WHO, WHICH, THAT*

• The verb *modify* means "change" or "limit the meaning." Thus, the traditional grammarian says that an adjective modifies a noun. Students can be referred to Appendix 1, Chart A-3, for an understanding of the terms "modify" and "adjective." Point out that an adjective changes or limits the meaning of a noun slightly (*a friendly woman, an old woman, a tall woman*) and that an adjective clause likewise changes or limits the meaning of a noun slightly (*the woman who helped me, the woman I saw in the park, the woman the teacher was talking to*).

• Stylistically and idiomatically, *who* is usually preferred to *that*, and *that* is preferred to *which* when used as subject relative pronouns. At this point, the students are being asked to learn all possible correct patterns.

• Point out that the adjective clause comes immediately after the noun it modifies. This may interrupt the main clause. (Advise students that an adjective clause should be put as close as possible to the noun it modifies, but at times there may be an interrupting element, usually a modifying prepositional phrase: *I didn't recognize the man **in the blue suit** who waved at me. The student **from Rome** who lives down the hall has invited me to a party.*)

☐ EXERCISE 1, p. 239. *Using subject pronouns in adjective clauses.*

ANSWERS: **2.** The girl ***who/that*** *won the race* is happy.
    3. The student ***who/that*** *sits next to me* is from China. [Point out subject-verb agreement: In item 3, *who/that* refers to a singular noun (*student*), so the adjective clause verb (*sits*) is singular. In item 4, *who/that* refers to a plural noun (*students*), so the adjective clause verb (*sit*) is plural.

Also note that the main verbs (*is* and *are*) agree with the noun subjects at the beginning of the sentences; incorrect subject-verb agreement is a common error when there is an interrupting adjective clause.]

4. The students *who/that sit in the front row* are from China.
5. We are studying sentences *that/which contain adjective clauses.*
6. I am using a sentence *that/which contains an adjective clause.*
7. Alegebra problems contain letters *that/which stand for unknown numbers.*
8. The taxi driver *who/that took me to the airport* was friendly.

CHART 6-3 (1): USING OBJECT PRONOUNS: *WHO(M),* **   *WHICH, THAT***

• Review the difference between *subject* and *object* if necessary.

• Discuss informal vs. formal usage (e.g., informal = everyday conversation, letter to a friend; formal = business or school report, academic journal, encyclopedia). Ask your students when or if they need to use formal English.

• The object form *whom* is used primarily in formal writing. Even in nonrestrictive clauses (Chart 6-8), *who* seems to be preferred to *whom* by many native speakers in certain situations (e.g., *My best friend, **who** nobody else seems to like, needs to learn how to get along with people.*).

• In everyday English, an object relative pronoun is usually omitted from a restrictive clause. Students should have control of all possibilities, however, so that they understand what they are omitting. Also, they will learn in Chart 6-8 that in nonrestrictive clauses they cannot omit the object pronoun.

• Some languages connect clauses similar to these with a conjunction, not a pronoun. Those languages, therefore, keep the object pronoun in its normal position in the dependent clause. For some students, transferring this pattern may lead to an ungrammatical sentence in English. For example:

INCORRECT: *The book that I read **it** yesterday was enjoyable.*
INCORRECT: *I didn't know the man who(m) I spoke to **him.***

☐ EXERCISE 2, p. 239.   *Using object pronouns in adjective clauses.*

ANSWERS: **1.** The book *that/which/Ø I read* was good.
2. I liked the woman *who(m)/that/Ø I met at the party last night.*
3. I liked the composition *that/which/Ø you wrote.*
4. The people *who(m)/that/Ø we visited yesterday* were very nice.

CHART 6-3(2): A PRONOUN AS THE OBJECT OF A **   PREPOSITION IN AN ADJECTIVE CLAUSE**

• Common problems: (1) repeating the preposition: *. . . the woman about whom I told you about.*
    (2) omitting the preposition: *. . . the music that we listened last night.*

☐ EXERCISE 3, p. 240.   *Object of a preposition in an adjective clause.*

ANSWERS: **1.** The meeting *to which I went* was interesting.
    The meeting *which/that/Ø I went to* was interesting.
2. The man *to whom I talked yesterday* was very kind.
    The man *who(m)/that/Ø I talked to yesterday* was very kind.

3. I must thank the people **from whom** *I got a present.*
   I must thank the people **who(m)/that/Ø** *I got a present* **from.**
4. The picture **at which** *she was looking* was beautiful.
   The picture **which/that/Ø** *she was looking* **at** was beautiful.
5. The man **about whom** *I was telling you* is standing over there.
   The man **who(m)/that/Ø** *I was telling you* **about** is standing over there.

CHART 6-4: USING *WHOSE*

• *Whose* can be troublesome for students. It has a relatively low frequency, so they aren't as familiar with these adjective clauses as with the ones in the preceding charts. Emphasize that *whose* functions as a possessive **adjective** and needs to be paired with a noun.

☐ **EXERCISE 4, p. 241.** *Using* whose *in an adjective clause.*

> Word order is difficult for students. Take time with this exercise and use the chalkboard so that they can see the patterns.

> ANSWERS: **1.** I apologized to the woman **whose coffee** *I spilled.* [no *it*]
> **2.** The man **whose wallet** *was stolen* called the police.
> **3.** I met the woman **whose husband** *is the president of the corporation.*
> **4.** The professor **whose course** *I am taking* is excellent. [There is no masculine/feminine difference with *whose.*]
> **5.** Mr. North teaches a class for students **whose native language** *is not English.* [There is no singular/plural difference with *whose.*]
> **6.** I come from a country **whose history** *goes back thousands of years.*
> **7.** The people **whose house** *we visited* were nice.
> **8.** I live in a dormitory **whose residents** *come from many countries.*
> **9.** I have to call the man **whose umbrella** *I accidentally picked up after the meeting.*
> **10.** The man **whose beard** *caught on fire when he lit a cigarette* poured a glass . . . .

◇ **WORKBOOK:** Practices 1, 2, 3, 4, and 5.

☐ **EXERCISE 5, p. 241.** *Cumulative review of adjective clauses.*

> ANSWERS: **2.** *who/that* examined the sick child   **3.** for *whom* I was waiting OR *who(m)/that/Ø* I was waiting for   **4.** *that/which* David is writing   **5.** *whose* opinions I respect most
> **6.** *who(m)/that/Ø* I met last night   **7.** *that/which* occurred in California   **8.** with *whom* I was dancing OR *who(m)/that/Ø* I was dancing with

☐ **EXERCISE 6, p. 242.** *Cumulative review of adjective clauses.*

> Students can discuss these answers in small groups or prepare them individually as written seatwork. You should walk around the classroom as they work and answer any questions they have.

> ANSWERS: **2.** . . . topic **about which** *I know very little.* OR topic **which/that/Ø** *I know very little* **about.**   **3.** The students **who/that** *were absent from class* missed . . . .   **4.** . . . friend **who(m)/that/Ø** *I hadn't seen for years.*   **5.** . . . teacher **whose** *class I had missed.*   **6.** . . . women **who(m)/that/Ø** *we met at the meeting last night* are . . . .   **7.** . . . book **that/which** *was written by Jane Austen.*   **8.** The man **to whom** *I spoke* OR **who(m)/that/Ø** *I spoke* **to** gave . . . .   **9.** The instructor **whose** *course I failed* gives . . . .   **10.** . . . .money **which/that/Ø** *I had borrowed from my*

roommate.   **11.** . . . dog *that/which* bit my neighbor's daughter.   **12.** The people *whose* house I *am staying at* OR *at whose* house I am staying are very kind.

◇ WORKBOOK: Practices 6, 7, and 8.

CHARTS 6-5 and 6-6: USING *WHERE* AND *WHEN*

• *Where* and *when* substitute for prepositional phrases and serve as the link between an adjective clause and the noun that it modifies.

☐ EXERCISE 7, p. 243.   *Using* where *in adjective clauses.*

    ANSWERS: **1.** The city *where we spent our vacation* was beautiful.
          in which we spent our vacation
          which/that/Ø we spent our vacation in
  2. That is the restaurant *where I will meet you.*
       in which I will meet you.
       that/Ø/which I will meet you in.
  3. The town *where I grew up* is small.
      in which I grew up
      that/Ø/which I grew up in
  4. That is the drawer *where I keep my jewelry.*
       in which I keep my jewelry.
       that/Ø/which I keep my jewelry in.

☐ EXERCISE 8, p. 243.   *Using* when *in adjective clauses.*

    This exercise also provides a good opportunity to remind students of some prepositions of time: *at* a specific time of day; *in* a year, month, or week; *on* a day.

    ANSWERS: **1.** Monday is the day *when we will come.*
         on which we will come. [not *which . . . on*]
         that/Ø we will come. [no preposition]
  2. 7:05 ["Seven-oh-five"] is the time *when my plane arrives.*
          at which my plane arrives. [not *which . . . at*]
         that/Ø my plane arrives. [no preposition]
  3. 1960 is the year *when the revolution took place.*
       in which the revolution took place.
       that/Ø the revolution took place.
  4. July is the month *when the weather is usually the hottest.*
       in which the weather is usually the hottest.
       that/Ø the weather is usually the hottest.

◇ WORKBOOK: Practice 9.

☐ EXERCISE 9, p. 244.   *Using* where *in adjective clauses.*

    You may want to lead the class through the first five items, then divide them into pairs or small groups. One student in each group is the "leader" who has an open book. The others must listen and respond with their books closed. (See the INTRODUCTION, pp. x–xviii, for suggestions for using various exercise types.)
    Ask the students to omit the pronoun and include the preposition for at least some of the items.

ANSWERS: **1.** That is the room where we have class. [Also: That's the room we have class in.]
2. That's the restaurant where we ate dinner.   **3.** That's the building where he works.
4. That's the street where he lives.   **5.** That's the cafeteria where I [change *you* to *I*] eat
lunch.   **6.** That's the bank where I keep my money.   **7.** That's the store where I do my
grocery shopping.   **8.** That's the island where I spent my vacation.   **9.** That's the lake where
I went swimming.   **10.** That's the town where I grew up.   **11.** That's the room where the
examination will be given.   **12.** That's the country where the earthquake occurred.
13. That's the university where my sister went to graduate school.   **14.** That's the park where
we're going to have a picnic.   **15.** That's the city where I lived until I was ten years old.

☐ **EXERCISE 10, p. 244.**   *Omitted pronoun patterns.*

The exercise provides practice on two important points. First is the use of articles. Each item
is a **general** statement using the indefinite article *a(n)*. Adding an adjective clause after a noun can
change that noun to a **definite,** identified concept requiring the definite article *the*. (It is, of
course, also possible for an adjective clause to follow an indefinite noun: *She told me about a letter
she had written.*)

The second focus of this exercise is the omission of the object pronouns, in other words, the
choice of the "Ø" option—the option that native speakers most often choose in everyday English.

You might begin by writing on the chalkboard: *Did she tell you about the letter that she wrote?*
Give the cue: "She wrote a letter." Then point out the change from *a* to *the*. Next, erase the word
that from the chalkboard, reminding students of this option and encouraging them to use "Ø" in
their responses (though accepting any correct response). Finally, erase *the letter she wrote*, and tell
the students to begin their answers with the words *Did she tell you about . . . .*

ADDITIONAL SUGGESTION: This exercise becomes more like a dialogue if you identify "she" (a
female student or teacher) and follow this pattern:

> TEACHER to STUDENT A: *Yoko wrote a letter. Does Ali know that?*
> STUDENT A to STUDENT B (Ali): *I'll ask him. Ali, did Yoko tell you about the letter she wrote?*
> STUDENT B to STUDENT A: *Yes, she did. She told me about the letter she wrote.* OR *No, she didn't.
> She didn't tell me about the letter she wrote.*

Don't interrupt to make corrections until the dialogue is completed by both students.

ANSWERS: *Did she tell you about . . . .*   **1.** the report she wrote?   **2.** the letter she got?
3. the party she went to?   **4.** the people she met?   **5.** the trip she took?   **6.** the movie she
went to?   **7.** the program she saw on TV?   **8.** the test she took?   **9.** the book she read?
10. the furniture she bought?   **11.** the accident she saw?   **12.** the man she met?   **13.** the
woman she talked to?   **14.** the problem she had?   **15.** the physics course she took?

☐ **EXERCISE 11, p. 244.**   *Omitted pronoun patterns.*

These sentences are longer than those in Exercise 10. Repeat as necessary. This exercise is
good practice for listening comprehension skill and for fluency of oral production.

ANSWERS: *Yes. She told me about . . . .*   **1.** the letter she wrote/had written to the President of
the United States.   **2.** the letter she got from her brother yesterday.   **3.** the party she went to
yesterday.   **4.** the people she met at that party.   **5.** the trip she took to Mexico last summer.
6. the experiences she had in Mexico.   **7.** the small town she used to live in.   **8.** the presents
she got for her birthday.   **9.** the experiment she did in (the) chemistry lab yesterday.   **10.** the
term paper she had to write for her English course.   **11.** the American history course she took
last semester.   **12.** the science fiction book she's reading.

EXPANSION: Add other items, using your students' names. Students sometimes have fun trying to
remember longer items, e.g., *Did she meet an interesting young man at the party Roberto had at his
aunt's house last Saturday?* Approximations in the responses are fine.

As always, adapt the items to your particular students as much as possible, changing the vocabulary (such as, from "chair" to "desk"), omitting some items, making up other items of your own. The text gives only affirmative responses in the examples; however, students can give negative responses if they wish.

Instead of being teacher-led, this exercise could be done by pairs or small groups.

ANSWERS: **1.** Yes, the chair I'm sitting *in* is comfortable. **2.** Yes, the man I saw was wearing a brown suit. **3.** Yes, the woman I talked *to* answered my question. **4.** Yes, the meat I had for dinner last night was good. **5.** Yes, the coat I bought keeps me warm. **6.** Yes, the soccer game I went *to* was exciting. **7.** Yes, the TV program I watched last night was good. **8.** Yes, the _____ I'm wearing are comfortable. **9.** Yes, the hotel I stayed *at* was in the middle of the city. **10.** Yes, the cafeteria I eat *at* has good food. **11.** Yes, the package I got in the mail was from my parents. **12.** Yes, the exercise I'm doing is easy.

□ **EXERCISE 13, p. 245.** *Cumulative review of adjective clauses.*

ANSWERS: [Affirmative answers are given; students may give negative answers if they wish.] *Yes, . . .* **1.** the waiter who served me at the restaurant was polite. **2.** the barber who cut my hair did a good job. **3.** the clerk who cashed my check asked for identification. **4.** the man who stopped me on the street asked me for directions. **5.** the student who stopped me in the hall asked me for the correct time. **6.** the woman who stepped on my toe apologized. **7.** the car that drove through the red light hit another car. **8.** most of the students who took the test passed. **9.** all of the students who are sitting in this room can speak English. **10.** the woman who shouted at me was angry. **11.** I thanked the police officer who helped me. **12.** I know the person who is sitting next to me. **13.** I like the professor who teaches Chemistry 101. [You might substitute the name of another course in your school.] **14.** I had a conversation with the taxi driver who took me to the bus station. **15.** I recognized the woman who came into the room. **16.** I thanked the man who opened the door for me. **17.** I'm sitting next to the student who is wearing a/the . . . **18.** I joined the students who were sitting on the grass outside the classroom building. **19.** I finished the book that I was reading. **20.** I enjoyed the party that I went to last night. **21.** I found the book that I was looking for. **22.** I believed the story that (. . .) told me. **23.** I opened the present that (. . .) gave me. **24.** I returned the pen that I borrowed from (. . .). **25.** I laughed at the joke that (. . .) told me.

□ **EXERCISE 14, p. 246.** *Prepositions in adjective clauses.*

Encourage omission of relative pronouns, but accept any correct pattern the student produces.

POSSIBLE ANSWERS: [Depend on students' creativity.] **1.** The person I'm looking at is/has/speaks/looks/(etc.) . . . . **2.** The desk I'm sitting at . . . . **3.** The student this book belongs to . . . . **4.** The field of study I'm interested in . . . . **5.** The music (. . .) and I listened to . . . . **6.** The movie (. . .) and I went to last night . . . . **7.** The movie (. . .) was talking about . . . . **8.** The man the police are looking for . . . .(etc.)

□ **EXERCISE 15, p. 247.** *Adjective clauses with* whose.

ANSWERS: **1.** There is the woman whose husband is a football player. **2.** There is the boy whose father is a doctor. **3.** There is the girl whose mother is a dentist. **4.** There is the person whose picture was in the newspaper. **5.** There is the man whose dog bit me. **6.** There is the man whose daughter won . . . . **7.** There is the woman whose car was stolen. **8.** There is the student whose lecture notes I borrowed. **9.** There is the woman whose keys I found. **10.** There is the teacher whose class I'm in. **11.** There is the author whose book I read. **12.** There is the man whose wife we met.

□ EXERCISE 16, p. 247.   *Adjective clauses with* whose.

> ANSWERS: **1.** (. . .) is the student whose book I found.   **2.** (. . .) is the student whose dictionary I borrowed.   **3.** Mark Twain is the author whose books I like best.   **4.** I thanked the woman whose phone I used.   **5.** The child whose toy I broke started to cry.   **6.** The family at whose house I stayed were very kind.   **7.** The woman whose purse was stolen called the police.   **8.** (. . .) is the singer whose music I like best.   **9.** The girl whose leg is in a cast has trouble climbing stairs. [A cast is a covering that keeps a broken bone from moving. It is made of thick white plaster.]   **10.** Everyone tried to help the family whose house had burned down.

□ EXERCISE 17, p. 247.   *Cumulative review of adjective clauses.*

> Students should use *the* in their responses.

> ANSWERS: [Depend on students' creativity.]

□ EXERCISE 18, p. 248.   *Cumulative review of adjective clauses.*

> Follow the instructions in the textbook. The idea is to make this as much like a natural conversation as possible. It is not necessary to use exactly the words in the book. Use ideas and things that occur naturally in your classroom with your students. Encourage them to exchange real information, to tell the truth, or to invent an interesting fact.

> TEACHER (looking around the room):   *Who got a letter yesterday?*
> A STUDENT: *I did.*
> TEACHER: *Who was it from?*
> THE STUDENT: *My brother.*
> TEACHER (to another student):   *Can you summarize this information?* [Point to the word "The" that you have written on the chalkboard as a way of reminding the student how to begin.]
> THE SECOND STUDENT: *The letter (. . .) got yesterday was from his brother.*

> ANSWERS: [Depend on students' creativity.]

CHART 6-7: USING ADJECTIVE CLAUSES TO MODIFY PRONOUNS

• Discourage students from using adjective clauses to modify personal pronouns. Sometimes students get enthusiastic about gaining control of adjective clauses and want to use them everywhere, including following personal pronouns, for example, *I, who am a student from Malaysia, am studying English.* Explain that such structures, even though grammatically logical, rarely occur idiomatically.

□ EXERCISE 19, p. 249.   *Using adjective clauses to modify pronouns.*

> Using adjective clauses to modify indefinite pronouns is a very common pattern; it is assumed that the students are familiar with it and will have little difficulty with idiomatic responses for items 2 through 9. The pronouns to be modified in 10 through 13 are included mainly for advanced students and may be difficult for intermediate students.

> POSSIBLE ANSWERS: **2.** . . . I need to ask you.   **3.** he can depend on.   **4.** I can do.   **5.** [Depends on students' creativity.]   **6.** she meets.   **7.** she said.   **8.** the teacher says.   **9.** he says is true.   **10.** who is standing.   **11.** we had today.   **12.** I took last semester.   **13.** who were late.

◇ WORKBOOK: Practices 10 and 11.

CHART 6-8: PUNCTUATION OF ADJECTIVE CLAUSES

• The use of commas with adjective clauses is rather difficult to learn. In fact, native speakers of English are sometimes uncertain about this point.

• This chart contains several important points, so you should plan to spend time discussing them and providing additional examples. The following exercises should help students understand the usage more easily.

☐ **EXERCISE 20, p. 251.** *Using commas with adjective clauses.*

You should read the first two items aloud as examples for students to follow. Demonstrate to them how to pause and lower the voice between commas. Read the complete sentence, then comment on the punctuation, as illustrated in items 1 and 2.

ANSWERS: **3.** no commas; *who* can be *that* **4.** commas (before *who* and after *night*); *who* cannot be *that* **5.** no commas; *who* can be *that* **6.** commas (before *who* and after *Russian*); *who* cannot change **7.** no commas; *which* can be *that* [In formal English, *which* may be considered stylistically unacceptable in restrictive clauses.] **8.** commas (before *which* and after *countries*); *which* cannot change **9.** comma (before *which*); *which* cannot change **10.** no comma; *which* can be *that* **11.** commas (before *which* and after *Mexico*); *which* cannot change **12.** no commas; *which* can be *that* **13.** commas (before *whose son* and after *contest*; no commas in the second sentence; *whose* cannot change in either sentence) **14.** commas (before *which* and after *Asia*); *which* cannot change **15.** no commas; *which* can be *that*

◇ WORKBOOK: Practices 12 and 13.

☐ **EXERCISE 21, p. 252.** *Understanding (non)restrictive clauses.*

ANSWERS: **1.** b **2.** a **3.** a **4.** b **5.** a **6.** a **7.** Only some apples were rotten. **8.** All the apples were rotten. **9.** Only some students were excused. **10.** All the students were excused. **11.** Cindy got one present. **12.** Cindy got several presents. **13.** There were other maps in the room, hanging on other walls. **14.** They were the only maps in the room.

◇ WORKBOOK: Practice 14.

☐ **EXERCISE 22, p. 253.** *Punctuating adjective clauses.*

This is a summary exercise. Students should do it at home, where they have plenty of time to ponder. Then in class you can lead a discussion of each item as students check their work. Also possible is group work, where students can discuss the punctuation among themselves.

ANSWERS: **1.** no commas **2.** comma (before *where*) **3.** commas (before *which* and after *mammal*) **4.** no commas; *which* can be *that* or Ø **5.** comma (before *which*) **6.** no additional comma; *which* can be *that* **7.** comma (before *which*) **8.** commas (before *which* and after *land*) **9.** no commas; *who* can be *that* **10.** commas (before *which* and after *gold*) **11.** comma (before *which*) **12.** no commas; *who* can be *that* **13.** comma (before *where*) **14.** no commas; *who* can be *that* **15.** no commas in the first sentence; *which* can be *that* or Ø; *who* can be *that*; second sentence needs commas (before *who* and after *jeans*) **16.** first sentence: no commas; second sentence: commas (before *who* and after *bees*); third sentence: no commas; *who* can be *that*

◇ **WORKBOOK:** Practice 15.

CHART 6-9: USING EXPRESSIONS OF QUANTITY IN ADJECTIVE CLAUSES

• This is a pattern where *whom* is always used (not *who*), even in speech.

☐ **EXERCISE 23, p. 254.** *Understanding expressions of quantity in adjective clauses.*

ANSWERS: **2.** . . . symphonies, *one of which* was Beethoven's Seventh. **3.** . . . pairs of shoes, *none of which* I liked. **4.** . . . people, *the majority of whom* are farmers. **5.** . . . employees, *all of whom* are computer experts. **6.** After the riot, over one hundred people, *many of whom* had been innocent bystanders, were taken to the hospital.

☐ **EXERCISE 24, p. 254.** *Using expressions of quantity in adjective clauses.*

ANSWERS: [Depend on students' creativity.] **2.** one of which **3.** all of whom **4.** one of which **5.** neither of whom **6.** most of which **7.** some of whom **8.** several of which

◇ **WORKBOOK:** Practice 16

CHART 6-10: USING *NOUN + OF WHICH*

• This pattern does not occur often, but students should understand its meaning.

• Sometimes the choice between using *whose* and *of which* is not clear when the clause modifies a nonhuman noun. We can use both:

*the table, the top **of which** . . . .* OR *the table, **whose** top . . . .*

☐ **EXERCISE 25, p. 255.** *Understanding NOUN + of which.*

ANSWERS: **2.** . . . painting, the value of which is over a million dollars. **3.** . . . magazine, the title of which is *Contemporary Architectural Styles.* **4.** . . . coffee, the price of which varies according to fluctuations in the world market. **5.** . . . experiments, the results of which will be published in the *Journal of Science.* **6.** . . . paper, the purpose of which is to acquaint them with methods of scholarly inquiry.

CHART 6-11: USING *WHICH* TO MODIFY A WHOLE SENTENCE

• Another way to explain this usage is to consider the first sentence as a fact. It could be illustrated this way:

*Tom was late. **That (fact)** surprised me.*
*Tom was late, **(a fact) which** surprised me.*

• Make sure that students understand that *that* and *this* are used here as demonstrative pronouns that refer to a whole sentence.

□ **EXERCISE 26, p. 256.** *Understanding* which *as a sentence modifier.*

> *ANSWERS:* **2.** . . . job, which surprised . . . .   **3.** . . . herself, which irritates me.
> **4.** . . . right away, which I appreciated very much. [no object pronoun *that*]   **5.** . . . on
> Highway 5, which means (that [noun clause]) I'll be . . . .   **6.** . . . necktie, which was really . . . .

□ **EXERCISE 27, p. 256.** *Using* which *as a sentence modifier.*

> *ANSWERS:*   [Depend on students' creativity.]

◇ **WORKBOOK:** Practices 17, 18, and 19.

CHARTS 6-12 and 6-13: REDUCTION OF ADJECTIVE CLAUSES TO PHRASES

• *Clause* and *phrase* are traditional terms in grammar. As usual, it is not our purpose to teach students the terminology. The purpose is to show them how to use English correctly. In this case, they benefit by seeing two related structures together. Each structure has a name, but students should focus on the structures, not on their names. (They could just as well be called "A" and "B" or "long" and "short" instead of "clause" and "phrase.") Therefore, on a test, it is not advisable to ask learners to identify clauses and phrases; it is more useful to have them **produce** alternative forms of one structure or the other.

• Some other terms used for adjective phrases (Chart 6-13) are

> modifying participial phrase: *The man **talking to John** . . . .*
> *The ideas **presented in that book** . . . .*
> appositive: *George Washington, **the first president,** was . . . .*

In these exercises, these types are simply called adjective phrases.

□ **EXERCISE 28, p. 258.** *Understanding adjective phrases.*

> This exercise is intended as immediate followup to explanation of Chart 6-13. Give students a few minutes to make the necessary changes, then open the discussion, reviewing each sentence carefully.
>
> *ANSWERS:*   **2.** The people waiting for the bus . . . .   **3.** I come from a city located in . . . .
> **4.** The children attending that school . . . .   **5.** The scientists researching the causes . . . .
> **6.** The fence surrounding our house . . . . [The fence surrounds the house; the house is surrounded by the fence.]   **7.** They live in a house built in 1890.   **8.** We have an apartment overlooking the park.

◇ **WORKBOOK:** Practice 20 and 21.

□ **EXERCISE 29, p. 258.** *Understanding adjective phrases.*

> After it is clear that the students understand the grammar in Exercise 28, they can do this exercise more independently. Students may work in pairs to decide on their answers, or may be assigned to do it for out-of-class preparation.
>
> *ANSWERS:*   **1.** (omit *who is*)   **2.** the message concerning   **3.** (omit *that are*)
> **4.** (omit *which is* and *which are*)   **5.** The rules allowing   **6.** (omit *which were*)   **7.** the problems facing   **8.** (omit *who was*)   **9.** The psychologists studying   **10.** (omit *which was*)
> **11.** Pictures showing   **12.** (omit *which is*)   **13.** The Indians living   **14.** the students hoping . . . one-tenth of those applying   **15.** persons possessing the technical skill required [Ask

the students to paraphrase sentence 15. In all probability, their paraphrase will be clearer and more to the point than the sentence in the text, which is an example of "academese." A possible paraphrase: *Today repairmen (repair people?) are important in our society because people's daily comforts depend on inventions such as cars, refrigerators, and hot water heaters.*]

☐ **EXERCISE 30, p. 259.** *Understanding adjective phrases and clauses.*

In this exercise, the reverse of the last two exercises, students must expand phrases into clauses. When they read books and articles, it can be important for them to be able to determine what key structure words have been omitted from a complicated sentence.

ANSWERS: **2.** one of the agricultural products *that/which was/were* introduced [Traditional grammar would require a plural verb (*were*) to agree with *products*, but in actual usage, many native speakers prefer the singular verb (*was*) in an adjective clause that modifies a plural noun following *one of*.] . . . Some of the other products *that/which were* introduced **3.** a novel *that/which was* written **4.** The sunlight *that/which comes* **5.** Mercury, *which is* the nearest **6.** The pyramids, *which are* the monumental tombs **7.** The sloth, *which is* a slow-moving animal *which/that is* found in [If a student asks, "What is a sloth?", tell him/her to try to figure it out alone before you give any further information. Point out that one of the main functions of adjective clauses is to provide definitions.] **8.** those *who are* arrested **9.** St. Louis, Missouri, *which is* known as . . . Pierre Laclede, *who was* a French fur trader **10.** Any student *who/that does not want* to go

☐ **EXERCISE 31, p. 259.** *Using adjective phrases.*

Students who find this exercise difficult might prefer to make an adjective clause first, then reduce it to a phrase. Or you can ask the students to make the appositive first, then change it to an adjective clause.

ANSWERS: **2.** John Quincy Adams, the sixth president of the United States, was born on July 11, 1767. **3.** . . . used in Helsinki, the capital of Finland. **4.** The Washington National Monument, a towering obelisk made of white marble, is . . . . **5.** Honolulu, best known to the traveler for Waikiki Beach, has . . . . [No *the* is used with *best* because *best* does not modify a noun here; it is the superlative form of the adverb *well*.] **6.** Libya, a country in North Africa, is a leading producer of oil.

◇ **WORKBOOK:** Practices 22, 23, 24, and 25.

☐ **EXERCISE 32, p. 260.** *Cumulative review.*

Students might work individually or in small groups to identify and remedy the errors they find. Perhaps ask them to count the number of errors they find.

ANSWERS: [Words in parentheses may be omitted.]
1. It is important to be polite to people who **live** in the same building.
2. She lives in a hotel (that/which is) restricted to senior citizens.
3. My sister has two **children, whose** names are . . . .
4. He comes from Venezuela, (which is) a Spanish-speaking country. [Note the comma.]
5. . . . Thailand, seven of **which are located** in Bangkok, (which is) the capital city. [Note the comma.]
6. . . . several problems (which/that) I have faced [no *them*] since I **came** to the United **States.**
7. There is a small wooden screen **separating** [OR which/that separates] the bed from the rest of the room. OR A small wooden screen separates the bed from the rest of the room.
8. . . . relatives **who(m)/that** I had never met [no *them*] before.
9. It is almost impossible to find two peopel [OR persons] whose opinions are the same.
10. On the wall, there is a colorful poster that/which [no *it*] consists of [OR poster consisting of] a group of young people (who are) dancing.

◇ **WORKBOOK:** Practices 26, 27, 28, and 29. Practice Tests A and B.

☐ **EXERCISE 33, p. 260.** *Using prepositions.*

Prepositions are listed in Appendix 2, pp. A24–A28. Students should try to complete this exercise before looking at the lists.

ANSWERS: **1.** known for   **2.** faithful to   **3.** counting on you   **4.** prohibited from   **5.** afraid of   **6.** take good care of   **7.** worried about   **8.** agree with   **9.** decided on   **10.** vote for   **11.** absent from   **12.** be polite to   **13.** hoping for   **14.** aware of   **15.** fight for

☐ **EXERCISE 34, p. 261.** *Using phrasal verbs.*

After deciding on their answers, pairs of students could read the dialogues aloud.

ANSWERS: **1.** get through [= finish a task]   **2.** give up   **3.** passed out [*got dizzy* = had a whirling sensation in the head; *revive* = return to normal breathing; *out cold* = unconscious, in a faint]   **4.** took over [*passed out* = fainted, became suddenly unconscious]   **5.** keep up with   **6.** cross it out [= make a line through it with pen or pencil]   **7.** get it back   **8.** call on   **9.** got on . . . got off   **10.** got into . . . got out of   **11.** got on . . . got off [*Des Moines* (a city in the state of Iowa) is pronounced with NO final -*s*/-*es* sounds: /di moin/.]   **12.** gets on . . . gets off

Chapter 7: NOUN CLAUSES

ORDER OF CHAPTER	CHARTS	EXERCISES	WORKBOOK
Noun clauses: Introduction	7-1		
Survey of noun clauses	7-2 → 7-5	Ex. 1 → 13	Pr. 1 → 10
Quoted speech vs. reported speech	7-6 → 7-7	Ex. 14 → 21	Pr. 11 → 15
Cumulative review and practice		Ex. 22 → 25	Pr. 16 → 19
Using the subjunctive in noun clauses	7-8	Ex. 26 → 27	Pr. 20
Using *-ever* words	7-9	Ex. 28	Pr. 21
Cumulative review and practice			Pr. Tests A & B

General Notes on Chapter 7:

• OBJECTIVE: One of the most common uses of conversation and writing is to report what was said by someone else. Another very common use is to express one's own opinion about or reaction to some situation. Therefore, speakers begin many sentences with "he/she/they said" and "I think" (or their equivalents) followed by a noun clause. Learners should pay special attention in this chapter to **the order of words** in a noun clause and **punctuation** with quoted speech.

• APPROACH: The chapter focuses attention on the words that introduce noun clauses. It begins by focusing on the use of question words and the confusing similarity between noun clauses and questions. The students transform questions into noun clauses. Then, many of the variations in the use of "*that* clauses" are presented. Next, the students learn to punctuate quoted speech, and then to make adjustments in verb forms and pronouns as they change it into reported speech. Added to the end of the chapter are two short sections, one on the subjunctive in noun clauses and one on words such as *whatever, whoever, whenever,* etc.

• TERMINOLOGY: **Noun clauses** are referred to variously as embedded sentences, embedded questions, indirect speech, nominal clauses, or certain kinds of complements. **Words used to introduce noun clauses** are labeled *conjunctions* in dictionaries. **Quoted and reported** speech is also called direct and indirect address/speech/discourse. **Question words** are also called "Wh-words" or interrogatives (interrogative pronouns, interrogative adjectives, interrogative adverbs). **Information questions** are also called "Wh-questions."

```
┌─────────────────────────────────────────────────────────────────────────┐
│   CHARTS 7-1 and 7-2:  INTRODUCTION: NOUN CLAUSES WHICH                    │
│                        BEGIN WITH A QUESTION WORD                          │
└─────────────────────────────────────────────────────────────────────────┘
```

• It is often useful to substitute the pronoun *something* in the place of noun clauses. Then students replace a pronoun with a clause. For example:

Something *was interesting.*
What he said *was interesting.*

I heard **something.**
I heard **what he said.**

• The main problem for most learners is word order. Also, they may try to use *do* or *did*, as in a question.

☐ EXERCISE 1, p. 264.   *Understanding noun clauses.*

      Ask students to write the complete sentences on the chalkboard, then use these to identify the noun clauses, discuss their grammatical function in the sentence, and label the subjects and verbs in both the independent and dependent clauses.

      If your students have difficulty with this exercise, you might suggest that they use a two-step approach to developing an answer:

      Step 1: *I don't know* **something.** Step 2: *I don't know* **how old he is.**
      Step 1: **Something** *was interesting.* Step 2: **What he was talking about** *was interesting.*

ANSWERS: **3.** Please tell me *where you live.*   **4.** *What she said* wasn't true.   **5.** Do you know *when they are coming?* [Note the question mark; however, there is no change of word order in the noun clause. The independent clause contains the question word order.]   **6.** I can't remember *how much it costs.*   **7.** Let's ask him *which one he wants.*   **8.** I don't know *who is coming to the party.*   **9.** I don't know *who those people are.*   **10.** Do you know *whose pen this is?*   **11.** *Why they left the country* is a secret.   **12.** *What we are doing in class* is easy.   **13.** *Where she went* is none of your business.   **14.** I don't remember *how many letters there are in the English alphabet.* [There are 26 letters.]   **15.** I don't know *who the mayor of New York City is.*   **16.** I need to find out *how old a person has to be to get a driver's license.*

☐ EXERCISE 2, p. 265.   *Word order in noun clauses.*

      Substitute familiar names between parentheses. You might also want to change some of the items so that they are related to information about your students' lives.

      This exercise can start slowly and get faster as the students become accustomed to the pattern. There's no need to rush, however. Allow spontaneous interchanges to develop if students have interesting things they want to say.

      You may wish to select students at random instead of in a predictable order, or sometimes have the whole class respond in chorus to one or two items for a change of pace.

      Alternative formats: Have the students tell you to ask someone else the question.

      TEACHER: *Where does Ali live?*
      STUDENT: *I don't know. Ask Ali/him where he lives.*

Or start a chain involving 3 students.

      TEACHER: *Maria, what is Ali's favorite color?*
    STUDENT A (Maria): *I don't know. Roberto, ask Ali what his favorite color is.*
  STUDENT B (Roberto): *Ali, what's your favorite color?*
     STUDENT C (Ali): *Blue.*

Write the pattern on the board: A: I don't know. _____, ask _____.
                                               B: _____, _____?
                                               C: (answer)

ANSWERS: [The noun clauses are given.] **1.** . . . where (. . .) lives.   **2.** . . . what country (. . .) is from.   **3.** . . . how long (. . .) has been living here.   **4.** . . . what (. . .)'s telephone number is.   **5.** . . . where the post office is.   **6.** . . . how far it is to (. . .)   **7.** . . . why (. . .) is absent.   **8.** . . . where your book is.   **9.** . . . what kind of watch (. . .) has.   **10.** . . . why (. . .) was absent yesterday.   **11.** . . . where (. . .) went yesterday.   **12.** . . . what (. . .)'s favorite color is.   **13.** . . . how long (. . .) has been married.   **14.** . . . how (. . .) met his wife/her husband.   **15.** . . . what the capital of (. . .) is.   **16.** . . . what the population of (. . .) is.   **17.** . . . why (. . .) was late to class.   **18.** . . . why we are doing this exercise.   **19.** . . . what kind of government (. . .) has.   **20.** . . . where (. . .) is going to eat lunch/dinner.   **21.** . . . when the semester ends.   **22.** . . . when (. . .) vacation starts.   **23.** . . . where (. . .) went after class yesterday.   **24.** . . . why (. . .) is smiling.   **25.** . . . how many questions you have asked in this exercise.   **26.** . . . how often (. . .) goes to the library.   **27.** . . . whose book that is.   **28.** . . . how much that book cost. [*cost* = past tense; *costs* = present]

EXPANSION: Exercise 2 can also be used for an oral review of question forms (in preparation for the next two exercises, in which the students have to produce questions). The teacher gives the noun clause, and the students give the questions:

    TEACHER: *Yoko, ask Maria where **Ali lives.***
    STUDENT A: *Maria, where **does Ali live?***
    STUDENT B: *In the dorm.* (OR *I don't know where he lives.*)

◇ **WORKBOOK:** Practice 1, 2, and 3.

☐ **EXERCISE 3, p. 266.** *Word order in questions and noun clauses.*

One purpose of this exercise is to review question forms. Use it to make sure the students have control of word order differences in questions and noun clauses. Have the students write the answers on the board so that you can compare the important features of the two structures. Refer students to Appendix 1, Unit B, or review the question unit with the whole class.

ANSWERS: **2.** Where does George live? I want to know where George lives.   **3.** What did Ann buy? Do you know what Ann bought?   **4.** How far is it to Denver from here? I need to know how far it is to Denver from here.   **5.** Why was Jack late to class? The teacher wants to know why Jack was late to class.   **6.** Whose pen is that? Tom wants to know whose pen that is.
7. Who(m) did Alex see at the meeting? I don't know who(m) Alex saw (at the meeting).
8. Who saw Mrs. Frost at the meeting? I don't know who saw Mrs. Frost (at the meeting).
9. Which book does Alice like best? I want to know which book Alice likes best.   **10.** What time/When is the plane supposed to land? Could you tell me what time/when the plane is supposed to land?

☐ **EXERCISE 4, p. 267.** *Using questions and noun clauses.*

One option: Appoint a Student A and a Student B for each item. A's book is open; B doesn't look at the book. The rest of the class can listen.

Another option: Divide the class into pairs. A and B can switch roles halfway through. Follow the pair work with a quick quiz in which you give about 5 items from the exercise and the students write the answers.

As another option, you might set this up as follows: In a real situation, people sometimes fail to understand what was said, then they turn to another person for clarification. So you—with your book open—say the sentence to Student A, who "misunderstands" you. A turns to Student B and asks the question "for clarification." B "doesn't know" the answer, so B reports the question to

Student C. C, who listened carefully to what you said, gives the answer to A. [Note that C's answer will normally use pronouns because everyone by that time knows the situation.]

TEACHER: *Ali lives in an apartment.*
STUDENT A [to Student B]: *Where does Ali live?*
STUDENT B [to Student C]: *Yoko, Maria wants to know where Ali lives. Do you know?*
STUDENT C [to Student B]: *Yes. He lives in an apartment.*

Write on the board:

A: _____?
B: _____ wants to know _____. Do you know?
C: Yes. _____.

The same chain could be set up in a group of students. Only the leader has an open book. The leader should change the direction of the chain after two or three items. Different students could become leaders for groups of items.

ANSWERS: **3.** A: *What* does Tom want for his birthday? B: (. . .) wants to know what Tom wants for his birthday. C: He wants a watch. **4.** A: *How* does Jane get to school? B: (. . .) wants to know how Jane gets to school. C: By bus. **5.** A: *When* does vacation start? B: . . . know when vacation starts. C: On June 3rd [= *third*]. **6.** A: *Why* did Sue leave class early? B: . . . know why Sue left class early. C: Etc. **7.** A: *How long* is the movie going to last? B: . . . know how long the movie is going to last. **8.** A: *Who(m)* did Mary call? B: . . . know who(m) Mary called. **9.** A: *Who* called Jim? B: . . . know who called Jim. **10.** A: *What* did Alice talk to the teacher about? B: . . . know what Alice talked to the teacher about. **11.** A: *Who(m)* did Alice talk to about the test? B: (. . .) wants to know who(m) Alice talked to about the test/know to whom Alice talked about the test. **12.** A: *Who* talked to the teacher about the test? B: (. . .) wants to know who talked to the teacher about the test. **13.** A: *When/At what time* will Sue's plane arrive? B: (. . .) wants to know when/at what time Sue's plane will arrive. **14.** A: *How many* students will be absent from class tomorrow? B: (. . .) wants to know how many students will be absent from class tomorrow. **15.** A: *How many* lakes are there in Minnesota? B: (. . .) wants to know how many lakes there are in Minnesota. **16.** A: *How far/How many miles* is it to Springfield from here? B: (. . .) wants to know how far/how many miles it is to Springfield from here. **17.** A: *What* did Jane do last night? B: (. . .) wants to know what Jane did last night. **18.** A: *Which* book are we supposed to buy? B: (. . .) wants to know which book we're supposed to buy. **19.** A: *What kind of* ice cream does Ann like the best? B: (. . .) wants to know what kind of ice cream Ann likes the best. **20.** A: *What* color is a robin's egg? B: (. . .) wants to know what color a robin's egg is. [*turquoise* is pronounced /tərkwɔiz/.] **21.** A: *Who* is that woman? B: (. . .) wants to know who that woman is. **22.** A: *Who* is talking on the telephone? B: (. . .) wants to know who is talking on the telephone. **23.** A: *Whose* notebook is that? B: (. . .) wants to know whose notebook that is. **24.** A: *Whose* car was stolen? B: (. . .) wants to know whose car was stolen.

◇ **WORKBOOK:** Practices 4 and 5.

CHART 7-3: NOUN CLAUSES WHICH BEGIN WITH
          WHETHER* OR *IF

- The word *whether* always implies a choice—in this case, between "yes" and "no."

- To avoid any problems with formal sequence of tenses in noun clauses, the main verbs in any additional material you might make up should not be in a past form until the students reach Chart 7-7.

□ **EXERCISE 5, p. 268.** *Beginning noun clauses with* if/whether *or question words.*

This exercise can be done rather quickly if you are the first speaker and a student merely gives the response. If, however, you set it up like the alternative formats discussed for Exercise 4, the interactions will be more realistic and students' responses will be a little less mechanical. For example:

TEACHER: *Where is Yoko?*
    A to B: *I wonder where Yoko is.*
    B to C: *B wants to know where Yoko is. Do you know?/What do you think?*
    C to B: *She's at home./I don't know where she is.*

ANSWERS: [Begin with ''I wonder . . . .''] **1.** [Items 1 to 3 are related.] . . . where my friend is. **2.** . . . if/whether we should wait for him. **3.** . . . if/whether I should call him. **4.** [Items 4 to 7 are related.] . . . where my dictionary is. **5.** who took my dictionary. **6.** if/whether (. . .) borrowed my dictionary. **7.** if/whether I left my dictionary at the library. **8.** [Items 8 and 9 are related.] . . . who that woman is. **9.** if/whether she needs any help. **10.** [Items 10 to 13 are related.] . . . who that man is. **11.** what he's doing **12.** if/whether he's having trouble. **13.** if/whether I should offer to help him. **14.** [Items 14 and 15 are related.] . . . how far it is to (. . .). **15.** if/whether we have enough time to go to (. . .) over vacation. **16.** [Items 16 and 17 are related.] . . . whose book this is. **17.** if/whether it belongs to (. . .). **18.** . . . why the sky is blue. **19.** . . . how long a butterfly lives. **20.** . . . what causes earthquakes. **21.** . . . when the first book was written. **22.** . . . why dinosaurs became extinct. **23.** . . . if/whether there is life on other planets. **24.** . . . how life began. **25.** . . . if/whether people will live on the moon someday. [Continue the exercise by asking the students what they wonder about.]

□ **EXERCISE 6, p. 269.** *Beginning noun clauses with* if/whether *or question words.*

ANSWERS: [Begin with ''Could you please tell me . . . .''] **1.** . . . where the library/nearest phone/rest room is? [Note: In American English, a *rest room* is a public toilet.] **2.** . . . how much this book costs? **3.** . . . when Flight 62 is expected to arrive? **4.** . . . if/whether this bus goes downtown? **5.** . . . if/whether this word is spelled correctly? **6.** . . . what time it is? **7.** . . . if/whether this information is correct? **8.** . . . how much it costs to fly from (. . .) to (. . .)? **9.** . . . where the bus station is? **10.** . . . whose pen this is?

◇ **WORKBOOK:** Practices 6 and 7.

CHART 7-4: QUESTION WORDS FOLLOWED BY INFINITIVES

• This is an example of language flexibility—two ways to say exactly the same thing. Learners benefit greatly from practicing such alternatives. The emphasis here is on the meaning of the infinitives in this structure.

□ **EXERCISE 7, p. 269.** *The meaning of infinitives after question words.*

The first six items require only a change from noun clause to infinitive, but items 7 to 13 require students to supply an appropriate infinitive phrase. Those items also contain some challenging vocabulary, so they might require some discussion.

ANSWERS: **2.** The plumber told me *how to fix* the leak in the sink. [*plumber* = a person who installs and repairs water pipes, etc.; *fix* = repair, mend; *leak* = water dripping slowly through a hole; *sink* = a wash basin in a kitchen or bathroom] **3.** Please tell me *where to meet* you. **4.** . . . but Sandy didn't know *whether to believe* him (or not). **5.** . . . but he had trouble

deciding *which one to buy.*
normal; *else* = additional]

6. . . . I don't know *what else to do.* [*straightened out* = in order,
7. through 13. [Depend on students' creativity.]

◇ **WORKBOOK:** Practice 8.

CHART 7-5: NOUN CLAUSES WHICH BEGIN WITH *THAT*

• Again, as with Chart 7-1, it may be helpful to substitute the pronoun *something* in these examples:
   (c) *We know **something**.*
       *We know **(that) the world is round**.*
   (d) ***Something** is obvious.*
       ***That she doesn't understand spoken English** is obvious.*

• Sentences beginning with a "that clause," such as (d) and (f), are much more common in written than in spoken English.

• Compare uses of *that*:

   (1) *This coat is mine. **That** coat/one/Ø is yours.* [***That*** is a demonstrative adjective/pronoun; pronounced /ðæt/ with stress.]

   (2) *I don't have a coat. **That** is a problem in cold weather.* [The demonstrative pronoun ***that*** refers to a whole sentence. It is pronounced /ðæt/ with stress.]

   (3) *I bought a coat **that** has a hood. I showed my friend the coat **(that)** I bought.* [***That*** is an adjective clause pronoun referring to the noun *coat.* It is pronounced /ðət/ without stress.]

   (4) *I think **(that)** Bob bought a new hat.* [***That*** marks a noun clause and links it to the independent clause. It refers to nothing. It has no semantic meaning. It is not a pronoun. It is pronounced /ðət/ without stress.]

☐ **EXERCISE 8, p. 271.** *Understanding noun clauses beginning with* that.

This exercise may proceed slowly with false starts and discussion. You might point out that A's responses are typical in both spoken and written English, while B's are usually written. Perhaps also include in the exercise the more informal structure shown in (2) above: e.g., *The world is round. **That** is a fact.* (= *It is a fact that the world is round.* = *That the world is round is a fact.*)

Encourage students to vary their responses by using words from the list. They should use the unstressed pronunciation /ðət/ in all these items.

ANSWERS: [Words from the list should be substituted in the blanks.]
   2. A: It is _____ (that) drug abuse can ruin one's health.   B: That drug abuse can ruin one's health is _____.
   3. A: It's _____ (that) Tim hasn't been able to make any friends.   B: That Tim hasn't been able to make any friends is _____.
   4. A: It's _____ (that) some women do not earn . . . . [etc.]
   5. A: It's _____ (that) the earth revolves around the sun. [etc.]
   6. A: It's _____ (that) Irene failed her entrance examination. [*Irene* is pronounced /ai-ri:n/]
   7. A: It's _____ (that) smoking can cause cancer.
   8. A: It's _____ (that) English is the principal language . . . .

☐ **EXERCISE 9, p. 271.** *Using noun clauses with* it *and* that.

Give the class about three quiet minutes to think of some good ideas for their responses using *it.* Then begin the exercise.

ANSWERS: [Depend on students' ideas.]

Students might produce some interesting personal responses to this exercise. If you think they are shy about expressing their opinions in class, you could have them write their responses to be seen only by you. Then you might respond with your agreement or a differing point of view, in addition to marking their grammatical structures.

ANSWERS: [Depend on students' ideas.]

□ EXERCISE 11, p. 272. *Using "that clauses."*

It's assumed the students are familiar with this common pattern: *subject (a person) + **be** + adjective/past participle + "**that** clause"*. Other words used in this pattern: *delighted, relieved, sad, upset, proud, ashamed, astonished, shocked, stunned, alarmed, angry, furious, irritated, worried, satisfied, fascinated, interested, impressed, intrigued, aware, sure, certain, lucky, fortunate.* Students aren't expected to have difficulty with the pattern, but they might enjoy practicing additional vocabulary.

ANSWERS: [Depend on students' ideas.]

□ EXERCISE 12, p. 272. *Using "that clauses."*

This exercise contains basics of English rhetoric: topic sentence followed by supporting sentences. Items 3, 4, and 5 could be turned into full compositions if your students are interested in the organization of writing.

When discussing item 4 in class, take some time to let the students share the problems they are having. Ask for completions from several or many students.

ANSWERS: [Depend on students' ideas.]

□ EXERCISE 13, p. 272. *Using "that clauses."*

ANSWERS: **2.** *The fact that Mary didn't come* made me angry.   **3.** I feel fine except for *the fact that I'm a little tired.*   **4.** She was not admitted to the university *due to the fact that she didn't pass the entrance examination.*   **5.** *The fact that many people in the world live in intolerable poverty* must concern all of us.   **6.** *The fact that he is frequently absent from class* indicates his lack of interest in school.   **7.** I was not aware of *the fact that I was supposed to bring my passport to the examination for identification.* As a result, I was not allowed to take the test.   **8.** *Due to the fact that the people of the town were given no warning of the approaching tornado,* there were many casualties.

◇ WORKBOOK: Practices 9 and 10.

┌───┐
│ **CHART 7-6: QUOTED SPEECH** │
└───┘

• As an example of the importance of using quotation marks correctly, you might put the following sentence on the chalkboard and ask students to add punctuation marks:
  My dog said Mary needs a new home.
If the punctuation is incorrect, the dog might appear to be speaking!
  INCORRECT: *My dog said, "Mary needs a new home."*
   CORRECT: *"My dog," said Mary, "needs a new home."*

• In the chart, *said* and *asked* are used as the reporting verbs. Some other reporting verbs are: *announce, cry, exclaim, mutter, reply, respond, reflect, shout, snarl.*

□ **EXERCISE 14, p. 274.**   *Using punctuation with quoted speech.*

Point out the exact placement of each punctuation mark. Make sure the students are writing the quotation marks above, not on, the line. A good approach in this exercise is to have the students write the items on the chalkboard to provide a focus for class discussion.

ANSWERS: **1.** Henry said, "There is a phone call for you."   **2.** "There is a phone call for you," he said.   **3.** "There is," said Henry, "a phone call for you."   **4.** "There is a phone call for you. It's your sister," said Henry.   **5.** "There is a phone call for you," he said. "It's your sister."   **6.** I asked him, "Where is the phone?"   **7.** "Where is the phone?" she asked.
8.   When the police officer came over to my car, he said, "Let me see your driver's license, please."
"What's wrong, officer?" I asked. "Was I speeding?"
"No, you weren't speeding," he replied. "You went through a red light at the corner of Fifth Avenue and Main Street. You almost caused an accident."
"Did I really do that?" I said. "I didn't see the red light."
EXPANSION ACTIVITY: Comic strips in a newspaper can be used to practice writing quotations; the students can describe a comic strip in writing, using quoted speech as appropriate.

◇ **WORKBOOK:** Practice 11.

□ **EXERCISE 15, p. 274.**   *Using quoted speech.*

The conversation should be brief, a maximum of six sentences. The two speakers will probably have to repeat their dialogue, for some of the listeners will miss the exact words at first. The speakers must repeat it exactly, so it's a good idea for them to work from a script that they have written.

Have the students compare their written conversations. Emphasize the importance of accuracy in direct quotations.

If your class is very large or the room is noisy, it might be difficult for everyone to hear the conversation. In that case, you might divide the class into groups, or simply ask students to imagine a conversation and write it down in order to practice quoted speech.

CHART 7-7: REPORTED SPEECH AND THE FORMAL SEQUENCE OF TENSES	

• Tense usage in noun clauses is by no means as regular and consistent as this chart may indicate. Rules for sequence of tenses are helpful, but there are many exceptions. Encourage your students to practice the sequence of tenses as presented in this chart, but accept any viable responses in the exercises.

• You might have Student A read a quoted speech sentence in the chart, then ask Student B (book closed) to paraphrase that in reported speech. Invite comments from the class about the grammatical differences.

□ **EXERCISE 16, p. 276.**   *Changing quoted speech to reported speech.*

This exercise requires students (1) to form noun clauses and (2) to adjust verb forms. The same student should read aloud both sentences in one item.

ANSWERS: **4.** . . . if I was hungry.   **5.** . . . (that) she wanted a sandwich.   **6.** . . . (that) he was going to move to Ohio. [*Ohio* is pronounced /ohaio/.]   **7.** . . . if/whether I had enjoyed my trip.   **8.** . . . what I was talking about.   **9.** . . . if/whether I had seen her grammar book.
10. . . . (that) she didn't want to go.   **11.** . . . where Amanda was.   **12.** . . . if/whether I could come to his party.   **13.** . . . (that) he might be late.   **14.** . . . (that) I should study

harder.   **15.** . . . (that) she had to go downtown.   **16.** . . . why the sky is blue. [reporting verb is present, so the noun clause verb doesn't change]   **17.** . . . why I was tired.   **18.** . . . (that) he would come to the meeting.   **19.** . . . if/whether I will be in class tomorrow.   **20.** . . . (that) the sun rises in the east.

◇ **WORKBOOK:** Practices 12 and 13.

☐ **EXERCISE 17, p. 277.** *Changing quoted speech to reported speech.*

> *ANSWERS:* **2.** . . . (that) he was going to postpone the examination.   **3.** . . . (that) someday we would/will be in contact with beings from outer space.   **4.** . . . (that) he thought (that) he would go to the library to study. [Note that there are two noun clauses.]   **5.** . . . if/whether there was anything (that/which) she could do to help. [Note that the adjective clause verb changes too.]   **6.** . . . if/whether Jim knew what he was doing. [Note that there are two noun clauses.]   **7.** . . . if/whether what I had heard was true. [Note that the two tenses in the quoted speech remain in the same relationship in reported speech. Also note that a noun clause (*what I had heard*) is the subject of another noun clause (*if/whether* [*it*] *was true*).]   **8.** . . . if/whether what she had written was correct.   **9.** . . . (that) she needed to go to the market before it closed. [Note that a time clause (adverb clause of time) is attached to a noun clause.]   **10.** . . . (that) sentences with noun clauses are a little complicated. [no changes]

☐ **EXERCISE 18, p. 278.** *Using parallel noun clauses in reported speech.*

> This exercise anticipates Exercise 1 in Chapter 8, which practices parallel structures. Students must notice whether the two statements are similar (use *and*) or in a contrasting relationship (use *but*).

> *ANSWERS:* **2.** . . . She said *that* she was excited about her new job *and that* she had found a nice apartment. [Encourage the inclusion and repetition of *that* for the sake of clarity in written English.]   **3.** . . . that my Uncle Harry was in the hospital and that my Aunt Sally was very worried about him.   **4.** . . . that he expected us to be in class every day and that unexcused absences might affect our grades.   **5.** . . . that Highway 66 would be closed for two months and that commuters should seek alternate routes.   **6.** . . . that he was/is getting good grades but that he had/has difficulty understanding lectures. [Because his studies are continuing, present tense is possible.]   **7.** . . . that she would/she'd come to the meeting but that she couldn't stay for more than an hour.   **8.** . . . that every obstacle is a steppingstone to success and (that) I should view problems in my life as opportunities to prove myself. [A general truth, but past (*was*) is also possible.]

◇ **WORKBOOK:** Practices 14 and 15.

☐ **EXERCISE 19, p. 279.** *Using reported speech in writing.*

> Before assigning this exercise, you might want to set a limit on its length—e.g., a minimum of five sentences and a maximum of eight. Students could be asked to underline the sentences that include the assigned pattern so that you can find them easily.
>
> When you mark the students' papers, focus mainly on sentences that include reported speech. Reward their grammatical successes, and perhaps comment on their interesting information.

☐ **EXERCISE 20, p. 279.** *Using reported speech in conversation.*

> You might set this up as chain conversation. (See the notes on Exercise 4 in this chapter.) You or the leader asks Student A a question. A turns to Student B and reports the question, perhaps in a tone of surprise or disbelief. B responds to A with curiosity ("Really? What are you going to

say?'' or "Well, what are you going to say to him/her?"). Then A adds a response to B ("I'm going to say (that) . . .").

> TEACHER [to Student A]: *Where is Pierre?*
> STUDENT A [to Student B]: *The teacher asked me where Pierre is/was.*
> STUDENT B: *Really? What are you going to say?*
> STUDENT A: *I'm going to say that Pierre is home in bed with a cold.*

You might suggest that the students use formal sequence, but in this kind of conversation, an unchanged verb may be equally or even more appropriate than the use of the formal sequence of tenses because the situation is immediate.

ANSWERS: [Begin each response with *She/He asked me* . . . Students use *she* or *he* depending upon who (female or male) is giving the cues.] **1.** . . . what time it was/is. [*is* = at this moment; *was* is equally correct] **2.** . . . what my name was/is. **3.** . . . if I could/can speak Arabic **4.** . . . if I had/have met her/his brother. **5.** . . . where I was/I'm living. **6.** . . . if I would/will be here tomorrow. **7.** . . . what kind of camera I had/have **8.** . . . how tall I was/am. **9.** . . . what courses I was/I'm taking. **10.** . . . if/whether I felt/feel okay. **11.** . . . if/whether I had/have read any good books lately. **12.** . . . how I liked/like living here. **13.** . . . if/whether I had finished/finished my assignment. **14.** . . . what I was/I'm doing. **15.** . . . whose briefcase that was/is. **16.** . . . if/whether s/he might/could borrow my dictionary. **17.** . . . if/whether I would/will be here tomorrow around three o'clock. **18.** . . . if/whether I had gone/went to class yesterday. **19.** . . . what I was/I'm going to do during vacation. **20.** . . . what the capital of my country was/is. **21.** . . . if/whether I went/had gone to a party last night. [The simple past is often not changed to the past perfect in everyday informal English.] **22.** . . . how many people I'd/I've met in the last couple of months. **23.** . . . if s/he could/can use my pen. **24.** . . . where s/he should meet me after class. **25.** . . . if/whether I understood/understand what s/he was/is saying. [Here, a noun clause is the object within another noun clause.] **26.** . . . what country I was/I'm from. **27.** . . . if/whether what I had said/said was really true. [Here, a noun clause is the subject within another noun clause] **28.** . . . how I knew/know that it was/is true. **29.** . . . who I thought/think would/will win the game. **30.** . . . if/whether what I wanted/want to talk to her/him about was/is important.

☐ EXERCISE 21, p. 279. *Using reported speech.*

This can be done as either seatwork or homework. (*Michigan* is pronounced /mɪšɪgən/.)

ANSWERS: The passenger sitting next to me on the plane **asked** me where I **was** from. I **told** her I **was** from Chicago. She **said** that she **was** from Mapleton, a small town in northern Michigan. She wondered if I **had heard** of it, and I told her that I **had** [British: *had done*]. I went on to say that I thought Michigan **was** a beautiful state and explained that I **had been** there on vacations many times. She **asked** me if I **had been** in Michigan on vacation this year. I replied that I **hadn't (been)** and **told** her that I **had gone** far away, to India. Then she asked me if it **was** a long drive . . . .

☐ EXERCISE 22, p. 280. *Cumulative review and practice.*

If students take time to use their knowledge and creativity, they can produce very interesting sentences. Encourage them to do this, then reward their successes.

ANSWERS: [Depend on students' creativity.]

☐ EXERCISE 23, p. 281. *Cumulative review and practice.*

Students can have fun with this exercise if they use their creativity. The "reporter" has to have a good memory!

ANSWERS: [Depend on students' creativity.]

As an ongoing activity, have one or two students per day give their one-minute speeches until everyone in the class has had an opportunity to speak. Allow writing time in class. Suggestion: Give the written reports to the student who spoke and ask her/him to correct them. It is enlightening for a speaker to read what others think s/he said.

One problem here is to encourage students to speak in front of the whole class, and to speak clearly so that their classmates can take notes and report on what was said. On the other hand, it may be difficult to keep some eager speakers within the one-minute limit.

If some students object to listening to each other's imperfect English, you might remind them that in future years they will probably use English to communicate with people who, like themselves, are not native speakers of English.

◇ WORKBOOK: Practices 16, 17, 18, and 19.

□ EXERCISE 25, p. 281. *Error analysis: cumulative review.*

Students usually enjoy this type of exercise where they can be the "expert."

ANSWERS: **1.** Tell the taxi driver **where you** want to go. [no *do*] **2.** My roommate came into the room and asked me why I **wasn't** in class. I said I **was** waiting for a telephone call from my family. **3.** It was my first day at the university, and I **was** on my way to my first class. I wondered who else **would** be in the class **and** what the teacher would be like. **4.** He asked me [no *that*] what **I intended** to do after I **graduate(d).** **5.** Many of the people in the United States **don't** know much about geography. For example, people will ask you where **Japan is** located. **6.** What **a patient tells** a doctor [no *it*] is confidential. **7.** The reason I decided to come here **is that** this university has a good meteorology department. **8.** We looked back to see where **we were** and how far **we were** from camp. We **didn't** know, so we decided to turn back. We **were** afraid that we **had wandered** (OR **might/would** wander) too far. **9.** After the accident, I opened my eyes slowly and **realized** that I was still alive. **10.** My country is prospering **due to the fact** that it has become a leading producer of oil. **11. It is** true that one must know **E**nglish in order to study at an **A**merican university. [*University* does not begin with a capital letter because it is not part of a name.] **12.** My mother told me what [no *it*] the purpose of our visit **was.**

CHART 7-8: USING THE SUBJUNCTIVE IN NOUN CLAUSES

• The subjunctive is referred to as a "mood" in traditional grammar books. This is unimportant for your students to know. The important point is for them to understand and use the subjunctive appropriately.

□ EXERCISES 26 & 27, pp. 282–284. *Understanding the subjunctive.*

Give students a moment to read and think before they answer.

EX. 26 POSSIBLE ANSWERS: **2.** play loud music/make noise/cook, etc. **3.** tell **4.** speak/talk/go **5.** write/send/submit **6.** talk to/meet (with)/see **7.** be/talk to/write (to) **8.** be/get/come/arrive

EX. 27 ANSWERS: [*should* is optional before these verbs] **1.** take **2.** be named [passive] **3.** stay **4.** be postponed **5.** be permitted **6.** be controlled . . . (be) eliminated [not necessary to repeat the auxiliary] **7.** have **8.** be **9.** know **10.** be **11.** be admitted **12.** not be late **13.** return **14.** be built **15.** not tell . . . be told

◇ WORKBOOK: Practice 20.

CHART 7-9: USING -EVER WORDS

• These words are fairly frequent and deserve a moment's notice. Concentrate on meaning here. The text treats these words principally as vocabulary items. The underlying structures are complicated. Distinctions between noun and adverb clauses blur; the simplified terminology is inadequate.

• Mention that "so" might be added with no change in meaning: *whosoever, whatsoever, wheresoever, howsoever.* This is more common in legal or religious contexts than in everyday speech or writing.

☐ **EXERCISE 28, p. 284.** *Understanding -ever words.*

Lead the class through this exercise fairly quickly, but discuss any questions that arise.

ANSWERS: **2.** whenever **3.** whatever **4.** whichever **5.** whatever **6.** Whoever
7. whatever **8.** however **9.** whoever **10.** wherever [Note that one "e" is omitted in spelling this word.] **11.** whoever . . . who(m)ever **12.** whatever **13.** whichever
14. whatever . . . wherever . . . who(m)ever . . . however

◇ **WORKBOOK:** Practice 21. Practice Tests A and B.

☐ **EXERCISE 29, p. 285.** *Phrasal verbs.*

Phrasal verbs are listed in Appendix 2.

ANSWERS: **1.** call on [perhaps *call up*] **2.** go over . . . handed it in . . . looked it over
3. made it up **4.** pick up **5.** passed away **6.** try on **7.** thinking it over
8. get out of **9.** dropped out of **10.** take off . . . get in [= arrive] **11.** put up with
12. brought about . . . get along with

Chapter 8: SHOWING RELATIONSHIPS BETWEEN IDEAS—PART I

ORDER OF CHAPTER	CHARTS	EXERCISES	WORKBOOK
Parallel structure	8-1	Ex. 1 → 4	Pr. 1 → 2
Using paired conjunctions	8-2	Ex. 5 → 8	Pr. 3 → 4
Cumulative review and practice		Ex. 9	Pr. 5 → 6
Combining independent clauses	8-3	Ex. 10 → 11	Pr. 7 → 8
Adverb clauses and time relationships	8-4 → 8-5	Ex. 12 → 17	Pr. 9 → 15
Cause and effect relationships	8-6 → 8-10	Ex. 18 → 31	Pr. 16 → 23
Expressing purpose	8-11	Ex. 32 → 34	Pr. 24 → 25
Cumulative review and practice		Ex. 35	Pr. 26
Reduction of adverb clauses to phrases	8-12 → 8-16	Ex. 36 → 44	Pr. 27 → 36
Cumulative review and practice		Ex. 45 → 46	Pr. 37 → 39 Pr. Tests A & B

General Notes on Chapter 8:

• OBJECTIVE: Continuing the focus in Chapters 6 and 7, this chapter gives students more choices for expressing related ideas. They will learn how English connects bits of information that are in a relationship of equality, of time, or of cause and effect. The more they understand such relationships, the clearer and more precise their communication will be.

• APPROACH: The chapter begins with the concept of parallelism. Two or more similar bits of information should be expressed in similar grammatical forms, according to the preferred style of written English. This introduces coordinating conjunctions and related rules for punctuation.

   The second part of the chapter introduces two important functions of adverb clauses: expressing the relationships of time and of cause and effect. Other expressions of cause and effect are introduced and their sentence patterns practiced. Finally, reductions of adverb clauses to phrases are covered.

• TERMINOLOGY: A conjunction is a connector or linking word used to show relationships. In the text, the word **conjunction** is used to refer to coordinating conjunctions (e.g., *and, but*). Correlative conjunctions (e.g., *both . . . and*) are called **paired conjunctions.** Subordinating conjunctions (e.g., *when, because*) are called **words that introduce adverb clauses** or **adverb clause words.** Coordinating and correlative conjunctions link similar elements; subordinating conjunctions link a dependent structure to an independent one. Words like *therefore*, which the text calls **transitions** (labeled ''adverbs'' in dictionaries), are also called conjunctive adverbs or a type of logical connector.

CHART 8-1: PARALLEL STRUCTURE

• Using parallel structure is an economical way to include several bits of information in a single phrase or clause. The ability to use parallel structure is highly valued in spoken and written English, for conciseness is a cultural value in English-speaking countries.

• Problems with parallel structure are common in student writing.

• To understand parallel structure, learners need to understand the concept of ellipsis: that certain words have been omitted from a sentence. The sentence can be understood without them because the omitted words are repetitive. English rhetoric does not value repetitiveness. Wordy and repetitive: *Steve is coming to dinner and his friend is coming to dinner.* In ellipsis, the repeated words (*be + coming to dinner*) are omitted, and the verb is made to agree with the subject: *Steve and his friend are coming to dinner.*

Write sentences without ellipsis on the board (e.g., *The man is wearing a hat, and the man is wearing a coat. Bob talked to Susan, and I talked to Susan.*) Ask the students to omit any unnecessarily repeated words. Explain the grammatical source of the parallel structure.

• In a series of parallel elements, the last item is preceded by a conjunction (usually *and* or *or*). Many people place a comma before that conjunction (e.g., *an apple, a banana, and a pear*), but that is a matter of choice. Grammar books and style guides do not agree on whether that comma is required. This text uses the final comma so that the students can more clearly see each element of a serial parallel structure. Furthermore, spoken English patterns usually have a pause before the conjunction in this instance, and the comma reflects the pause.

☐ **EXERCISE 1, p. 287.** *Understanding parallel structure.*

> *ANSWERS:* **3.** angrily and bitterly [adverb + adverb] (Point out the ellipsis, the words omitted from, *She spoke angrily about the war and she spoke bitterly about the war.*) **4.** looked . . . but couldn't find [main verbs] **5.** to go . . . and (to) study [infinitives] **6.** reading . . . or watching [gerunds] **7.** will leave . . . and (will) arrive [verbs in simple form following a modal] **8.** should have broken . . . and (should have) married [past participles in a past modal]

◇ **WORKBOOK:** Practice 1.

☐ **EXERCISE 2, p. 288.** *Understanding parallel structure.*

Ask the students to explain the grammatical functions of the parallel words. This may lead to a review of basic terminology (noun, verb, adjective, preposition, etc.) and how to recognize the various forms. Anyone having difficulty should review Appendix 1, pp. A1–A6.

> *ANSWERS:* **2.** Mary *is opening* the door and *greeting* her guests. **3.** Mary *will open* the door and *greet* her guests. **4.** Alice is *kind, generous,* and *trustworthy.* **5.** Please try to speak more *loudly* and *clearly.* **6.** He gave her *flowers on Sunday, candy on Monday,* and *a ring on Tuesday.* **7.** While we were in New York, we *attended* an opera, *ate* at marvelous restaurants, and *visited* some old friends. **8.** He decided *to quit* school, *go* to California, and *find* a job. [*To* is usually not repeated in parallel infinitives (unless the sentence is long and complicated). In a series, if the second *to* (*to go* in item 8) is included, the third *to* (*to find*) should be included also.] **9.** I am looking forward to *going* to Italy and *eating* wonderful pasta every day. [Point out that *to* is a preposition here, followed by a gerund. The preposition does not need to be repeated but may be.] **10.** I *should have finished* my homework and *cleaned* up my room. **11.** The boy was old enough *to work* and *earn* some money. **12.** He preferred *to play* baseball or *spend* his time in the streets with the other boys. **13.** I like *coffee but not tea.* **14.** I have met *his mother but not his father.* **15.** Jake would like to live *in Puerto Rico but not (in) Iceland.*

☐ **EXERCISE 3, p. 289.** *Using parallel structure.*

Students might enjoy working in pairs to complete these sentences. Then you can ask for several versions of each item from the class. Exercises 3 and 4 can also be assigned as out-of-class homework now that the students understand parallel structure.

POSSIBLE ANSWERS: **2.** I like to become acquainted with the people, (the) customs, and (the) ___**noun phrase***___ [e.g., *places*] of other countries.   **3.** I dislike living in a city because of the air pollution, (the) crime, and (the) ___**noun phrase**___. [e.g., *heavy traffic*].   **4.** We discussed some of the social, political, and ___**adjective**___ [e.g., *economic*] problems of the United States. [Compare *economic* (relating to the economy) and *economical* (not wasteful).]   **5.** Hawaii has ___**noun phrase**___ [e.g., *pleasant weather*], many interesting tropical trees and flowers, and beautiful beaches.   **6.** Mary Hart would make a good president because she ___**verb phrase**___ [e.g., *is a strong leader*], works effectively with others, and has a reputation for integrity and independent thinking.

☐ **EXERCISE 4, p. 290.** *Recognizing parallel structure.*

Ask the students to explain how they made their choices.

ANSWERS: **1.** E [prepositional phrase]   **2.** F [noun]   **3.** A [noun]   **4.** C [adverb]
5. J [gerund]   **6.** I [adjective]   **7.** B [prepositional phrase + adjective clause]
8. K [adjective]   **9.** L [adjective clause]   **10.** D [noun + preposition]   **11.** G [verb]
12. H [infinitive]

CHART 8-2: USING PAIRED CONJUNCTIONS

• There are two important grammatical points here: (1) subject-verb agreement and (2) parallel structure. Both are practiced in the following exercises. Some native speakers of English have trouble using these structures grammatically, so learners too can expect to be confused sometimes. (In actual usage of *neither . . . nor*, native speakers often use a plural verb with two singular subjects, e.g.: *Neither my mother nor my sister* **are** *here. Neither my brother nor* **I** **were** *interested.*)

☐ **EXERCISE 5, p. 292.** *Subject-verb agreement with paired conjunctions.*

ANSWERS: **1.** are   **2.** is   **3.** is   **4.** are   **5.** is   **6.** are

☐ **EXERCISE 6, p. 292.** *Recognizing parallel structure.*

The three sentences in this exercise are ungrammatical and therefore unclear in meaning. Point out the importance of proper placement of correlative conjunctions.

ANSWERS: **1.** Either John or Bob will call Mary. OR John will call either Mary or Bob.
2. Not only Sue but also the cat saw the mouse. OR Sue saw not only the mouse but also the cat.
3. Both my mother and my father talked to the teacher. OR My mother talked *to both* the teacher and my father/My mother talked *both to* the teacher and *to* my father.

◇ **WORKBOOK:** Practices 2, 3, and 4.

---

*The term "noun phrase" is used in linguistics to refer to any single word or group of words that can function as a subject or an object in a sentence.

□ **EXERCISE 7, p. 292.** *Using paired conjunctions.*

For an advanced class, do this exercise with books closed. Group work is also possible; follow the group work with a quick written quiz using one item from each section.

Both . . . and is used more frequently than *not only . . . but also*. *Not only . . . but also* tends to mean that something is surprising or especially interesting. Note that "Yes" is the required answer in the first three groups of items, but "No" is the answer with *neither . . . nor.*

ANSWERS: **2.** Yes, *both* **the driver** *and* **the passenger** were injured in the accident.   **3.** Yes, *both* **wheat** *and* **corn** are grown in Kansas. [*Kansas is pronounced /kænzəs/.*   **4.** Yes, he *both* **buys** *and* **sells** used cars. [*Used cars have been owned and sold at least one time.*]   **5.** Yes, I had *both* **lunch** *and* **dinner** . . . .   **6.** Yes, . . . from *both* **air** (pollution) *and* **water** pollution.   **8.** Yes, *not only* **his cousin** *but also* **his mother-in-law** *is* . . . .   **9.** Yes, *not only* **my country** *but also* **the United States** has . . . .   **10.** Yes, I lost *not only* **my wallet** *but also* **my keys**.   **11.** Yes, she *not only* **goes** to school *but also* **has** a full-time job.   **12.** Yes, he bought *not only* **a coat** *but also* **a new pair of shoes**.   **14.** Yes, . . . friend *either* **a book** *or* **a pen** for . . . .   **15.** Yes, *either* **my sister** *or* **my brother** will . . . .   **16.** Yes, they can *either* **go** swimming *or* **play** tennis.   **17.** . . . for *either* **Mr. Smith** *or* **Mr. Jones**.   **18.** Yes, I'll go *either* **to New Orleans** *or* **to Miami** for my vacation/go to *either* **New Orleans** *or* **Miami** for my vacation.   **20.** No, *neither* **her husband** *nor* **her children** speak English.   **21.** No, *neither* **the students** *nor* **the teacher** *is* . . . .   **22.** No, they have *neither* **a refrigerator** *nor* **a stove** . . . .   **23.** No, she enjoys *neither* **hunting** *nor* **fishing**.   **24.** . . . was *neither* **good** *nor* **bad**.

□ **EXERCISE 8, p. 293.** *Using paired conjunctions.*

This exercise can be done as seatwork or homework, giving students an opportunity to write these conjunctions and parallel structures. It can also be used as a summary oral review in class discussion.

POSSIBLE ANSWERS: **2.** *Both* **Ron** *and* **Bob** enjoy horseback riding.   **3.** You can have *either* **tea** *or* **coffee**.   **4.** *Neither* **Arthur** *nor* **Ricardo** is in class today.   **5.** *Both* **Arthur** *and* **Ricardo** are absent.   **6.** We can *either* **fix** dinner for them *or* **take** them to a restaurant. [*Fix dinner is American English meaning prepare dinner.*]   **7.** . . . buy *either* **a Chevrolet** *or* **a Toyota**.   **8.** *Not only* **the leopard** *but also* **the tiger** faces . . . .   **9.** *Neither* **the library** *nor* **the bookstore** has . . . .   **10.** We could *either* **fly** *or* **take** the train.   **11.** . . . will *neither* **confirm** *nor* **deny** the story.   **12.** *Both* **coal** *and* **oil** are irreplaceable natural resources.   **13.** *Both* **smallpox** *and* **malaria** are dangerous diseases.   **14.** *Neither* **her roommates** *nor* **her brother** knows where she is.   **15.** . . . will *either* **snow** *or* **rain** tonight.

□ **EXERCISE 9, p. 294.** *Cumulative review and practice.*

ANSWERS: **1.** . . . can save *energy, lives, and* **money/expense**.
   2. . . . feeling of *security,* **warmth,** *and love*.
   3. . . . labored *to clear* away the forest *and* **plant** crops.
   4. . . . she *became* very angry *and* **shouted** at me.
   5. . . . enjoy *taking care of* my aquarium *and* **working** on my stamp collection.
   6. . . . Wiggins *is* going to teach . . . .
   7. I enjoy **reading not only** *novels but also magazines*.
   8. Oxygen is plentiful. *Both* air *and* **water contain** oxygen. [The unacceptable sentence "Air contains both water and oxygen" doesn't make sense as support for the idea that "Oxygen is plentiful."]

◇ **WORKBOOK:** Practices 5 and 6.

```
┌─────────────────────────────────────────────────────────────────────────┐
│   CHART 8-3:  COMBINING INDEPENDENT CLAUSES WITH                           │
│               CONJUNCTIONS                                                 │
├─────────────────────────────────────────────────────────────────────────┤
```

• Formal English usually requires a comma preceding the conjunction.

• Another term for a "run-on sentence" is a "comma splice" when a comma is used in place of a period. Run-on sentences are a common problem in student writing.

• Advanced students may be interested to know that it is possible to use commas between independent clauses in a series: *Janet washed the windows, Bob swept the floor, and I dusted the furniture.* (But INCORRECT: *Janet washed the windows, Bob swept the floor.*)

☐ **EXERCISES 10 & 11, pp. 295–297.** *Using punctuation with conjunctions.*

Exercise 10 could be done as seatwork in about 5 to 8 minutes. After reviewing the answers with you, the students could continue with Exercise 11 as seatwork or homework. Exercise 10 is intended to help you explain the chart. Exercise 11 is intended as practice for the students.

EX. 10 ANSWERS: **2.** The teacher lectured. The students took notes. **3.** The teacher lectured, and the students took notes. [The comma is not required between two short clauses. Also possible informally: period and capitalized *And* . . . .] **4.** Jessica came to the meeting, but Ron stayed home. [The comma is not required. Also possible: period and capitalized *But* . . . .] **5.** Jessica came to the meeting. Her brother stayed home. **6.** Her academic record was outstanding, yet she was not . . . . **7.** I have not finished writing my term paper yet. I will not . . . . **8.** [No change; *for* is a preposition, not a conjunction, here.] **9.** We had to go to the grocery store, for there was . . . . **10.** . . . airplane ticket, so he couldn't . . . .

◇ **WORKBOOK:** Practice 7.

EX. 11 ANSWERS: **1.** . . . temperature. A barometer measures . . . . **2.** . . . promises, but he had . . . . **3.** . . . in high school, so I decided . . . . **4.** . . . good dentists. Archaeologists have found . . . . **5.** Both John and I had many errands to do yesterday. John had to go to the post office and the bookstore. I had to go to the drugstore, the travel agency, and the bank. **6.** . . . legal trouble, for she had no car insurance . . . . **7.** Last night, Martha had to study for a test, so she went . . . .[The comma after *night* is not required.] **8.** . . . actor, yet the movie was . . . . **9.** . . . the statistics yet. Their work will not . . . . **10.** We have nothing to fear, for our country is . . . . **11.** . . . in disgust. He had failed . . . . **12.** . . . above water. I tried to yell for help, but no sound . . . . **13.** The earthquake was devastating. Tall buildings crumbled and fell to the earth. **14.** It was a wonderful picnic. The children waded in the stream, collected rocks and insects, and flew kites. The teenagers played an enthusiastic game of baseball. The adults busied themselves preparing the food, supervising the children, and playing a game or two of volleyball. **15.** The butterfly is a marvel. It begins as an ugly caterpillar and turns into a work of art. **16.** Caterpillars eat plants and cause damage to some crops, but adult butterflies feed principally on nectar from flowers and do not cause any harm. **17.** Some people collect butterflies for a hobby. These collectors capture them with a net and put them in a jar that has poison in it. The dead butterflies are then mounted on a board. **18.** The sight of a butterfly floating from flower to flower on a warm sunny day brightens anyone's heart. A butterfly is a charming and gentle creature. [It's possible to put a comma between *warm* and *sunny* to separate two descriptive adjectives; it would replace the word *and* between two adjectives of equal status.]
NOTE: Items 19 and 20 are intended to help you introduce the patterns and punctuation of adverb clauses, as explained in the chart that follows.
19. *When cold weather comes*, some butterflies travel great distances to reach tropical climates.
20. Butterflies are admired throughout the world *because they are beautiful.* They can be found on every continent except Antarctica. [Point out that the period after *beautiful* shows which

independent clause the adverb clause should be linked to. With improper punctuation, the reader doesn't know exactly what relationships the writer intended. Examples of IMPROPER PUNCTUATION: *I should have stayed home. Because I wanted to see my friends. I went to the meeting.* OR *I should have stayed home because I wanted to see my friends I went to the meeting.*]

◇ **WORKBOOK:** Practice 8.

CHART 8-4: ADVERB CLAUSES: INTRODUCTION

• Students have learned about two other kinds of dependent clauses: adjective clauses (Chapter 6) and noun clauses (Chapter 7). You might review the characteristics of dependent clauses (must contain subject + verb, cannot stand alone as a sentence).

• Point out the four general functions of adverb clauses listed in the bottom half of the chart. These are especially useful in writing coherent paragraphs. Chapter 8 deals with ''time'' and ''cause and effect.'' Chapter 9 covers ''opposition'' and ''condition.''

• Incomplete sentences consisting of only an adverb clause are a common problem in student writing. INCORRECT: *He went to bed.* **Because he was sleepy.** Such incomplete sentences are common in conversation, however:
    A: *Why did he go to bed?*
    B: **Because he was sleepy.**

◇ **WORKBOOK:** Practices 9, 10, and 11.

CHART 8-5: USING ADVERB CLAUSES TO SHOW TIME RELATIONSHIPS

• Point out the punctuation rule in Chart 8-4, then show how it works in the examples in Chart 8-5.

• Also call attention to the first note in this chart: future tense is NOT used in the adverb clause. (See Chart 1-21.) Discuss the other tenses in the examples; refer the students to Chapter 1 (Verb Tenses) as necessary.

☐ **EXERCISE 12, p. 299.** *Verb tenses in adverb clauses.*

    This exercise provides a review of verb tenses while presenting adverb clauses. Students will probably have questions about both points. This exercise could be used as a summary overview of the English tense system as presented in Chapter 1.

POSSIBLE ANSWERS: **1.** had done/had finished/did/finished [The past perfect is slowly disappearing from everyday English when the meaning is clear without it.]   **2.** do/finish
3. have been   **4.** was playing [*a contact lens* = a corrective piece of glass or plastic worn on the surface of the eyeball]   **5.** hand/turn [no future tense in an adverb clause]   **6.** had delivered
7. was   **8.** was driving [One superstition holds that a black cat crossing one's path will bring bad luck. What other superstitions do the students know of that will bring bad luck? Walking under a ladder? Breaking a mirror?]   **9.** will have lived/will have been living/will have been
10. gets/is   **11.** used to go   **12.** [use simple present]   **13.** go   **14.** ate

◇ **WORKBOOK:** Practices 12 and 13.

☐ **EXERCISE 13, p. 300.** *Understanding* until.

The meaning and use of *until* are difficult for many learners. The meaning is something like "continuing to the moment when the situation changes." In this exercise, students must state the event that will change the situation. That statement is in the adverb clause that begins with *until*.

ANSWERS: **2.** We can't leave *until Nancy comes/gets here/arrives.* **3.** I'm not going to leave this room *until you tell me the truth.* **4.** It was/had been a dull party *until Donald arrived.* **5.** Let's just sit here by the fire *until dinner is ready.* [no future tense in an adverb clause] **6.** When I go to bed at night, I like to read *until I get sleepy.* [Note the two adverb clauses in the same sentence.]

☐ **EXERCISE 14, p. 300.** *Understanding* as soon as *and* once.

In this and other exercises that follow, the answers are given with the sentence order reflecting the order of the ideas in the cue sentences. The adverb clauses can, of course, be switched around.

POSSIBLE ANSWERS: **2.** *(Just) as soon as* the rice **is** done, we can eat. [*Once* is also possible, but *as soon as* communicates the immediacy of the situation.] **3.** *Once* I graduate, I can return home. [*As soon as*, though possible, is too "immediate" for this situation.] **4.** *Once* spring com**es** and the weather **is** nice again, we can start playing tennis every morning before class. **5.** *(Just) as soon as* my roommate walked into the room, I knew that something was wrong. **6.** *Once* your English **gets** better, you will begin to feel more comfortable living in the United States. **7.** *(Just) as soon as* the singer finished her song, the audience burst into applause. **8.** *(Just) as soon as* the baseball game is over, I'll take out the garbage.

☐ **EXERCISE 15, p. 301.** *Understanding* just *in adverb clauses.*

Just as = at the same moment, not before or after.

POSSIBLE ANSWERS: **2.** You shouldn't go to bed *just after* you eat a heavy meal. OR You shouldn't eat a heavy meal *just before* you go to bed. **3.** *Just after* I went to bed, my phone rang. **4.** *Just as* we were sitting down to eat, someone knocked on the door. **5.** *Just as* I was getting on the bus, I remembered that I had left my briefcase at home. **6.** *Just before* I got to give my speech, I got butterflies in my stomach. [*Butterflies in the stomach* describes a feeling of nervousness.] **7.** *Just before* the guests come (at 7:00), I'll light the candles. **8.** *Just as* I was bending over to pick up my pencil, my pants split. [*split* = tore]

☐ **EXERCISE 16, p. 302.** *Distinguishing between* after *and* afterwards.

Some learners tend to use *after* as an adverb, but this is incorrect. *After* can function only as the first word of a clause or phrase:

After I ate dinner, we went out. OR *We went out after I ate dinner.*
After dinner, we went out. OR *We went out after dinner.*

The adverb *afterwards* is complete by itself. It functions alone as an adverb, not as the first word of a phrase or dependent clause.

I ate dinner. Afterwards, we went out. OR *We went out afterwards.*

Afterward (no *-s*) is an American English variation, generally not used in British English.

POSSIBLE ANSWERS:
1. (a) I went to bed after I studied. OR After I studied, I went to bed. (b) I studied. Afterwards, I went to bed. OR I went to bed afterwards. [You might also mention the use of the adverb *later* (*I studied. Later I went to bed./I went to bed later.*) and of the prepositional phrase *after that* (*I studied. After that, I went to bed/I went to bed after that.*).]

2. (a) We went to the museum *after we had some lunch*. OR *After we had some lunch*, we went to the museum. (b) We had some lunch. *Afterwards*, we went to the museum. OR We went to the museum *afterwards*.

3. (a) *After he was in an automobile accident*, he had to walk on crutches for two months. OR He had to walk on crutches for two months *after he was in an automobile accident*. (b) He was in an automobile accident. *Afterwards*, he had to walk on crutches for two months. OR He had to walk on crutches for two months *afterwards*.

◇ **WORKBOOK:** Practices 14 and 15.

☐ **EXERCISE 17, p. 302.** *Cumulative review and practice.*

This can be done as seatwork while you walk around the classroom and offer help, or it could be assigned as homework.

ANSWERS: [No comma before the adverb clause in items 3, 5, 6, 7, 8, 11, 14, 16; in item 15 there is a period after the first sentence and a comma following *Afterwards*.]

◇ **WORKBOOK:** Practice 16 (used as a preview or pretest).

CHART 8-6: ADVERB CLAUSES: CAUSE AND EFFECT RELATIONSHIPS

• There are differences among the ways to say "because." *Because* makes the most direct or emphatic cause-and-effect statement. *Since* expresses a known cause; it means "because it is a fact that" or "seeing that it is true that" [e.g., *Since you've done this before* (a known fact), *could you please show me how?*]. *Because*, but not *since*, can ask about an unknown cause [e.g., *Did he stay home because he was tired?*]. *As*, *as/so long as*, and *inasmuch as* are similar to *since*; they also express a cause that is a known fact. *Now that* is special to present-time, known reasons and indicates that a situation has changed.

• *As* has many uses. Students should know that one use is to express cause and effect. In their own writing, however, they might prefer to use *because*, *since*, or *now that* in order to ensure clarity.

• By learning these synonyms, students can add variety to their use of English and understand the cause-and-effect relationships expressed in what they read and hear.

• Punctuation follows the same rules with these adverb clauses as with others.

☐ **EXERCISE 18, p. 303.** *Understanding* now that = because.

ANSWERS: **2.** Now that you are sixteen (years old), you can get a driver's license. **3.** We have to wear warm clothes now that it's winter. **4.** Now that Bob has moved into an apartment, he can cook his own food. ["A couple of weeks ago" is omitted; the present perfect is used to express an action that occurred at an unspecified time in the past.] **5.** Now that I've finally finished painting the house, I can go fishing. [The present perfect means that the action of painting was completed "before now," at an unspecified time in the past.] **6.** I can get a job as a bilingual secretary now that I know English. **7.** Now that my brother is a married man, he has more responsibilities. **8.** Do you want to go for a walk now that the rain has stopped? [Note that question word order occurs in the independent clause, not the adverb clause.] **9.** Now that final exams are finally over, we can relax. **10.** Now that the civil war has ended, a new government is being formed.

☐ **EXERCISE 19, p. 304.** *Understanding* as long as = because.

Each of these items is set up as a suggestion or a possible plan. [Suggestions and requests are covered in Chapter 2.] Students should use their imaginations in creating interesting sentences.

ANSWERS: [Depend on students' creativity.] In item 6, the "speaker" is probably sitting and is addressing a "listener" who has just stood up.

☐ **EXERCISE 20, p. 304.** *Understanding* since *and* inasmuch as.

ANSWERS: [Items 2, 4, and 6 are formal enough to use *inasmuch as*.] **1.** Since Monday is Bob's birthday, let's give him a party. **2.** Since/Inasmuch as Monday is a national holiday, all government offices will be closed. **3.** Since the guys [Guys is colloquial, that is, suitable for everyday conversation but not formal discourse.] I live with don't know any Arabic, I have to speak English with them. **4.** Since/Inasmuch as oil is an irreplaceable natural resource, we must do whatever we can in order to conserve it. **5.** Mary, maybe you could help me with this calculus problem since you're a math major. **6.** Many young people move to the cities in search of employment since/inasmuch as there are few jobs available in the rural areas.

◇ **WORKBOOK:** Practice 17.

☐ **EXERCISE 21, p. 305.** *Cumulative review and practice.*

ANSWERS: [Depend on students' ideas.]

CHART 8-7: USING PREPOSITIONS TO SHOW CAUSE AND EFFECT

• A common error is for a learner to begin an adverb clause with *because of*. (INCORRECT: *He stayed home because of he was ill.*)

• Traditionally, a distinction has been made between *because of* and *due to*: *because of* is used adverbially (*He stayed home because of illness.*) and *due to* is used adjectivally (*His absence is due to illness.*). In current usage, *due to* is also used with verbs: *He stayed home due to illness.* (But *because of* is not used adjectivally following *be*. INCORRECT: *His absence is because of illness.*) Students probably don't need to know this.

• Note that punctuation rules are the same for these phrases as for adverb clauses.

☐ **EXERCISE 22, p. 306.** *Understanding* because of *and* due to.

Students need to create noun phrases for these answers.

ANSWERS: **2.** . . . the heavy traffic. / . . . the fact that the traffic was heavy. **3.** . . . his wife's illness **4.** . . . Dr. Robinson's excellent research on wolves, we . . . . OR Due to the fact that Dr. Robinson has done . . ., we know . . . . **5.** . . . the noise in the next apartment. **6.** . . . circumstances (that are) beyond my control, . . .

◇ **WORKBOOK:** Practice 18.

CHART 8-8: USING TRANSITIONS TO SHOW CAUSE AND EFFECT

• Students sometimes ask, "Why are these two words so different from *so* if they mean the same?" There is no really satisfactory answer except: "It's traditional in English to use them in this way." Languages develop patterns; certain words fit certain patterns and certain other words do not.

• Students are learning structural distinctions in the use of coordinating conjunctions, subordinating conjunctions, adverbial prepositional phrases, and conjunctive adverbs by using "cause and effect" sentences as models. The patterns and terminology (conjunction, adverb clause, preposition, transition) they learn here will transfer to the units on opposition and condition in the following chapter.

• Have the students identify which of the related ideas is the "cause" and which is the "effect"—*not studying* is the cause; *failing* is the effect.

☐ EXERCISE 23, p. 307.   *Understanding* therefore *and* consequently.

Give the class time to write this exercise as seatwork. They need to practice all three forms of each sentence. Then you can ask several of them to explain what they wrote. As they explain, you might show the punctuation on the chalkboard or on pieces of cardboard (pasteboard):

~~~~~. Therefore, ~~~~~~~.   ~~~~~. Consequently, ~~~~~~~.

~~~~~. ~~~~~, therefore, ~~~~~.   ~~~~~. ~~~, consequently, ~~~.

~~~~~. ~~~~~~~, therefore.   ~~~~~. ~~~~~~~, consequently.

ANSWERS: 1. A storm was approaching. Therefore, the children stayed home.
A storm was approaching. The children, therefore, stayed home.
A storm was approaching. The children stayed home, therefore.
2. I didn't have my umbrella. Consequently, I got wet.
I didn't have my umbrella. I, consequently, got wet.
I didn't have my umbrella. I got wet, consequently.

☐ EXERCISES 24 & 25, p. 307.   *Cumulative review and practice.*

Students can write these items on the chalkboard for everyone to discuss, or they can read them aloud and indicate where they used punctuation and capital letters.

EX. 24 ANSWERS: 1. Because it was cold, she wore a coat.   2. [no change]   3. Because of the cold weather, she wore a coat.   4. [no change]   5. The weather was cold. Therefore, she wore a coat.   6. The weather was cold. She, therefore, wore a coat.   7. The weather was cold. She wore a coat, therefore.   8. The weather was cold, so she wore a coat.

EX. 25 ANSWERS: 1. . . . in high school. Therefore, she . . . .   2. . . . in the economy, fewer people . . . .   3. . . . the power lines. Consequently, the town . . . .   4. Because of the snowstorm, only five students came to class. The teacher, therefore, canceled the class.   5. [No change. Remind students that not every long sentence has commas; commas must be used judiciously. General guidelines: Use a comma after a phrase or clause that precedes the subject of the main clause. Use a comma in a parallel structure series. Use a comma in front of a conjunction that connects two independent clauses. (Restrictive-nonrestrictive use of commas is discussed in Chart 6-8.)]

◇ **WORKBOOK:** Practices 19 and 20.

CHART 8-9: SUMMARY OF PATTERNS AND PUNCTUATION

- A wall chart, cards, or a transparency of the patterns and punctuation may prove useful—not only for the remaining exercises in Chapter 8 but also for the charts and exercises in Chapter 9. For example:

Adverb clause, ～～～.	Prepositional phrase, ～～～.
～～～ adverb clause .	～～～ prepositional phrase .
～. Transition, ～～.	～～, conjunction ～～.
～. ～, transition, ～.	
～. ～～, transition .	

- When some students discover the semicolon (see the chart footnote), they tend to use it everywhere. You might point out that it is not often used, even by professional writers. (If students overuse it, tell them to look at any English text and see how many semicolons they can find. Chances are that they will find very few.) Many native speakers are unsure about its correct use. A period (full stop) is usually acceptable or even preferable.

☐ **EXERCISES 26 & 27, pp. 308–309.** *Cumulative review and practice.*

Assign each item to a student to write all the possible patterns on the board. Insist on perfect punctuation and capitalization. (Include the semicolon only with an advanced class.) Have the rest of the class offer suggestions and corrections. Let students who think they see an error go to the board and correct it.

Another option is to have the students work in small groups to produce one communal paper that everyone in the group agrees is perfect.

EX. 26 ANSWERS:
2. The weather was bad. Therefore, we postponed our trip. OR . . . bad. We, therefore, . . . OR . . . our trip, therefore.
3. Since the weather was bad, we . . . . OR We postponed our trip since . . . .
4. The weather was bad, so we . . . .
5. Because of the bad weather, we . . . . OR . . . trip because of the bad weather.
6. The weather was bad. Consequently, we . . . . [OR see item 2]
7. Due to [same as item 5]. OR Due to the fact that the weather was bad, we . . . . OR We postponed our trip due to the fact that the weather was bad.

EX. 27 ANSWERS:
1. She missed class because of (her) illness. OR Because of (her) illness, she . . . .
2. She missed class because she was ill. OR Because she was ill, she missed class.
3. She was ill. Consequently, she missed class. OR She was ill. She, consequently, missed class. OR She was ill. She missed class, consequently.
4. She was ill, so she missed class.
5. She missed class due to illness. OR She missed class due to the fact that she was ill. [OR begin with *due to*]
6. She was ill. Therefore, she missed class. [OR see item 3]

◇ **WORKBOOK:** Practice 21.

• Often in conversation we don't add a clause with *that* after using *so*. The word *so* then seems to mean *very* with additional emphasis. For example:

A: *Did you enjoy that book?*
B: *Yes, it was so interesting.*

This implies a clause with *that*, such as ". . . *so* interesting *that* I couldn't stop reading until I finished the whole book." This colloquial use of *so* is not appropriate in most expository writing.

◇ **WORKBOOK:** Practice 22.

☐ **EXERCISES 28 & 29, pp. 309–311.** *Understanding* so/such . . . that.

Exercise 28 is for class use to clarify the points in the chart. Exercise 29 is for seatwork or homework.

EX. 28 ANSWERS: **3.** The car was *so expensive (that)* we couldn't . . . . **4.** It was *such an expensive car (that)* we . . . . **5.** It was *such a cold day that* I . . . . **6.** The weather was *so hot that* you could fry an egg on the sidewalk. [This is a common saying in the United States. It is a humorous exaggeration.] **7.** We're having *such beautiful weather that* I . . . . **8.** Grandpa held me *so tightly* when he hugged me *that* I . . . . [*Grandpa* = a name for grandfather] **9.** She talked *so fast that* I . . . . **10.** It was *such a bad performance that* the audience booed the actors. [*boo* = the word that people shout when they are displeased with someone's actions, such as in a ballgame or, in this case, in a theater performance; pronounced /buːw/] **11.** I've met *so many people* in the last few days *that* I . . . . **12.** There was *so little traffic that* it took . . . . **13.** There were *so few people* at the meeting *that* it was . . . . **14.** Sally used *so much paper* when she was writing her report *that* the wastepaper . . . .

EX. 29 ANSWERS: **1.** The classroom has *such comfortable chairs that* the students find it easy to fall asleep. [*It* has no real meaning here; it anticipates the infinitive phrase.] **2.** Ted was *so worried* about the exam *that* he couldn't get to sleep last night. [The name is usually in the first clause.] **3.** Jerry got *so angry that* he put his fist throught the wall. [= He hit the wall so hard that he made a hole in it with his hand; this might prompt a cross-cultural discussion of appropriate or acceptable displays of anger.] **4.** I have *so many problems that* I can . . . . **5.** The tornado struck with *such great force that* it lifted . . . . **6.** . . . we had *such hot and humid weather that* it . . . . **7.** His handwriting is *so illegible that* I can't . . . . **8.** David has *so many girlfriends that* he can't . . . . **9.** *So many people* came to the meeting *that* there were . . . . **10.** In some countries, *so few students* are accepted by the universities *that* admission is virtually a guarantee of a good job upon graduation. [virtually = almost always; *upon* graduation = immediately after graduation]

☐ **EXERCISE 30, p. 311.** *Using* so/such . . . that.

Students should use their creativity in this exercise, even exaggerating some of their information. This is a common use of *so/such* . . . *that*, sometimes for a humorous effect.

ANSWERS: [Students complete the sentences.] **1.** so hot/cold/nice (that) **2.** such a good student (that) **3.** so softly (that) **4.** so tired (that) **5.** so heavy (that) **6.** so fast **7.** so much homework **8.** such a high temperature [= fever] **9.** such an easy test **10.** so frightened **11.** such a good movie **12.** so much noise **13.** so many students absent **14.** waited so long **15.** so nervous **16.** so angry **17.** so happy **18.** so exhausted **19.** so surprised **20.** so . . .

□ **EXERCISE 31, p. 312.** *Contrasting* so *and* too.

(You may wish to review Chart 4-12 in Chapter 4, which presents infinitives with *too*.) The purpose of this exercise is to point out that a clause beginning with *that* follows *so* but not *too*. Common error: *The test was too hard that I couldn't pass it.*

POSSIBLE ANSWERS: **3.** That car is too expensive (for me/us) to afford/buy/get. **4.** That car is so expensive that I/we could never afford (to buy) it. **5.** The coffee was too hot (for me) to drink. **6.** The coffee was so hot that it burned my tongue. **7.** It's so dark in here that I can't see my hand in front of my face. [a common saying] **8.** It's too dark in here (for me/us) to read.

◇ **WORKBOOK:** Practice 23.

CHART 8-11: EXPRESSING PURPOSE: USING *SO THAT*

• In **conversation,** it is common for a dependent "*so that* clause" to be used in answer to a "*why* question":

    A: *Why did you cut class yesterday?* [cut class = not go to class]
    B: *So (that) I could cram for the test.* [cram = study hard at the last possible moment]

In **writing,** a dependent clause must never stand alone; it must be joined grammatically to an independent clause: *I cut class yesterday so I could cram for the test.*

• The word *that* does not have full pronunciation as a conjunction. (This is perhaps why it is so often omitted.) It is said very quickly and with a lower voice. The vowel is reduced to a very short sound /ðət/.

• The difference between the coordinating conjunction *so* and the subordinating conjunction *so (that)* is a little tricky to explain. Students generally don't confuse the two in their own production. To avoid unnecessary confusion, the text does not compare the two; some students get too involved in trying to distinguish "purpose" from "cause and effect."

• Advanced students might want to know that *so as to* is a more formal, less frequent alternative to *in order to*. For example, *The law was changed so as to protect people more equitably.*

□ **EXERCISES 32 & 33, pp. 313–314.** *Understanding* so (that) *clauses.*

Begin with the four examples so that everyone gets accustomed to the pattern. Then give the students some seatwork time to work out the rest. During discussion, the responder should choose only one form of the answer, not try to say all the possible forms.

After Exercise 32, you could do Exercise 33 in any of several ways: Continue like Exercise 32, or assign it as written homework, or have students in small groups work out the answers, or assign it for independent study with a quiz the next day.

EX. 32 ANSWERS: **5.** Please be quiet so (that) I *can hear* what Sharon is saying. [Sharon is a woman's name pronounced /šɛrən/.] **6.** . . . quiet so (that) I *could hear* what . . . .
7. . . . check so (that) I *will have/have* enough . . . . **8.** . . . yesterday so (that) I *would have* enough . . . . **9.** . . . tonight so (that) they *can go* . . . . **10.** . . . babysitter so (that) they *could go* . . . . **11.** . . . at 5:00 so (that) it *will be/is* ready . . . . **12.** . . . at 5:00 so (that) it *would be* ready . . . .

EX. 33 ANSWERS: **1.** early so (that) I *can get* . . . . **2.** . . . umbrella so (that) he *wouldn't get* wet. **3.** . . . type so (that) you *can type* . . . . [Perhaps mention that language changes: The verb *type* is being replaced by the verb *keyboard* when the typing is done on a computer. Today one learns how "to keyboard."] **4.** . . . her finger so (that) she *wouldn't forget* to take . . . .

5. . . . his pocket so (that) he *could buy* a newspaper.   **6.** . . . sick so (that) he *could stay* home from school.   **7.** . . . tiptoes so (that) I *could see* the parade better (over the heads of the people standing in front of me).   **8.** . . . TV so (that) I *could listen* . . . .   **9.** . . . phone so (that) I wouldn't be interrupted . . . .   **10.** . . . she raised the hood [*bonnet* in British English] of her car so (that) other drivers *would know* that she had car trouble.

◇ **WORKBOOK:** Practices 24 and 25.

☐ **EXERCISE 34, p. 314.** *Using* so (that) *clauses.*

ANSWERS: [Depend on students' creativity.]

☐ **EXERCISE 35, p. 314.** *Cumulative review of cause and effect expressions.*

Encourage the students to think up interesting or humorous sentences. Some students have fun making up sentences about their class, using their classmates' names.

You could have students in small groups work out answers together. You could have students write sentences on the board. You could open each item to brainstorming, eliciting as many sentences as you can. You could assign the whole exercise as written homework to be handed in, or have the students correct each other's papers before they are handed in to you.

Another option is to have Student A give Student B a word to include in a sentence that Student B makes up.

STUDENT A: *Use "now that." Include the word "green."*
STUDENT B: *Now that chalkboards are green, they are no longer called blackboards.*

The students could be divided into two teams. A student from Team A could give a student on Team B a conjunction from Exercise 35 plus a word or phrase to include. B could write the sentence on the board. Team A could judge its correctness. If it's correct (in all aspects, including punctuation and spelling), Team B gets a point. If it's not correct and Team A recognizes that, Team A gets a point and Team B gets 0 points. If it's not correct and Team A does not recognize that, nobody gets any points. (You can make up any rules you wish, perhaps giving one point for correct spelling, one point for correct punctuation, and two points for correct sentence structure. Whatever the rules of the game, the purpose is for the students to be engaged and have fun while they're practicing English.)

ANSWERS: [Depend on students' creativity.]

◇ **WORKBOOK:** Practice 26.

CHARTS 8-12 and 8-13: REDUCTION OF ADVERB CLAUSES TO MODIFYING PHRASES

• These modifying phrases are often called **participial phrases** because the main word is a present participle or sometimes a past participle (conveying a passive meaning). If the phrase doesn't modify the subject of the main clause, the unacceptable result is called a "dangling participle"—the participle has nothing to modify, so it dangles (hangs) unattached to any other word. For example:

While walking by the lake, a fish jumped out of the water.

Obviously, the fish wasn't walking! But in this sentence *walking* must refer to *fish*, so the whole thing is ungrammatical (as well as unscientific).

• In Chart 8-13, the word *since* has its time-related meaning (see Chart 8-5), not its cause-effect meaning. Learners are sometimes confused about this. Just tell them that there are two different vocabulary items that have the same spelling, like *fall* (autumn) vs. *fall* (drop down).

• The English language, like all living languages, is slowly changing. As an example, it is losing any distinction between *after finishing* and *after having finished*. This phenomenon is related to sentence (c) in 8-13, which illustrates that the past perfect tense is beginning to disappear from common use, especially in informal English.

☐ EXERCISES 36 & 37, pp. 316–317.   *Changing clauses to modifying phrases.*

Use Exercise 36 for chart reinforcement and Exercise 37 for group work. In other words, after you explain a chart and discuss it with the class by using one exercise, the material can be turned over to group work, in which the students can teach each other.

EX. 36 ANSWERS: **3.** *Before coming* to class, I had a cup of coffee.   **4.** [no change]
5. *Since coming* here, *I* have learned a lot of English.   **6.** *After finishing/After having finished* breakfast, *he* left . . . .   **7.** *While living* in India last year, I learned . . . . [Earlier editions have *Burma* instead of *India*. Myanmar is now the name of what English-speakers used to call Burma.]   **8.** *Jennifer* looked . . . [no comma] *before driving* onto the main road.   **9.** *Since entering* the Institute of Technology, *Michael* has begun . . . .   **10.** [no change]

EX. 37 ANSWERS: **1.** *Before going* to Yellowstone . . ., I had never seen . . . .   **2.** *After completing/After having completed* her shopping, *she* went home.   **3.** *Alex* hurt his back *while chopping* wood. [no comma]   **4.** *You* . . . contract *before signing* your name.   **5.** [no change]
6. *The Wilsons* have . . . lifestyle *since adopting* twins.   **7.** [no change]   **8.** [no change]
9. *Since arriving* here, I have . . . .   **10.** *After hearing/After having heard* Mary . . . winter, *I* decided . . . .   **11.** *While climbing* the mountain, *Susan* lost . . . .   **12.** *Before asking* the librarian for help, *you* should . . . .

◇ **WORKBOOK:** Practices 27, 28, and 29.

CHART 8-14: EXPRESSING "DURING THE SAME TIME" IN MODIFYING PHRASES

• Compare modifying participial phrases at the beginning of a sentence with gerund subjects (sometimes a point of confusion for learners).

Gerund subjects: ***Walking*** *down that street alone at night* ***is*** *dangerous.*
     Hiking *through the woods* ***is*** *an enjoyable way to get exercise.*

• Point out that the position of certain modifying phrases can determine meaning. Compare those in (c) and (d) with the following:

I ran into an old friend (who was) walking down the street.
We saw a bear (that was) hiking through the woods.

```
┌─────────────────────────────────────────────────────────────────┐
│  CHART 8-15:  EXPRESSING CAUSE AND EFFECT IN                      │
│               MODIFYING PHRASES                                   │
├─────────────────────────────────────────────────────────────────┤
```

• The important point for learners to understand is that the grammatical structure itself (without function words) expresses a cause-and-effect meaning.

• In many cases, an initial modifying participial phrase combines the ideas of "during the same time" and "because"—as the students will discover in Exercise 38.

• To point out that *being* expresses cause and effect in this structure, have the students compare the meanings of the following two sentences.

   (1) *Chicago, a large city, has a crime problem.* [*a large city* = an appositive, reduced adjective clause, that gives identifying information about the noun: *Chicago, which is a large city, has . . . .* cause and effect possibly implied, but not stated.]

   (2) *Chicago, being a large city, has a crime problem.* [a clear cause-and-effect relationship]

```
└─────────────────────────────────────────────────────────────────┘
```

☐ **EXERCISE 38, p. 318.** *Understanding modifying phrases.*

See the INTRODUCTION to this *Guide*, p. xvii, for suggestions about using discussion-of-meaning exercises.

ANSWERS: **1.** thought *while* sitting   **2.** *because* she is a widow   **3.** forgot *while* lying   **4.** *because* he has already spent it   **5.** felt *while* I was watching and *because* I was watching [a fine line between *while* and *because*]   **6.** *because* they have brought up ten children   **7.** *because* she was surprised   **8.** saw *while* driving . . . *because* we wanted flowers   **9.** forced myself *while* struggling and *because* I was struggling   **10.** *because* I had guessed   **11.** *because* I realized   **12.** *while* and *because*

☐ **EXERCISES 39 & 40, pp. 318–319.** *Modifying phrases.*

Exercise 39 emphasizes that these modifying phrases convey a cause-and-effect meaning without the word *because*. In Exercise 40, the students have to make modifying phrases while being careful to avoid dangling participles. In both exercises, it is helpful to point out repeatedly that these phrases modify the subject of the main clause.

EX. 39 ANSWERS: **2.** *Believing* that no one loved him, the little boy . . . .   **3.** *Not paying* attention to where she was going, she stepped . . . .   **4.** *Having forgotten* to bring a pencil to the examination, I had . . . .   **5.** *Being* a vegetarian, she does . . . . [also possible: *A vegetarian,* she . . . . The use of *being* makes the cause-and-effect relationship clearer.]   **6.** *Having flunked* out of school once, he is determined . . . .

EX. 40 ANSWERS: **2.** *Hearing/Having heard* that Judy was in the hospital, I called . . . .   **3.** *Trying* his best not to cry, the little boy . . . .   **4.** *Not wanting to* inconvenience my friend . . . , I decided . . . .   **5.** *Sitting* on a large rock at the edge of a mountain stream, I felt . . . .   **6.** [no change]   **7.** *Being* a married man, I have . . . . [also possible: *A married man,* I . . . .]   **8.** *Reading* the paper last night, I saw . . . .   **9.** *Not having understood* what he said, I asked . . . . [also possible: *Having not understood*]   **10.** [no change]   **11.** *Being convinced* that . . . piano, Ann . . . . [also possible: *Convinced* that . . . .]

This exercise is a summary review of Charts 8-12, 8-13, 8-14, and 8-15.

ANSWERS: **1.** *Before talking* to you, I had . . . .   **2.** *Not wanting to* spend any more money this month, Alfred decided . . . .   **3.** *After reading/After having read* the chapter four times, I finally . . . .   **4.** *Remembering* that everyone makes mistakes, I softened . . . .   **5.** *Since completing* his Bachelor's degree, he has had . . . . [In the United States, a Bachelor's degree is earned upon graduation from college. Postgraduate degrees are a Master's (e.g., Master of Arts, Master of Science, Master of Music) and a Ph.D., which stands for Doctor of Philosophy.].
6. *Travel(l)ing/While travel(l)ing* across the United States, I could not help . . . .   **7.** *Before gaining* national fame, the union leader . . . .   **8.** *Enjoying* the cool . . . and *listening* . . . nature, we lost . . . . [Point out the parallel structure.]   **9.** *Never having flown/Having never flown* in an airplane before, the little girl . . . .   **10.** *Before becoming* vice-president of marketing and sales, Peter McKay . . . .

◇ **WORKBOOK:** Practices 30, 31, and 32.

CHART 8-16: USING *UPON* + *ING* IN MODIFYING PHRASES	

• These phrases are more common in formal writing than in conversation.

ANSWERS: **2.** *(Up)On crossing* the marathon finish line, *Tina* fell in exhaustion.   **3.** *(Up)On looking* in my wallet, *I* discovered . . . .   **4.** *(Up)On meeting* the king, *I* bowed my head.
5. *(Up)On re-reading* the figures, *Sam* . . . .   **6.** *(Up)On getting* an appraisal of my coin collection, *I* was . . . .   **7.** *(Up)On learning* that she had won the lottery, *Mrs. Alexander* . . . .
8. *(Up)On finishing* the examination, [*you*—implied imperative subject] bring . . . .   **9.** *(Up)On being elected* a member of the club, *I* found . . . .

◇ **WORKBOOK:** Practice 33.

Use Exercise 43 for brainstorming (with the students' attention focused on the subject that the phrase is modifying) and 44 for homework.

ANSWERS: [Depend on students' creativity.]

◇ **WORKBOOK:** Practices 34, 35, and 36.

ANSWERS: **1.** The weather was **so** cold that I **didn't** like . . . . [OR *is . . . don't*]
2. I have to study four **hours** every day because [**no of**] my courses are difficult.
3. . . . downstairs (in order) **to watch** television.
4. . . . sailed across a rough sea before **reaching** the shore.
5. . . . class. **Therefore,** my roommate . . . .
6. . . . village. **He** finally found it after **walking** two hundred **miles.**

7. Because my country is located in a subtropical area, [**no so**] the weather is hot. OR [**no Because**] My country is located in a subtropical area, so the weather is hot.

8. I will stay in the *United States* for two more *years* [**no period**] *because I* want to finish my degree before *going/I go* home.

9. After *I graduate* from college, my father . . . . [The assumption is that the daughter/son is graduating from college, not the father.]

10. We were floating far from the beach when suddenly my mother cried out, [**comma**] ''*Shark! A* shark is coming!'' *Seeing* a black fin cutting the water and coming toward us, we *were* paralyzed with fear. [Other changes are possible, such as using periods to create shorter sentences. However, dependent clauses and modifying phrases are preferable, as shown here.]

☐ **EXERCISE 46, p. 322.** *Using adverb clauses and modifying phrases.*

Of course, this exercise works best if the articles are written in English; students will not have to translate specialized words. However, they could summarize articles written in another language.

If you have access to a copying machine, you could distribute a few of the students' best summaries to the class as good examples. Students usually enjoy seeing their best writing ''in publication.'' Keep the authors anonymous. They can reveal their authorship if they want to.

Suggestion: Assign oral news summaries each day for the rest of the term. Limit the speaking time strictly (one to three minutes) before one of the class members tries to give an hour lecture on world politics. A student can act as timekeeper. Schedule also some question-and-answer time. Encourage lively discussion in whatever time is available.

◇ **WORKBOOK:** Practices 37, 38, and 39. Practice Tests A and B.

☐ **EXERCISE 47, p. 322.** *Using prepositions.*

ANSWERS: **1.** grateful *to you for*   **2.** escaped *from*   **3.** not content *with*   **4.** not relevant *to*   **5.** decided *(up)on*   **6.** made *of*   **7.** depending *(up)on*   **8.** applied *for* admission *to*   **9.** dreamed *about*   **10.** dreams *of*   **11.** innocent *of*   **12.** friendly *to(ward)/ with*   **13.** proud *of*   **14.** provided me *with*   **15.** compared . . . *to/with*

☐ **EXERCISE 48, p. 323.** *Phrasal verbs.*

Select two students for each item. For a humorous effect, you should read the last item!

ANSWERS: **1.** take *after*   **2.** cut it *out*   **3.** clean *up* . . . taking *out*   **4.** throw *up* [= get ill or sick]   **5.** hung it *up*   **6.** called me *in* [= into his office for an appointment]   **7.** checked *out/into*   **8.** torn *down*   **9.** kicked them *out* [*crash a party* = come without being invited, an impolite act]   **10.** put *away*

Chapter 9: SHOWING RELATIONSHIPS BETWEEN IDEAS—PART II

ORDER OF CHAPTER	CHARTS	EXERCISES	WORKBOOK
Expressing opposition	9-1 → 9-3	Ex. 1 → 10	Pr. 1 → 10
Expressing conditions	9-4 → 9-9	Ex. 11 → 21	Pr. 11 → 19
Cumulative review and practice	9-10	Ex. 22 → 28	Pr. 20 → 26
Giving examples	9-11	Ex. 29 → 30	Pr. 27
Continuing the same idea	9-12	Ex. 31 → 32	Pr. 28
Cumulative review and practice			Pr. 29 Pr. Tests A & B

General Notes on Chapter 9:

• OBJECTIVE: This chapter gives learners flexibility in expressing complex ideas in English. The structures presented here are useful both in formal writing and in conversation.

• APPROACH: This chapter continues the approach of Chapter 8 in presenting clauses and phrases that relate ideas to each other. This is a semantic as well as grammatical approach because it focuses on the meaning of certain conjunctions that are used for expressing opposition, conditions, and additions.

• TERMINOLOGY: (See Chapter 8.)

CHART 9-1: EXPRESSING UNEXPECTED RESULT: USING *EVEN THOUGH*

• The general category of "opposition" is labeled "unexpected result" here to help the students compare *because* and *even though*, and also to help them understand the meaning of "opposition" (i.e., that something is in some way "opposite" of something else) as used in the text.

• Other forms of *even though* are *although* and *though* (see Chart 9-2). The differences are minor.

☐ EXERCISE 1, p. 324. *Comparing* even though *and* because.

Discuss the related pairs of sentences.

ANSWERS: **3.** Because **4.** Even though **5.** Even though [assuming we don't like to walk in the rain] **6.** Because **7.** even though **8.** because **9.** even though **10.** because **11.** even though **12.** because [People protest because dolphins are killed.]

◇ **WORKBOOK:** Practices 1 and 2.

☐ **EXERCISE 2, p. 325.** *Using* even though.

Before responding, the students need a moment to decide whether the "truthful" answer is *Yes* or *No*. Then they must construct a complete sentence. The result is a fairly realistic dialogue between you and a student.

ANSWERS: [The adverb clause can come before or after the main clause.] **1.** Yes, even though I wasn't tired, I went to bed.   **2.** No, John didn't wake up even though the telephone rang many times.   **3.** Yes, even though the food was terrible, I ate it.   **4.** Yes, even though I didn't study, I passed the test.   **5.** No, I didn't stay home even though the weather is terrible (today).   **6.** No, even though I fell down the stairs, I didn't get hurt.   **7.** Yes, I still feel tired even though I took a nap. [*took a nap* = slept for a short time during the day]   **8.** No, even though I told the truth, no one believed me.   **9.** Yes, I still have a headache even though I took an aspirin.   **10.** Yes, even though I turned on the air conditioner, it's still hot in here.   **11.** No, even though I mailed the letter three days ago, it still hasn't arrived/it hasn't arrived yet.   **12.** No, I can't afford to buy an airplane even though I have a lot of money.   **13.** Yes, even though my grandmother is ninety years old, she's still young at heart.   **14.** Yes, I laughed at (. . .)'s joke even though I didn't understand it.   **15.** Yes, I'm still cheerful even though (all those terrible things happened).

CHART 9-2: SHOWING OPPOSITION (UNEXPECTED RESULT)

• This chart presents a number of synonyms. Point out their semantic similarities and grammatical differences. It is assumed that the students understand the structural differences and the grammatical labels from their study of Chapter 8.

• A common error is the use of both *although* and *but* to connect two ideas within a sentence. INCORRECT: ***Although*** it was raining, ***but*** *we went to the zoo.*

• The text does not mention that *though* can be used as a final position adverb: *I was hungry. I didn't eat anything though.* Advanced students may be curious about this usage.

☐ **EXERCISE 3, p. 326.** *Understanding expressions showing unexpected result.*

Use a wall chart (or something similar) of patterns and punctuation as suggested for use with Chart 8-9 (p. 150 of this *Guide*).

ANSWERS: (The variations in sentence order and punctuation as presented in 8-9 and 9-2 aren't given here but should be discussed with the class.)
1. Even though it was raining, we went to the zoo.
  It was raining, but we went to the zoo anyway.
  It was raining. Nevertheless, we went to the zoo.
  In spite of the rain, we went to the zoo.
  We didn't go to the zoo because it was raining.
2. Although his grades were low, he was admitted to the university.
  His grades were low, yet he was admitted to the university.
  His grades were low. Nonetheless, he was admitted to the university.
  He was admitted to the university despite (his) low grades.
  He was not admitted to the university because of (his) low grades.

□ **EXERCISE 4, p. 326.** *Using expressions showing unexpected results.*

Since students will have to think of logical completions, you might assign this to be written as seatwork or homework prior to discussion. Then the whole class can compare alternative answers, perhaps "voting" to choose the most creative ones.

ANSWERS: [Depend on students' creativity.]

□ **EXERCISE 5, p. 327.** *Understanding* nevertheless.

When they respond, students could read the sentence from the book aloud and then the version with *nevertheless*. They should explain how the punctuation changes.

You might want to model some patterns of sentence-level stress and intonation for the learners. (An unstressed word or syllable is spoken with lower and softer voice than a stressed segment.) Demonstrate that words like *but* and *although* are usually unstressed, whereas *nevertheless* and *despite* usually receive stress. In writing, the accompanying pauses and intonation are represented by periods and commas.

One point which the text does not mention but which may arise in an advanced class is that *nevertheless* can also be used as an adverb, like *still* or *anyway*. For example: *Although I don't agree with his actions, I nevertheless admire his courage. He wasn't tired, but he went to bed nevertheless.* To minimize possible confusion, the text teaches the use of *nevertheless* as a conjunctive adverb only.

ANSWERS: **2.** She was not hungry. *Nevertheless*, she ate . . . . [Use of *was not* instead of *wasn't* is possibly preferable because *nevertheless* is rather formal.] **3.** Jack was not feeling good. Nevertheless, he went . . . . **4.** He lied to me. Nevertheless, I still trust him. **5.** Sally was very sad. Nevertheless, she smiled and . . . . **6.** George was alone and lost in the woods. Nevertheless, he did not panic. **7.** Elizabeth . . . the United States. Nevertheless, she has to pay income taxes. [Omit *anyway* in formal English.] **8.** Henry . . . an honest politician. Nevertheless, I would never . . . . **9.** The local police . . . programs. Nevertheless, the crime rate . . . . **10.** Math . . . for him. Nevertheless, he understands that . . . .

□ **EXERCISE 6, p. 327.** *Understanding* in spite of *and* despite.

ANSWERS: **2.** . . . in spite of/despite its noise OR in spite of/despite the fact that it is noisy **3.** in spite of/despite the hard work [etc.] **4.** in spite of/despite the danger **5.** in spite of/despite the extremely hot weather **6.** in spite of/despite his vast fortune

◇ **WORKBOOK:** Practices 3, 4, 5, and 6.

□ **EXERCISE 7, p. 328.** *Cumulative review and practice.*

ANSWERS: [Depend on students' creativity.]

CHART 9-3: SHOWING DIRECT OPPOSITION

• *Whereas* and *while* can appear at the beginning of either clause with no change of meaning. *Whereas* is somewhat formal and of relatively low frequency. *While*, *but*, and *however* are used more frequently than *whereas*.

• *While* has two different meanings: (1) at the same time and (2) whereas.

    (1) *While (he was) swimming, he got very tired.*
    (2) *While fire is hot, ice is cold.*

□ **EXERCISE 8, p. 329.** *Understanding* whereas *and* while.

Two or more students should give different versions of each item. Every sentence should contain a comma before the second adverb clause.

POSSIBLE ANSWERS: **2.** Some people are tall, whereas others are short. [could move *whereas* to the first clause] **3.** . . . while others prefer to live in town/in the city. **4.** . . . others know one or more foreign languages. **5.** . . . a rat is large. **6.** . . . is always extremely cold. **7.** and **8.** [Depend on students' ideas.]

◇ **WORKBOOK:** Practice 7.

□ **EXERCISE 9, p. 329.** *Understanding* however *and* on the other hand.

The student who answers can decide which transition to use. He or she should also choose any correct punctuation and explain it.

POSSIBLE ANSWERS: **1.** Florida has a warm climate. Alaska, on the other hand, has a cold climate. **2.** Fred is a good student. However, his brother is lazy. **3.** . . . . Sue is hoping for a boy; Ron, however, is hoping for a girl. **4.** Old people . . . their children; on the other hand, the old . . . . **5.** . . . states. However, in my . . . .

◇ **WORKBOOK:** Practice 8.

□ **EXERCISE 10, p. 329.** *Cumulative review.*

In this exercise, focus primarily on the grammar and go through the items rather quickly, or develop the exercise into an activity designed to encourage the sharing of information about the students' countries in comparison with the United States. Some options: (1) Ask for volunteers for each item, concentrating on how to express direct opposition. (2) Assign one item per student to present orally to the class to initiate open discussion on each topic. (3) Assign national groups to make oral presentations. (4) Have the students discuss all of the items in small groups. (5) Open all of the items for "brainstorming" class discussion; follow with a composition that compares and contrasts the United States and the student's country. (You might point out that almost any one of these items alone could be the topic of an entire composition.) (6) In a multinational class, open discussion could also be followed by a composition in which the students write about what they learned and heard, both about the United States and about other countries represented in the class.

If students are not familiar with contrasts between their country and the United States, they could choose two other countries or perhaps regions within their own country.

ANSWERS: [Depend on students' ideas.]

◇ **WORKBOOK:** Practices 9 and 10.

CHART 9-4: EXPRESSING CONDITIONS IN ADVERB CLAUSES: "*IF* CLAUSES"

• As with adverb clauses of time (see Chapter 8), it is incorrect to use *will/be going to* in an "*if* clause." An exception, however, occurs when the speaker is trying to arrange an exchange of promises: *If you'll do it, I'll do it.*

• All of the examples and exercise items in this unit on "condition" (9-4 through 9-9) are in present or future time. Chapter 10 picks up the use of other verb forms in conditional sentences.

□ **EXERCISE 11, p. 330.** *Understanding "if clauses."*

Several students could give answers for each item. Encourage them to be creative or humorous. The main point is to use present verbs in the *"if* clause."

ANSWERS: [Depend on students' ideas.]

◇ **WORKBOOK:** Practice 11.

CHART 9-5: USING *WHETHER OR NOT* AND *EVEN IF*	

• Students sometimes wonder about the difference between *even though* and *even if. Even though* deals with actual events or states; *even if* deals with possible conditions. *Even though the weather is cold (today)* = the weather is cold. *Even if the weather is cold (tomorrow)* = the weather may be cold. In some contexts, the distinction blurs: *Even if you don't like pickles, you should try one of these.*

□ **EXERCISE 12, p. 331.** *Understanding* whether or not *and* even if.

You should read the cue to the class so they understand the situation. It isn't necessary to use the exact words from the book; just describe a situation. Then ask students to complete the sentences logically.

POSSIBLE ANSWERS: **2.** a: Sam laughs at the jokes whether they're funny or not. b. . . . even if they're not funny. **3.** a. You have to hand in your examination paper whether you're finished or not. b. . . . even if you're not finished. **4.** a. We're going to go camping in the mountains whether it snows or not. b. . . . even if it snows. **5.** a. Max can go to school whether or not his family has enough money to send him. b. . . . even if his family doesn't have enough money to send him. **6.** a. . . . whether or not the weather is cold. b. . . . even if the weather is hot. **7.** a. . . . whether you approve or not. b. . . . even if you disapprove/don't approve. **8.** Even if he apologizes, . . . **9.** to **12.** [Depend on students' ideas.]

◇ **WORKBOOK:** Practice 12.

CHART 9-6: USING *IN CASE (THAT)* AND *IN THE EVENT (THAT)*	

• British English uses *in the event* rather differently. It is not followed by a *"that*-clause"; it is a transition followed by a comma. It expresses an unexpected result or the idea that "this is what really happened instead." For example:

They had planned to go swimming. In the event, they went to a movie because it rained.

An American English speaker would use *instead* or *as it turned out* rather than *in the event* in this context.

□ **EXERCISE 13, p. 332.** *Understanding* in case *and* in the event that.

In these sentences, students should take the role of "I." In other words, they are just changing the form of your sentence, not having a dialogue with you. Responders can alternate between *in case* and *in the event that* or simply use whichever one seems more comfortable.

POSSIBLE ANSWERS: **2.** In case you need to see me, I'll be in my office tomorrow morning around ten. **3.** In the event that you need more information, you can call me. **4.** In case you have any more questions, ask Dr. Smith. **5.** In the event (that) you are not satisfied with your purchase, you can return it to the store. **6.** In case Jack calls, please tell him that I'm at the library. **7.** to **13.** [Depend on students' ideas.]

◇ **WORKBOOK:** Practice 13.

CHART 9-7: ADVERB CLAUSES OF CONDITION: USING
UNLESS

• Trying to distinguish between _until_ and _unless_ can be difficult for the students. _Unless_ expresses a condition that is required for a particular result. _Until_ expresses a time relationship—but also expresses a condition required for a result. It is no wonder that students may be confused when they compare the following: _You can't drive unless/until you're sixteen. Class can't start unless/until the teacher arrives. I don't eat unless/until I'm hungry._

• The verb in the "_unless_ clause" is usually positive, but it could be negative. For example:

  A: _Will I see you at the theater tonight?_
  B: _Yes, unless I can't go._

□ **EXERCISE 14, p. 333.** _Understanding_ unless.

ANSWERS: **2.** You can't travel abroad unless you have a passport. **3.** You can't get a driver's license unless you're at least sixteen years old. [If the focus were on time, not law, then _until_ would be an appropriate conjunction in 2 and 3.] **4.** Unless I get some film, I won't be able . . . . **5.** You'll get hungry during class unless you eat breakfast.

□ **EXERCISE 15, p. 334.** _Using_ unless.

ANSWERS: [Depend on students' creativity.]

◇ **WORKBOOK:** Practices 14 and 15.

CHART 9-8: USING _ONLY IF_ AND _PROVIDING/PROVIDED_
THAT

• Other subordinating conjunctions and prepositional phrases fronted by _only_ at the beginning of a sentence require subject-verb inversion in the main clause:

  Only when the teacher dismisses us **can we stand** and **leave** the room.
  Only after the phone rang **did I realize** that I had fallen asleep in my chair.
  Only in my hometown do I feel at ease.

• There is no difference between using _providing_ or _provided_, as in (c).

☐ **EXERCISE 16, p. 334.** *Understanding* only if.

You should set up the situation in each item so that students understand it. It is not necessary to use exactly the same words that are in the book; just explain it briefly and naturally. Make up similar items using your students' names and situations.

POSSIBLE ANSWERS: **2.** You can go to the party only if you have an invitation. **3.** You can attend this school only if you have a student visa. **4.** Jimmy can chew gum only if he's sure (that) his mother won't find out. **5.** We will go to the movie only if you want to. **6.** Water will freeze only if the temperature reaches 32 °F/0 °C. [F = Fahrenheit. C = Centigrade or Celsius.] **7.** Only if you study hard *will you pass* the exam. **8.** Only if you have a ticket *can you get* into the soccer stadium. **9.** Only if my homework is finished *can I watch* TV in the evening. **10.** Only if I get a job *will I have* enough money to go to school.
11. to **13.** [Depend on students' ideas.]

◇ **WORKBOOK:** Practice 16.

☐ **EXERCISE 17, p. 335.** *Comparing* only if *and* unless.

You can expect some hesitations and false starts in this exercise because these concepts are rather complex semantically. The sentences speak of events that have not yet occurred or don't usually occur; the events need a certain condition to "trigger" their occurrence. Two students could give different responses to each item, as in the example.

ANSWERS: **2.** a) I can pay my bills only if I get a job. OR Only if I get a job *can I pay* my bills. b) I can't pay my bills unless I get a job. OR Unless I get a job, I can't pay my bills. **3.** a) Your clothes will get clean only if you use soap. OR Only if you use soap *will your clothes get* clean. b) Your clothes won't get clean unless you use soap. OR Unless you use . . . . **4.** a) I can take pictures only if I buy some film. OR Only if I buy some film *can I take* pictures. b) I can't take pictures unless I buy some film. OR Unless I buy . . . . **5.** a) I wake up only if the alarm clock rings. OR Only if the alarm clock rings *do I wake* up. b) I don't wake up unless the alarm clock rings. OR Unless the alarm clock . . . .

☐ **EXERCISE 18, p. 335.** *Understanding* provided/providing that.

A comma can be used before *provided/providing that* when the adverb clause follows the main clause. This indicates a pause before adding the condition to the statement. (The text teaches that no comma is used when the adverb clause follows the main clause. There are, however, many exceptions; stylistic preferences in punctuation differ.)

ANSWERS: **2.** You are eligible for the insurance [optional comma] provided (that) you are a student. [Other answers depend on students' ideas.]

☐ **EXERCISE 19, p. 336.** *Cumulative practice.*

Do this exercise orally as a quick review. One student could answer and another could then indicate the necessary punctuation in the sentence.

POSSIBLE ANSWERS: **2.** The party will be held outside whether or not it rains. **3.** Even if it rains, the party will be held outside. **4.** In case it rains, . . . **5.** . . . in the event that it rains. **6.** Unless it rains, . . . **7.** Only if it rains [optional comma] will the party be held outside. **8.** . . . providing that it does not rain. **9.** Provided that it doesn't rain, . . .

◇ **WORKBOOK:** Practice 17.

CHART 9-9: EXPRESSING CONDITIONS: USING *OTHERWISE* AND *OR (ELSE)*

• As a transition, *otherwise* is common in contrary-to-fact conditional sentences. Its use is picked up again in Chapter 10 (Conditional Sentences).

• *Otherwise* can also function as an adverb meaning "differently" (e.g., *Johns thinks that Mars is inhabited. I believe **otherwise**.*). *Otherwise* can also mean "except for that/other than that" (*I have a broken leg, but **otherwise** I'm fine.*). The text asks the students to focus on the use of *otherwise* only as a conjunctive adverb, but advanced students might be curious about these other uses.

☐ **EXERCISE 20, p. 336.** *Understanding* otherwise.

Note that only the present tense is used in the "*if* clauses." When the "*if* clause" is transformed to a simple sentence in this exercise, a future modal (e.g., *will, must*) or future "similar expression"★ (e.g., *be going to, have to*) is needed.

Some responses could use *or else* for variety. Discuss punctuation.

POSSIBLE ANSWERS: **2.** I have to/should/had better/[etc.] wash my clothes tonight. *Otherwise,* I won't have any clean clothes to wear tomorrow. **3.** You'd better leave now. *Otherwise,* you'll be late for class. **4.** You should/ought to/[etc.] go to bed, *or else* your cold will get worse. **5.** You'd better [etc.] get a ticket. *Otherwise,* you can't get into the theater. **6.** You need a passport. *Otherwise,* you can't enter the country. **7.** Tom had better [etc.] get a job soon, *or else* his family won't . . . . **8.** Mary has to [etc.] get a scholarship. *Otherwise,* she can't go to school. **9.** You have to [etc.] speak both Japanese and Chinese fluently. *Otherwise,* you won't be considered for that job.

◇ **WORKBOOK:** Practices 18 and 19.

☐ **EXERCISE 21, p. 337.** *Cumulative review of conditions.*

ANSWERS: [Punctuation only] **1.** [no punctuation] **2.** ⌒⌒⌒choice. We have to ⌒⌒⌒. **3.** [optional comma before *providing*] **4.** ⌒⌒⌒ is very inconsiderate. He ⌒⌒⌒. **5.** [no punctuation] **6.** ⌒⌒⌒. Otherwise, ⌒⌒⌒. **7.** [no punctuation] **8.** [no punctuation] **9.** [no punctuation] **10.** ⌒⌒⌒. Otherwise, ⌒⌒⌒.

CHART 9-10: SUMMARY: CAUSE AND EFFECT, OPPOSITION, CONDITION

• Congratulate your students on knowing how to use all these expressions. Make them aware of how much they have accomplished.

★See Chapter 2 (Modal Auxiliaries and Similar Expressions).

□ **EXERCISES 22 & 23, pp. 338–339.** *Cumulative review and practice.*

These exercises should proceed rather easily because the students don't have to create any content, just manipulate word order and punctuation. Students generally treat this type of exercise as a word game.

You could go through the exercises quickly with the whole class, or the students could have fun working together. You might want to do the first few items with the whole class to show them how to proceed, then you could have them work in pairs or small groups. You should walk around to give assistance as needed, perhaps suggesting where students might look in the text to find the answer to a problem. As a final step, you could open the exercises for general class discussion, answering any questions and settling any disputes.

ANSWERS: [Depend on students' creativity. Refer to charts for punctuation.]

□ **EXERCISE 24, p. 339.** *Cumulative review and practice.*

This exercise could be turned into a game. A student could make a sentence (orally or on the chalkboard), and the rest of the class could "vote" on its correctness. (Weaker students should be assigned easy items or paired with stronger students.) The class should have fun with this exercise and be impressed with their own recently acquired skills in using these words and structures.

ANSWERS: [Depend on students' creativity. Refer to charts for punctuation.]

□ **EXERCISES 25 & 26, p. 340–341.** *Cumulative review and practice.*

After practicing the previous exercises, students could do these two as written seatwork or homework prior to discussion. Encourage them to use recently learned vocabulary and idioms in their answers. Later, you could copy some of their sentences for everyone to benefit from through discussion.

ANSWERS: [Depend on students' creativity.]

◇ **WORKBOOK:** Practices 20, 21, 22, and 23.

□ **EXERCISE 27, p. 341.** *Cumulative review.*

ANSWERS: 1. Unless I study very hard, I **won't** pass all of my exams. OR **If** I study very hard, I will pass all of my exams.
2. My shoes and pants got muddy [no period] **e**ven though I walked carefully through the wet streets.
3. My neighborhood is quiet and safe. **H**owever**,** I always lock my doors. OR . . . safe; however, I . . . .
4. Although I usually don't like **F**rench food, [no *but*] I liked the food I had at the **F**rench restaurant . . . . OR [no *Although*] I usually don't like . . . , but I liked . . . .
5. Although my room in the dormitory is very small, [no *but*] I like it [no period] **b**ecause it is a place where I can be by myself and study in peace and quiet. OR [no *Although*] My room . . . small, but I . . . because it is . . . quiet.
6. **Despite my preference/Despite preferring/Despite the fact that I prefer/Although I prefer/Even though I prefer** to be a history teacher, I am studying in the Business School **so (that) I can get/in order to be able to get** a job in industry.
7. A little girl approached the cage. **H**owever**,** when the tiger **showed** its teeth and **growled,** she **ran** to her mother [no period] **b**ecause she was frightened.
8. . . . battle [no period] **b**ecause . . .

□ **EXERCISE 28, p. 341.** *Review of noun, adjective, and adverb clauses.*

In this exercise, students should have fun creating very complex sentences with more than one dependent clause linked to an independent clause (like some of the items in Exercise 27). They must think of some logical information to include, make sure that every verb has a subject, and check on verb tenses.

Ask volunteers to write their best sentences on the chalkboard for analysis and discussion. Help the class to see how each sentence is constructed and linked together.

POSSIBLE ANSWERS: **1.** If what he said was true, he must have been in great danger. **2.** Because the man who came to dinner had not been invited, we didn't have enough food. **3.** Even though she didn't understand what I (had) asked, she tried to be helpful.   **4.** Now that all of the students who are my age have graduated, I am the oldest one in this class. **5.** Since the restaurant where we first met has burned down, we have only our memories of it.

◇ **WORKBOOK:** Practices 24, 25, and 26.

CHART 9-11: GIVING EXAMPLES	

- Giving examples is important in English rhetoric; general statements need specific support for clarity and persuasiveness.

□ **EXERCISE 29, p. 342.** *Understanding* such as.

Students can use their knowledge of many things to complete these sentences. You might ask more than one student to give relevant examples for an item. They enjoy giving examples from their own experience or knowledge.

The commas are already given so that students can concentrate on meaning.

ANSWERS: [Depend on students' ideas.]

□ **EXERCISE 30, p. 343.** *Using* such as.

In this exercise, too, students usually enjoy sharing their opinions. When you read an item, try to be as natural as possible, changing the wording as you wish.

ANSWERS: [Depend on students' ideas.]

◇ **WORKBOOK:** Practice 27.

CHART 9-12: CONTINUING THE SAME IDEA	

- One other transition in this pattern is *besides that*. Example:

  She's an excellent teacher. Besides that, students really like her.

This transition is usually used when listing points in an argument in order to persuade someone. (In this example, you might be trying to persuade an administrator to give the teacher a promotion or a salary increase.) Informally, *that* is sometimes dropped:

  She's an excellent teacher. Besides, students really like her.

- Ask the students to give additional examples using *beside* vs. *besides* in order to clarify the difference.

□ **EXERCISE 31, p. 344.** *Using expressions to continue an idea.*

Since these items are rather long and several answers are possible, students should prepare their answers (seatwork or homework). Then you can lead a discussion of good alternatives and the required punctuation.

POSSIBLE ANSWERS: **1.** I like to read that newspaper for several reasons. One is that the news is always reported accurately. *Furthermore/Moreover,* it has interesting special features.
2. . . . *Furthermore,* you should read . . . . *In addition,* watching television can be helpful.
3. . . . *Furthermore/Besides that/In addition,* a housing shortage has developed. *Moreover,* there are so many automobiles . . . . **4.** . . . a balanced diet. *Moreover,* the body needs . . . . *Besides* physical exercise, sleep and rest should not be neglected.

□ **EXERCISE 32, p. 345.** *Using expressions to continue an idea.*

A student should choose only **one** of the topics to develop. (If the topics are inappropriate for your students, you could use other general statements.)
When marking the papers, focus mainly on the use of connecting words, and praise good usage freely. If there are errors in other structures, treat them as a bit less important.

◇ **WORKBOOK:** Practices 28 and 29. Practice Tests A and B.

□ **EXERCISE 33, p. 345.** *Phrasal verbs.*

Students can work in pairs on these dialogues. Then you could have a pair read one dialogue to the whole class. Encourage them to speak expressively and with good enunciation.

ANSWERS: **1.** ran *into*   **2.** put it *off*   **3.** put *on*   **4.** call you *back* [They are talking on the telephone.]   **5.** point *out*   **6.** figure that *out* . . . came *across/upon*   **7.** brought them *up*   **8.** look *into* it . . . find *out*   **9.** make *up*   **10.** turning *on/off/out*

Chapter 10: CONDITIONAL SENTENCES

ORDER OF CHAPTER	CHARTS	EXERCISES	WORKBOOK
Basic verb form usage in conditional sentences	10-1 → 10-4	Ex. 1 → 4	Pr. 1 → 3
Cumulative review and practice		Ex. 5 → 7	Pr. 4 → 7
Other verb forms in conditional sentences	10-5 → 10-7	Ex. 8 → 10	Pr. 8 → 10
Conditional sentences without "*if* clauses"	10-8 → 10-9	Ex. 11 → 12	Pr. 11 → 13
Cumulative review and practice		Ex. 13 → 17	Pr. 14 → 17
Verb forms following *wish*	10-10 → 10-11	Ex. 18 → 22	Pr. 18 → 20
Using *as if/as though*	10-12	Ex. 23	Pr. 21 → 22
Cumulative review and practice of verb forms		Ex. 24 → 27	Pr. 23 Pr. Tests A & B

General Notes on Chapter 10:

• OBJECTIVE: Conditional sentences are among the most useful forms for communicating about possibilities, guesses, wishes, regrets, and other abstract notions. Students who learn to form these clauses correctly will add a very important dimension to their ability to understand and use English in order to communicate complex information in both speech and writing.

• APPROACH: Since verb forms are used for subtle distinctions of meaning in conditional sentences, the chapter begins with a summary of their use in presenting factual and contrary-to-fact information. Then variations in conditional sentences are introduced. The last two units deal with expressing wishes and using *as if/as though*. The chapter (and the book) ends with several exercises reviewing the use of verb forms in many contexts.

CHART 10-1: SUMMARY OF BASIC VERB FORM USAGE IN CONDITIONAL SENTENCES

• This chart summarizes the information in the next three charts. It is helpful to have a wall chart or transparency of these verb forms for you to point at and for the students to refer to during discussion of the exercises. When information about using progressives and other modals is introduced in later charts, this basic chart can be expanded to include them.

• It is assumed that the students are familiar with conditional sentences. You might introduce this chapter with an oral exercise in which you ask leading questions: *What would you do if there were a fire in this room? What would you have done if you hadn't come to class today? What would you do if I asked you to stand on your head in the middle of the classroom? If you were a bird/cat/mouse/etc., how would you spend your days? What would you be doing if you weren't in class?*

• Some students seem to think that conditional sentences are odd and unimportant. Assure them that conditionals are common, even in daily conversation. They are the only way to express certain ideas.

◇ **WORKBOOK:** Practice 1.

**CHARTS 10-2 and 10-3: TRUE OR UNTRUE IN THE PRESENT
OR FUTURE**

• Conditional sentences have a "truth value" in the mind of the speaker. The "*if* clause" contains a condition under which, **in the speaker's opinion,** an expected result might or might not occur. The "result clause" can state the speaker's prediction of an outcome.

• Like adverb clauses of time, an "*if* clause" cannot contain a future tense verb. This fact about English usage must be learned, even though it might seem illogical to some students. A language is not a logical set of scientific formulas or rules; it is a complex, flexible instrument of communication based on traditions and preferences—as much art as science. Students should understand this point by the time they complete this book.

• In everyday conversation, the subjunctive use of *were* instead of *was* with singular subjects is more typical of American than British English. The text encourages the use of *were*, but either is correct.

☐ **EXERCISE 1, p. 348.** *Understanding the truth value of conditionals.*

Pairs of items in this exercise are related, showing true and untrue conditional statements. ("Untrue" does not mean that the speaker is lying, of course. It means that he or she is speaking of some situation that does not or cannot truly exist. The situation is hypothetical, not real.)

Perhaps students should work on two items at a time. Lead them in a discussion of the correct forms and the differences in meaning. Try to help them understand that the speaker communicates an opinion about the truth value by his/her choice of verb forms. Ask leading questions about the truth value throughout: e.g., *Am I* (the speaker) *going to bake an apple pie? Do I have enough apples? Do I want to bake an apple pie?*

ANSWERS: **1.** *will bake* [First, I will count the apples.] **2.** *would bake* [Truth: I don't have enough apples.] **3.** *have* [I will look for one.] **4.** *had* [Truth: I don't have one.] **5.** *will make* **6.** *would make* [Truth: The tomatoes are not ripe.] **7.** *had* [Truth: He doesn't have one.] **8.** *has* [First, he must look for one.] **9.** *is* **10.** *were/was* **11.** *would not be . . . were/was* [Truth: English is not my native language; therefore, I am in this class.]

◇ **WORKBOOK:** Practice 2.

CHART 10-4: UNTRUE (CONTRARY TO FACT) IN THE PAST

• Looking back at past times, we know whether events really occurred or not. We can still talk about events that did not occur, using conditional sentences.

• Native speakers (even educated speakers) at times use *would* in "*if* clauses." Examples: *If you'd try harder, you'd learn more. If you would've told me about it, I could've helped you.* This is generally considered nonstandard, especially in formal English.

☐ **EXERCISE 2, p. 349.** *Understanding contrary-to-fact in the past.*

In this exercise, three similar sentences are grouped together. Lead students in a discussion of the differences in form and meaning among the grouped sentences.

ANSWERS: **1.** *have* [First, I must count my money.]   **2.** *had* [Truth: I don't have enough.]
3. *had had* [Truth: I didn't have enough.]   **4.** *will/are going to go* [a plan or promise]
5. *would go* [Truth: The weather is bad.]   **6.** *would have gone* [Truth: The weather was bad, so we didn't go.]   **7.** *is*   **8.** *were/was . . . would visit*   **9.** *had been . . . would have visited*

☐ **EXERCISE 3, p. 349.** *Understanding conditional sentences.*

These items are past, present, and future. Students must identify the time and also the truth value, then use appropriate verb forms. They should be given time to do this as seatwork or homework before discussing their answers.

ANSWERS: **1.** were/was . . . would know   **2.** had studied . . . would have passed
3. throw   **4.** were [In the expression "if I were you," *was* is rarely used, even in British English.] . . . would tell   **5.** had had . . . would have taken   **6.** have . . . will give
7. would not have got(ten) . . . had remembered   **8.** would change . . . were/was   **9.** is
10. had . . . would not have to   **11.** were/was . . . would accept   **12.** had been . . . would not have bitten

☐ **EXERCISE 4, p. 351.** *Understanding conditional sentences.*

Substituting an auxiliary for a verb phrase to avoid unnecessary repetition isn't explained in the text, as the students are assumed to be familiar with these patterns. However, some students may have difficulty with this exercise. Its purpose is to prepare for the next two oral exercises, so you should take time now for discussion of the patterns.

There are some minor differences between British and American usages:
1. *British*: if I had—*American*: if I did (have one)
2. *British*: if he wasn't/weren't—*American*: if he weren't/wasn't
3. *British only*: had done—*American*: had

ANSWERS: **4.** did [British: *had*]   **5.** weren't/wasn't   **6.** had (come) [British: *had done*]
7. were/was   **8.** didn't (have to)   **9.** had (gone) [British: *had done*]   **10.** didn't
11. weren't/wasn't   **12.** hadn't (called) [British: *hadn't done*]

◇ **WORKBOOK:** Practice 3.

☐ **EXERCISES 5 & 6, pp. 351–352.** *Using conditional sentences in present and past.*

You could call on students in random order, perhaps beginning with some of the quicker ones, and ask each one an appropriate question. If some of the questions in the book aren't suitable, change them or substitute others.

Give the responder enough time to comprehend the question (repeat it if necessary), to think of an interesting response, and to say it grammatically. Keep the pace moving by calling on a more advanced student after one who takes a lot of time to answer.

Exercise 5 is in the present, and Exercise 6 is in the past.

ANSWERS: [Depend on students' creativity.]

☐ **EXERCISE 7, p. 352.** *Cumulative review and practice of conditionals.*

Students should be able to respond orally. If that is too difficult, they could do the exercise as written seatwork, then read their answers aloud.

ANSWERS: [Clauses may appear in either order.] **2.** But I*'d buy* it if I *had* enough money. OR But if I *had* enough money, I*'d buy* it. **3.** But you *wouldn't have gotten* [British: *got*] into so much trouble if you*'d listened* to me. **4.** But she *would have died* if she *hadn't received* immediate medical attention. **5.** But if he *hadn't come*, I *would've been* disappointed. **6.** But she *would've been admitted* to the university if she*'d passed* the entrance examination. **7.** But if we*'d stopped* at the service station, we *wouldn't've run* out of gas. **8.** But there *wouldn't be* so many bugs in the room if there *were/was* a screen on the window.

EXPANSION ACTIVITY: Have Student A make a statement about his/her future activities. Have Student B say what s/he would do if s/he were Student A. Student B is using a conditional sentence to make a suggestion. Example:

STUDENT A: *I'm going to eat lunch after class.*
STUDENT B: *If I were you, I'd eat at Luigi's Italian Restaurant on 5th Street.*

◇ **WORKBOOK:** Practices 4, 5, 6, and 7.

CHART 10-5: USING PROGRESSIVE VERB FORMS

• If students are unclear about the function and meaning of progressive verb forms, you might conduct a review of the relevant parts of Chapter 1. A "progressive situation" is one in which an activity is (was/will be/would be) in progress during or at a particular time.

☐ **EXERCISE 8, p. 353.** *Using progressive verb forms in conditionals.*

ANSWERS: [Clauses may appear in reverse order.] **2.** But the child *wouldn't be crying* if his mother *were/was* here. **3.** But if *you'd been listening*, you *would've understood* the directions. **4.** But Joe *wouldn't've got(ten)* a ticket if he *hadn't been driving* too fast. **5.** But if I *hadn't been listening* to the radio, I *wouldn't've heard* the news bulletin. **6.** But Grandpa *would be wearing* his hearing aid if it *weren't/wasn't* broken. **7.** But if you *hadn't been sleeping*, I *would've told* you the news as soon as I heard it. **8.** But if I *weren't/wasn't enjoying* myself, *I would leave*.

CHART 10-6: USING "MIXED TIME" IN CONDITIONAL SENTENCES

• Most books don't point out this usage, but it is very common in both speech and writing. It is assumed the students have control of the basic conditional verb forms outlined in 10-1 and are ready to practice variations that are common in actual usage: progressive verb forms, mixed time, use of other modals, omission of *if*, implied conditions.

□ **EXERCISE 9, p. 354.** *Understanding "mixed time" in conditional sentences.*

> *ANSWERS:* [Clauses can occur in reverse order.] **2.** But if you *hadn't left* the door open, the room *wouldn't be* full of flies. **3.** But you *wouldn't be* tired . . . if you *had gone* to bed . . . . **4.** But if I *had finished* my . . . , I *could begin* a new . . . . [Point out that *could* is used in conditional sentences to express "ability."] **5.** But Helen *wouldn't be* sick if she *had followed* the . . . . **6.** But if I *were* [Note: *was* is almost never used in this particular expression, even in British English.] you, I *would've told* him the truth. **7.** But I *would've fixed* the leak . . . if I *knew* anything . . . . **8.** But if I *hadn't received* a good . . . , I *would* seriously *consider* taking . . . .

> EXPANSION ACTIVITY: Have Student A make a statement about his/her past activities. Have Student B say what s/he would have done if s/he were Student A. Example:
> > STUDENT A: *I ate dinner at the student cafeteria last night.*
> > STUDENT B: *If I were you, I would have eaten at Luigi's Italian Restaurant on 5th Street.*

◇ **WORKBOOK:** Practices 8 and 9.

CHART 10-7: USING *COULD, MIGHT,* AND *SHOULD*	

• In (a), compare *I could fly home* with *I would fly home. Could* expresses ability or possibility, but doesn't include desire or willingness. *Would* indicates that the speaker wants to do something.

• Review the meaning of *might* as necessary (see Charts 2-13 through 2-16).

• The use of *should* in conditional sentences is different from its other uses as presented in Chapter 2; in conditional sentences it indicates that a possibility exists but is unlikely to occur.

□ **EXERCISE 10, p. 354.** *Using modals in conditional sentences.*

> Ask the students to explain differences of meaning between *could* and *would*.

> *ANSWERS:* [Depend on students' ideas.]

◇ **WORKBOOK:** Practice 10.

CHART 10-8: OMITTING *IF*	

• Of the three examples in this chart, the one with *had* is the most commonly used in both conversation and writing.

• The example with *should* is somewhat formal usage.

• The example with *were* is less frequent than the others, especially in conversation. *Was* is not substituted for *were* in this pattern.

☐ **EXERCISE 11, p. 355.** *Understanding the omission of* if.

This is a simple transformation exercise designed to help students become familiar with the pattern. You or a student could read the item aloud, then another could change it to the new pattern. Or students could do this in pairs.

ANSWERS: [No contractions are used when *if* is omitted.] **2.** *Were I* you, I would look . . . . **3.** *Had you used* a computer, you could have finished . . . . **4.** *Should you need* to reach me, . . . **5.** *Had it gone* out of business, . . . **6.** . . . *had Thompson caught* the ball. [You might mention to the students that the use of *had* in this structure is especially common in sports broadcasting.] **7.** *Had Thompson not dropped* the ball, . . . **8.** *Had they not dared* to be different, . . . **9.** *Should there be* a global war, . . . **10.** *Had Tom told* the truth about his educational background, . . . **11.** However, *were you* to finish your education, . . . [Notice the pattern **were you to finish**/if you **were to finish.** Subjunctive *be* (i.e., *were*) + infinitive has a special meaning: "if this should happen." See Chart 2-10 for the usual meaning of *be* + infinitive (*be to/be supposed to*).] **12.** *Had I not been* there, . . .

◇ **WORKBOOK:** Practices 11 and 12.

CHART 10-9: IMPLIED CONDITIONS

• These examples show one of the most common uses of conditional verb forms. A "result clause" does not always come neatly attached to an "*if* clause" in actual usage. Many of the uses of *would* and *could* in daily conversation express results of implied conditions. In writing, one condition expressed near the beginning of a composition can affect verb forms throughout.

☐ **EXERCISE 12, p. 356.** *Understanding implied conditions.*

Like Exercise 11, this exercise asks students to substitute one expression for another with the same meaning. This expands their communicative repertoire.

ANSWERS: **3.** . . . if I had heard it ring. **4.** . . . if you hadn't helped me. **5.** . . . if I had had enough money. **6.** If I hadn't stepped on the brakes, I would've hit the child on the bicycle. **7.** If Cathy hadn't turned down the volume on the tape player, the neighbors . . . . **8.** . . . if he hadn't had to quit school and find a job . . . .

◇ **WORKBOOK:** Practice 13.

☐ **EXERCISE 13, p. 357.** *Cumulative review of verb forms in conditional sentences.*

ANSWERS: **1.** would spend OR could spend [discuss difference in meaning] **2.** would have sent **3.** is completed **4.** would you be . . . had been born **5.** weren't snowing **6.** would've gone (also possible: *could've gone*) **7.** would have . . . hadn't spent **8.** would've been hit . . . hadn't pulled **9.** would be **10.** were/was . . . would be **11.** hadn't been sleeping **12.** would forget . . . weren't/wasn't [humorous exaggeration] **13.** didn't outnumber . . . couldn't eat [Ask a student to explain in his/her own words the meaning of item 13.]

EXERCISE 14, p. 358. *Cumulative review of conditionals.*

The class should divide into pairs to practice dialogues. Then you can have some of them read their answers aloud expressively.

ANSWERS: **1.** weren't . . . I'd/I would be sleeping.   **2.** would've been   **3.** would've/could've taken   **4.** would think   **5.** were/was . . . wouldn't be ["Boy" is an informal American English interjection here. It is similar to *wow, gee, gosh.* Also, the inverted word order signifies an exclamation here, not a question.]   **6.** wouldn't be . . . had   **7.** would have graduated **8.** would've been   **9.** wouldn't ride   **10.** wouldn't have come had I known   **11.** would've done/could've done   **12.** wouldn't say . . . meant OR wouldn't have said . . . had meant **13.** I'll tell   **14.** had been driving . . . would have been

◇ **WORKBOOK:** Practices 14 and 15.

EXERCISE 15, p. 360. *Using conditional sentences.*

This could be written, then read aloud and discussed by the class. Alternative versions could be presented and evaluated.

ANSWERS: [Depend on students' creativity.]

EXPANSION ACTIVITY: Summarize an event from the front page of today's newspaper. Have students discuss their reactions to this event by using conditional sentences. Example:
> SUMMARY: *There was an election yesterday. The people of this city voted against an increase in taxes to improve the school system.*
> STUDENT REACTION: *I would have voted for the tax increase because quality education is very important to the children of this city.*

If all the students have copies of today's newspaper, each one can be asked to summarize an article (in one or two sentences). For each oral summary, other students can volunteer their reactions using conditional sentences.

EXERCISE 16, p. 360. *Using conditional sentences.*

The purpose of this exercise is to prompt spontaneous, interactive use of conditional sentences. Your task is to set up a situation for a student to respond to. It isn't necessary to use the exact words in the book, and you may wish to substitute other situations that are more familiar to your students. Use your students' names in place of "John" and "Mary." The responses should usually begin: "I would (have) . . . ."

You could ask for more than one response to an item. Sometimes people have quite different reactions to the same situation.

This exercise could be done in small groups, with only the leaders having open books.

ANSWERS: [Depend on students' ideas.]

◇ **WORKBOOK:** Practices 16 and 17.

EXERCISE 17, p. 361. *Using conditional sentences.*

When assigning this exercise, you may want to set some limits such as how many topics each student should write about, how long the writing should be, and how many conditional sentences should be included.

It's excellent practice for **you** also to write this assignment. If you do it before you assign it to the students, you can get some idea of how challenging it is for them. This helps you design reasonable limits for the length of their writing.

CHART 10-10: VERB FORMS FOLLOWING *WISH*

• Noun clause verbs following *wish* are in a past form. The past form signifies "contrary to fact"—just as it does in conditional sentences in "*if* clauses." Discuss verb relationships:

"true" situation	→	"wish" situation
simple present	→	simple past
present progressive	→	past progressive
simple past	→	past perfect
present perfect	→	past perfect
will	→	*would*
am/is/are going to	→	*was/were going to*
can	→	*could*
could + simple form	→	*could have* + past participle

• *Wish* can also be followed by an infinitive, e.g., *I wish to know the results of the test as soon as possible.* In this instance, *wish* is usually a more formal way of saying *want*, or a more direct (possibly impolite or imperious) way of saying *would like*.

• The subjunctive use of *were* instead of *was* with *I/he/she/it* is considered formal by some, standard by others.

• Some teachers like to compare *hope* and *wish*. See notes for Chart 10-11.

☐ EXERCISE 18, p. 362. *Understanding verb forms with* wish.

ANSWERS: **1.** had **2.** were/was shining **3.** had gone **4.** knew **5.** had told **6.** were/was wearing [also possible: *had worn*] **7.** had **8.** had gone **9.** could go **10.** would lend **11.** were/was coming [also possible: *would come, could come*] **12.** weren't/wasn't going to give [also possible: *weren't giving, wouldn't give*] **13.** could meet **14.** had come **15.** were/was lying

☐ EXERCISE 19, p. 363. *Using* wish.

Only an auxiliary (helping) verb is required in each item. British and American English differ somewhat in usage. For example:

3. *I can't sing well, but I wish* **could** [American] OR . . . *I wish I* **could do** [British].
4. *I didn't go, but I wish I* **had** [American] OR . . . *I wish I* **had done** [British].
5. *He won't . . . , but I wish he* **would** [American] OR . . . *I wish he* **would do** [British].
    The answers given here are American usage, also understandable in Britain.

ANSWERS: **6.** had **7.** could **8.** did **9.** had **10.** could **11.** would **12.** were/was **13.** had **14.** did **15.** were/was

CHART 10-11: USING *WOULD* TO MAKE WISHES ABOUT THE FUTURE

• When speakers want something to happen in the future and think it is possible, they use *hope* to introduce their idea: *I hope they will come.* When they want something to happen but think it is probably not possible, they use *wish*: *I wish they would come.*

• A common mistake is the use of *will* in the noun clause following *wish*: INCORRECT: *I wish they will come.*

☐ **EXERCISE 20, p. 364.** *Understanding wishes about the future.*

Would is used in every answer in order to illustrate its meaning.

ANSWERS: **1.** would change   **2.** would shave   **3.** would send   **4.** would end   **5.** would pick

◇ **WORKBOOK:** Practices 18, 19, and 20.

☐ **EXERCISE 21, p. 364.** *Expressing wishes.*

Give the class a few minutes to prepare their answers. Then you might have individuals answer the first four items, and have pairs read the dialogues.

ANSWERS: **1.** were/was . . . were/was   **2.** had come . . . had come . . . would have had   **3.** were/was not . . . weren't/wasn't . . . would go   **4.** had paid   **5.** did [Brit. *had*]   **6.** had [Brit. *had done*]   **7.** would turn   **8.** were/was lying . . . were/was   **9.** had told   **10.** would go   **11.** didn't have . . . were/was   **12.** had [Brit. *had done*]

☐ **EXERCISE 22, p. 365.** *Expressing wishes.*

You should set up the questions so that students are eager to share their wishes and dreams with the class. If some of the items are not appropriate to your students, you might substitute others. It isn't necessary to use the exact words in the book; just ask the question in an interesting way.

ANSWERS: [Depend on students' ideas.]

CHART 10-12: USING *AS IF/AS THOUGH*

• The word *like* is often difficult for learners because it has many functions and meanings. The notes in this chart are useful in pointing out two common uses of *like*.

☐ **EXERCISE 23, p. 367.** *Understanding* as if/as though.

Be sure that students understand what they are doing in this exercise. Even though they change a negative statement to a positive form, they do not change its meaning or "truth value." The example should make this clear, but you might want to be sure the students understand it correctly.

ANSWERS: [Ask responders to alternate between *as if* and *as though*, as in these answers.]   **2.** She speaks English as if it were her native tongue.   **3.** . . . as though they were people.   **4.** You look as if you'd/you had seen a ghost.   **5.** . . . as though he were a general in the army.   **6.** . . . as if I had climbed Mt. Everest . . . . [*winded* = out of breath; *Mt.* = Mount]   **7.** . . . as though he didn't have [Amer.]/he hadn't [Brit.] a brain in his head. [This sentence is intended as humorous exaggeration. In some cultures, this sentence might be interpreted as a terrible insult, but in English it is not when it is said with humor.]   **8.** . . . we felt as if we had known each other all of our lives.   **9.** After the tornado, the town looked as though a bulldozer had driven down Main Street. [*bulldozer* = a huge vehicle for pushing dirt and trees aside]   **10.** . . . I felt as if I had wings and could fly.   **11.** . . . he looked as though he would burst.   **12.** would [in every blank]

◇ **WORKBOOK:** Practices 21, 22, and 23. Practice Tests A & B.

☐ EXERCISES 24 → 26, pp. 368-374.   *General review of verb forms.*

At the end of the book, these three exercises give students an opportunity to evaluate their understanding and control of verb forms in English. The exercises cover verbs forms presented in Chapters 1 through 10. All three should be prepared before discussion, whether as seatwork or homework.

EX. 24 ANSWERS: [structure is identified in brackets]   **1.** had never spoken [past perfect] **2.** had not come [past conditional]   **3.** be [subjunctive] (Brit. *should be*)   **4.** would not have come [past conditional]   **5.** was stamped [past passive]   **6.** will probably continue [future] . . . lives [no future in a time clause]   **7.** will have been [future perfect]   **8.** going [reduced time clause]   **9.** Having heard [reduced from clause: *because I had heard*]   **10.** sitting [reduced adjective clause: *who is sitting*]   **11.** have been produced [present perfect passive]   **12.** would give/was going to give [reported speech, future] (also possible in immediate reporting: *will give/is going to give*)   **13.** have known [present perfect] . . . met [past] . . . was working [past progressive] (The use of the simple past for *know—I knew Beth for six years*—would indicate Beth is dead.)   **14.** had been . . . would have met [past conditional]   **15.** were/was made [present conditional, passive]   **16.** have been standing [present perfect progressive] . . . are **17.** would change . . . and decide [*wish* conditional, parallel]   **18.** had understood [past conditional] (also possible: *understood*)   **19.** Being [reduced clause] . . . is respected [present, passive] (also possible: *Being/Having been . . . was respected*—if Dr. Barnes is dead.) **20.** could/would not exist [implied conditional, present]

EX. 25 ANSWERS: **1.** coming [reduced from time clause: *since she came*] . . . has learned [present perfect]   **2.** had already given [past perfect]   **3.** apply [subjunctive] (also possible, principally British: *should apply*)   **4.** would have been [implied conditional, past]   **5.** would be/was going to be/could be [reported speech, future] (also possible, immediate reporting: *will be, is going to be, can be*)   **6.** Sitting . . . and watching [parallel reduced time clauses]   **7.** had been informed [past *wish* conditional, passive]   **8.** was completely destroyed [past, passive] . . . had gone [past perfect]   **9.** embarrassing [participial adjective]   **10.** were/was [present conditional] **11.** (who were/had been) invited [reduced adjective clause]   **12.** puzzled [participial adjective] . . . puzzling [participial adjective] . . . give [subjunctive] . . . figure [subjunctive]   **13.** has been [present perfect]   **14.** working [reduced adjective clause] . . . can/will be solved [future, passive]   **15.** call [time clause, no future]

EX. 26 ANSWERS: Next week, when I ***finish taking/have finished taking*** my final examinations, I ***will also finish*** (also possible: ***will also have finished***) one of the best experiences I ***have ever had*** in my lifetime. In the last four months, I ***have learned*** more about foreign cultures than I ***had anticipated*** (also possible: ***anticipated***) before ***coming*** to the United States. ***Living*** in a foreign country and ***going*** to school with people from various parts of the world ***have given*** [also possible: *has given*, considering the double subject as one unit] me the opportunity ***to encounter*** and ***interact*** with people from different cultures. I ***would like*** to share some of my experiences and thoughts with you.

When I first ***arrived***, I ***knew*** no one and I ***needed*** all of my fingers ***to communicate*** what I was trying to say in English. All of the international students were in the same situation. When we ***could not find*** the right word, we ***used/would use*** strange movements and gestures ***to communicate*** our meaning. ***Knowing*** some common phrases, such as ''How are you?'' ''Fine, thank you, and you?'' and ''What country are you from?'', ***was*** enough for us in the beginning ***to make*** friends with each other. The TV room in the dormitory ***became*** our meeting place every evening after dinner. ***Hoping to improve*** our English, many of us tried to watch television and ***understand*** what the people ***appearing*** on the screen ***were saying,*** but for the most part their words were just a strange mumble to us. After a while, ***bored*** and a little sad, we slowly began to disappear to our rooms. I ***think*** (also possible: *thought*) that all of us ***experienced/were experiencing*** some homesickness. However, despite my loneliness, I had a good feeling within myself because I ***was doing*** what I ***had wanted*** (also possible: ***had been wanting***) to do for many years: ***living*** and ***studying*** in a foreign country.

After a few days, classes **began** and we **had** another meeting place: the classroom. **Not knowing** quite what **to expect** the first day of class, I was a bit nervous, but also **excited.** After **finding** (also possible but not idiomatic: *having found*) the right building and the right room, I walked in and **chose** an empty seat. I **introduced** myself to the person **sitting** next to me, and we sat **talking** for a few minutes. Since we **were** from different countries, we **spoke** in English. At first, I was afraid that the other student **would not understand/did not understand/had not understood** what I **said/was saying,** but I **was pleasantly surprised** when she **responded** to my questions easily. Together we **took/had taken** the first steps toward **building** a friendship.

As the semester **progressed,** I **found** out more and more about my fellow students. Students from some countries were reticent and shy in class. They almost never **asked** questions and **spoke** very softly. Others of different nationalities **were** just the opposite: They spoke in booming voices and never **hesitated to ask** questions—and sometimes they **even interrupted** the teacher. I **had never been** in a classroom with such a mixture of cultures before. I learned **not to be surprised** by anything my classmates might say or do. The time we spent **sharing** our ideas with each other and **learning** about each other's customs and beliefs **was** valuable and fun. As we progressed in our English, we slowly learned about each other, too.

Now, several months after my arrival in the United States, I **am** able to understand not only some English but also something about different cultures. If I **had not come** here, I **would not have been able** to attain these insights into other cultures. I wish everyone in the world **could have** (also possible: *had*) the same experience. Perhaps if all the people in the world **knew** more about cultures different from their own and **had** the opportunity to make friends with people from different countries, peace **would** be secure.

☐ **EXERCISE 27, p. 374.** *Composition.*

You should set some limits on the length of this assignment. Specify the "audience" of readers as either fellow students or teachers and other educated adults. Encourage the writers to use dependent clauses and phrases, new vocabulary and idioms, and an appropriate level of formality for their audience. In marking their papers, try to make some encouraging comment on the interest, accuracy, or range of their information—that is, on the message. Then focus mainly on clause structures and verb forms. Other problem areas—articles, prepositions, and word choice—might be given a bit less attention.

EXPANSION ACTIVITIES: (1) Open the topics to class discussion. (2) Have the students interview each other to gather information for their compositions.

Appendix 1: SUPPLEMENTARY GRAMMAR UNITS

Unit A: Basic Grammar Terminology
Unit B: Questions
Unit C: Negatives
Unit D: Articles

General Notes on Appendix 1:

• PURPOSES: Teachers and students need a common vocabulary of grammar terms so that they can identify and discuss the patterns they are using in English. Also, every language learner needs to use a dictionary, and every dictionary uses grammar terms. Appendix 1 presents basic terms and patterns with some short exercises for clarification of chart information and a few longer ones for practice.

• USES: At the beginning of the English course, you could show your students the appendices and suggest how to use them. Also refer them to the Selfstudy Practices in the *Workbook*. The textbook assumes that your students are already familiar with basic grammar terminology, but often it is helpful for them to review these concepts, either on their own or at your direction. You may want to cover some of the Appendix 1 units in connection with related units in the chapter material.

Unit A: Basic Grammar Terminology

CHART A-1: SUBJECTS, VERBS, AND OBJECTS

• Write simple sentences on the board and have the students identify subjects, verbs, and objects until you're satisfied that this basic grammar is thoroughly understood by all.

• Some common verbs that are usually or always intransitive: *agree, appear, arrive, come, cost, cry, die, exist, fall, flow, go, happen, laugh, live, occur, rain, rise, seem, sit, sleep, sneeze, snow, stand, stay, talk, wait, walk.*

• Not all languages employ the same categories of grammar in the same ways. For example, the verb *enjoy* must always be transitive in English, but in some languages its equivalent is intransitive. (A good dictionary identifies each verb as transitive or intransitive.)

	S	V	O
TRANSITIVE:	*I enjoyed*	*the party*	*very much.*

	S	V	O
	I enjoyed	*myself*	*at the party.*

INTRANSITIVE: [*I enjoyed very much.* = ungrammatical English]

• Have the students look in their dictionaries to find the abbreviated labels **n, v, vi, vt, adj, adv, prep.** (Warn them that not all dictionaries use the same abbreviations.)

◇ **WORKBOOK:** Practices 1 and 2.

CHART A-2: PREPOSITIONS AND PREPOSITIONAL PHRASES

• A preposition is a kind of "cement" that connects a noun or pronoun to the other parts of an English sentence. Many languages have no prepositions, so these small English words can be very difficult to understand and explain. To get across the importance of these words, take a simple sentence such as "I walked _____ my father" and complete it with as many different prepositions as possible: *I walked with, toward, into, beside, behind, like, on (!), under (?), around (etc.) my father.*

• In (d) notice that a comma is customary before the subject of the sentence. This comma signals that an element has been moved to the front of the sentence, and the speaker's voice will rise a bit before the comma.

• A few prepositions consist of short phrases; for example:

because of	*in the middle of*	*out of*
instead of	*in (the) back of*	*according to*
in (the) front of	*ahead of*	*due to*

◇ WORKBOOK: Practices 3 and 4.

☐ EXERCISE 1, p. A2.   *Identifying subjects, verbs, objects, and prepositions.*

Most students should be able to identify each structure quickly. If not, perhaps they need to review a more basic English textbook. Only #6 is intended to be at all challenging.

ANSWERS:

        S   **V**   **PP**
2. The children   walked   to school.
      S   **V**   **O**
3. Beethoven   wrote   nine symphonies. [*Nine* is an adjective here.]
   S **V**   **O**   **PP**
4. Mary   did   her homework   at the library. [*Her* is a possessive adjective here (see p. A6).]
   S   **V**   **PP**
5. Bells   originated   in Asia.
         S   **V**   **O**   **PP**
6. Chinese printers   created   the first paper money   in the world.
   [*Chinese* = an adjective here.]
   [*the first* = an ordinal or counting expression.]
   [*paper* = a noun adjunct (a noun that modifies the next noun); see Chart 5-4 in Chapter 5.]

CHART A-3: ADJECTIVES and CHART A-4: ADVERBS

• Have the class call out words they think are adjectives and make sentences with these words.

• In general, adjectives are placed before nouns in English.

• Another common pattern places an adjective after the verb *be* or other linking verbs. (See Charts A-5 and A-6.)
   (a) *The student is intelligent.*
   (b) *The children were hungry.*

• Chart A-4 summarizes only the basic form and placement of adverbs. There are many other phenomena related to adverbs, but they are not included here.

◇ WORKBOOK: Practices 5, 6, 7.

□ EXERCISES 2 & 3, pp. A3–A4. *Adjectives and adverbs.*

> EX. 2 ANSWERS: **1.** careless...carelessly **2.** easy...easily **3.** softly...soft **4.** quietly **5.** well...good

> EX. 3 ANSWERS: **2.** Chinese [adj.]...beautiful [adj.] **3.** old [adj.]...wooden [adj.]...skillfully [adv.] **4.** busy [adj.]...usually [midsentence frequency adv.]...short [adj.] **5.** young [adj.]...very [adv.] good [adj.]...yesterday [adv.] [Note: Prepositional phrases *from jade* (item 2) and *on the telephone* (item 4) might also be called adverbial expressions.]

□ EXERCISE 4, p. A4. *Midsentence adverbs.*

Ask the students to use these adverbs in their usual positions. Point out that using them in other positions is possible and focuses attention on them; e.g., **Never has Erica seen snow.** (See Chart C-3.) **Often** *Ted studies at the library in the evening. Ann* **often** *is at the library in the evening, too. Fred has finished studying for tomorrow's test* **already.**

> ANSWERS: **2.** Ted often studies.... **3.** Ann is often at the library.... **4.** Fred has already finished.... **5.** Jack is seldom at home. **6.** Does he always stay here? **7.** He often goes...[*hang around* = enjoy idle time, leisure; *buddies* = close friends, pals, mates] **8.** You should always tell the truth.

CHART A-5: THE VERB *BE* and CHART A-6: LINKING VERBS

- Some grammar books call *be* a linking verb.

- It is important for learners to understand that *be* can function in two ways:
  —as the main verb in a sentence (a, b, c)
  —as the auxiliary element in a verb phrase (d, e, f)

□ EXERCISE 5, p. A5. *Adjectives and adverbs.*

> ANSWERS: **1.** easy...easily **2.** comfortable **3.** carefully **4.** sad **5.** cheerfully...cheerful **6.** carefully...good [*The soup tasted good* = it had a delicious flavor.] **7.** quiet [*got* = became]...quietly **8.** dark [*grew* = became]

◇ WORKBOOK: Practices 8, 9, 10.

CHART A-7: PERSONAL PRONOUNS

- The use of apostrophes can be a problem for second language learners as well as for native speakers of English. Call attention to the note below the chart.

- The "antecedent" may also be called the "referent."

- The term "possessive adjective" is useful to distinguish *my* from *mine*, but a "possessive adjective" is still a "pronoun." The terminology is awkward.

◇ WORKBOOK: Practices 11 and 12.

☐ **EXERCISE 6, p. A6.** *Pronouns and antecedents.*

> ANSWERS: **2.** *they* (pronoun): monkeys (antecedent)   **3.** *She*: teacher... *them*: papers
> **4.** *It*: cormorant... *it*: cormorant... *them*: fishermen [Note that the antecedent for *it* is not ''a
> diving bird''; *it* refers specifically to ''the cormorant,'' for it is not true that any diving bird is able
> to stay under water for a long time. And it is the cormorant, not ''a diving bird,'' that is used to
> catch fish for fishermen.] [Your students might be interested in how English has changed
> recently: *policeman* has become *police officer*, *fireman* has become *firefighter*, *mailman* has become
> *letter carrier*. *Fisherman* has not yet developed a widely accepted alternative expression, but some
> people use *fisherperson*.]   **5.** *him*: Tom... *He*: Tom... *it*: apple

☐ **EXERCISE 7, p. A6.** *Possessive pronouns and possessive adjectives.*

> ANSWERS: **1.** my....   **2.** mine...yours   **3.** their...hers   **4.** its   **5.** It's (It is)...
> its...its   **6.** Its...It's (It is)...It's (It has)

CHART A-8: CONTRACTIONS

• This chart is useful with Chapter 1: Verb Tenses.

• Make sure the students understand that the contractions in quotation marks are NOT written.

• Mention the possibility that learners may have difficulty with auxiliary verbs in their own speech and
writing because they don't always hear them in normal, rapid spoken English. Unstressed contracted
forms may be barely discernible to the inexperienced, unaware ear.

◇ **WORKBOOK:** Practice 13.

☐ **EXERCISE 8, p. A7.** *Contractions.*

> Have the students listen carefully to your oral production. Students enjoy trying to copy the
> teacher's model, but the emphasis should be on their <u>hearing</u> the contractions you say.
>
> ANSWERS: **1.** My *friend's* here.   **2.** My *friends're* here.   **3.** *Tom's* /tamz/ been   **4.** The
> *students've* /studəntsəv/   **5.** *Bob'd* /''Bob''-əd/   **6.** Bob'd   **7.** *Don'll*/''Don''-əl/   **8.** The
> *window's* /windouz/ open.   **9.** The *windows're* /windouzər/ open.   **10.** *Jane's* never....
> **11.** *boys've* /boizəv/   **12.** *Sally'd* /sælid/ forgotten   **13.** *Sally'd* forget   **14.** *Who's* /hu:z/ that
> woman?   **15.** *Who're* /huər/ those people?   **16.** *Who's* been taking   **17.** *What've* /hwətəv/
> you been doing   **18.** *What'd* /hwətəd/ you been doing   **19.** *What'd* you like....
> **20.** *What'd* you do....   **21.** *Why'd* /hwaid/ you stay   **22.** *When'll* /hwenəl/ I see you again?
> **23.** How *long'll* /lɔŋəl/ you   **24.** *Where'm* /hwerəm/ I   **25.** *Where'd* /hwerd/ you stay?

Unit B: Questions

Every chapter in the textbook requires students not only to understand but to produce question
forms. Students need to be able to ask and answer them grammatically. Even advanced students
can profit from review. Unit B can be a useful lesson with Chapter 1 (Verb Tenses) and/or Chapter
7 (Noun Clauses). It can also be allotted its own slot in a syllabus.

CHART B-1: FORMS OF YES/NO AND INFORMATION QUESTIONS

• The chart gives a statement of fact—(a) to (k)—on the left. In the center are two forms of questions about that given fact. On the right are notes about word forms and order, the main points of difficulty for learners of English.

• To reinforce the word order, you might copy the center of the chart on the chalkboard. Students can look there instead of in their books as they do the exercises, and you can point to the correct position for each word.

• Note the special form of questions with *who* as subject.

◇ **WORKBOOK:** Practice 14.

☐ **EXERCISE 9, p. A9.** *Forming questions.*

The purpose of this mechanical exercise is for students to review the word order of questions using a variety of verb forms.

SUGGESTION: Draw a chart on the chalkboard with the following headings:

Q Word + Auxiliary + Subject + Main Verb + Rest of the Sentence

Then ask students to fit each element of a question sentence into the chart. This makes clear the position of each element in a question. For example:

Q Word +	Auxiliary +	Subject +	Main Verb +	Rest of the Sentence
	Does	she	stay	there?
Where	does	she	stay?	

As a variation, you could divide the class into thirds. Group 1 reads the cue, Group 2 asks the yes/no question, then Group 3 asks the information question. You could have four groups, with Group 4 asking the question with *who*. Rotate the groups occasionally so that everyone has a chance to use each question type. The exercise is mechanical, but it can be turned into a game.

ANSWERS: [all three types]
1. Does she stay there? Where does she stay? Who stays there?
2. Is she staying there? Where is she staying? Who is staying there?
3. Will she stay there? Where will she stay? Who will stay there?
4. Is she going to stay there? Where is she going to stay? Who is going to stay there?
5. Did they stay there? Where did they stay? Who stayed there?
6. Will they be staying there? Where will they be staying? Who will be staying there?
7. Should they stay there? Where should they stay? Who should stay there?
8. Has he stayed there? Where has he stayed? Who has stayed there?
9. Has he been staying there? Where has he been staying? Who has been staying there?
10. Is John there? Where is John? Who is there?
11. Will John be there? Where will John be? Who will be there?
12. Has John been there? Where has John been? Who has been there?
13. Will Judy have been there? Where will Judy have been? Who will have been there?
14. Were Ann and Tom married there? Where were . . . ? Who was married there?
15. Should this package have been taken there? Where should this . . . ? What should have . . . ?

• This chart is for consolidation and review. It is intended for reference, not memorization. In order to acquaint the students with its contents, spend a little time discussing it in class, including modeling spoken contractions (e.g., *When'd they arrive?*). After you discuss it, have the students close their books. Give answers from the ANSWER column (adapting them to your class), and have the students supply possible questions. Examples:

TEACHER: David's. [OR Yoko's, Olga's, Ali's, Roberto's, etc.]
STUDENT: Whose...?
TEACHER: Yesterday.
STUDENT: When...?
TEACHER: Dark brown.
STUDENT: What color...?

◇ **WORKBOOK:** Practices 15, 16, 17, 18, 19, 20, 21.

☐ **EXERCISES 10 → 12, pp. A12–A13.** *Forming information questions.*

Of course, changing a statement into a question is not part of normal communication. Nevertheless, learners need to understand the grammatical relationships between statements and questions. These exercises practice those relationships.

To make the exercise more like a dialogue, you could follow this pattern:

1. TEACHER (to STUDENT B): You need five dollars.
   STUDENT A to B: How much money do you need?
   STUDENT B to A: I need five dollars.

2. TEACHER (to STUDENT D): (...) was born in (...). [Use real information.]
   STUDENT C to D: Where was (...) born?
   STUDENT D to C: S/He was born in (...).

EX. 10 ANSWERS: **2.** Where was Roberto born? / In what country/city was...? / What country/city was Roberto born in? **3.** How often do you go out to eat? **4.** Who(m) are you waiting for? [*For whom are you waiting?* is very formal and seldom used.] **5.** Who answered the phone? **6.** Who(m) did you call? **7.** Who called? **8.** What does the boy have in his pocket? [British: *What has the boy (got) in his pocket?*] **9.** What does "deceitful" mean? **10.** What is an abyss? **11.** Which way did he go? **12.** Whose books and papers are these? **13.** How many children do they have? [British or regional American: *How many children have they?*] **14.** How long has he been here? **15.** How far is it/How many miles is it to New Orleans? ["New Orleans" has at least two commonly used pronunciations. Whatever pronunciation your students are familiar with is correct.]

EX. 11 ANSWERS: **1.** How much gas/How many gallons of gas/What did she buy? [In British English, gas = *petrol*.] **2.** When/At what time can the doctor see me? **3.** Who **is** her roommate? **4.** Who **are** her roommates? **5.** How long/How many years have your parents been living there? **6.** Whose book is this? **7.** What made her sneeze? **8.** Who's coming over for dinner? **9.** What color **is** Ann's dress? **10.** What color **are** Ann's eyes? **11.** Why **were you** late? / How come **you were** late? **12.** Who can't go...? **13.** Why **can't Bob** go? / How come **Bob can't** go? **14.** Why **didn't you**/ How come **you didn't** answer...? [formal and rare: *Why **did you not** answer the phone?*] **15.** What kind of music do you like? **16.** What don't you understand? **17.** What **is** Janet **doing** right now? **18.** How do you spell "sitting"? [*you* = impersonal pronoun] **19.** What **does** Tom **look like**? **20.** What **is** Tom **like**? **21.** What does Ron do (for a living)? **22.** How far/How many miles is Mexico from here?   **23.** How do you take/like your coffee?   **24.** Which (city) is farther north, Stockholm or Moscow? / Of Stockholm and Moscow, which (city/one) is farther north?   **25.** How are you getting along?

EX. 12 ANSWERS: [There is more than one possible response to most items.]
1. How far/How many miles is it to (...)? [Use a familiar place name.]
2. When does fall semester begin? / What begins on...?
3. Which pen did...?
4. Who typed...? / What did the secretary type?
5. How many courses did...?
6. What does "rapid" mean?
7. Who went...? / Where did (...) go?
8. Who telephoned you?
9. Where is the post office?
10. How far is it to...?
11. How long did you...? / How many hours did you...?
12. Who gave a speech? / What did (...) do?
13. & 14. Who talked about...? / What did (...) talk about? / About what did (...) talk?
15. How much money / What do you need?
16. Which floor does (...) live on? / On which floor does (...) live?
17. Where will you be...?
18. Whose pen is this?
19. How often do you go to the library? / Where do you go every day?
20. When / On what day is...?
21. How long have you been...?
22. Why did you laugh?
23. Who dropped...?
24. Who(m) should I give this book to? / To whom should I...?
25. Why didn't you come... / How come you didn't come...?

☐ **EXERCISE 13, p. A13.**   *Forming questions.*

Many items in this exercise could become a dialogue in the following way:

> TEACHER to STUDENT A: "I had a sandwich for lunch."
> STUDENT A to STUDENT B: "The teacher had a sandwich for lunch. What did *you* have?"
> STUDENT B to STUDENT A: "I had (...)."

> TEACHER to STUDENT A: "These are my books."
> STUDENT A to STUDENT B: "These are the teacher's books. Whose are *those*?" (pointing)
> STUDENT B to STUDENT A: "These are mine/my books/(...'s)."

ANSWERS: **1.** What did you have for lunch?   **2.** Whose books are those?   **3.** Which chapter are we supposed...?   **4.** Who(m) did you talk to?/To whom did you talk?   **5.** What did you talk to (...) about?   **6.** Why did you fall asleep...?   **7.** Who(m) does that book belong to?/To whom does that book belong?   **8.** What does "request" mean?   **9.** How far is it to (...)?   **10.** How many languages can you speak?   **11.** Who opened...?   **12.** Why didn't you go...?   **13.** Which house do you live in?   **14.** Where did you hang...?   **15.** Who(m) is the letter addressed to? / To whom is...?   **16.** How long did it take (you) to finish your assignments?   **17.** Where did Mr. Smith teach English? / What did...teach in Japan? / Who taught English in Japan?   **18.** When/What time should I be here? [*be here* = arrive for an appointment.]   **19.** Whose keys did you find? / What did you find?   **20.** How often/How many times a year do you visit your aunt and uncle?

CHART B-3: NEGATIVE QUESTIONS

• Negative questions are seldom found in nonfiction writing (other than as rhetorical questions). They are principally conversational, expressing emotions and opinions.

• The speaker of a negative question has an opinion about a situation. Asking the negative question is a signal to the listener. The speaker expects a certain answer, but the listener has to answer truthfully. Sometimes, therefore, the answer is unexpected. Even with native speakers, this can cause confusion, so the questioner may have to ask another question for clarification. For example:
   (e) A: "What happened? Didn't you study?"
       B: "Yes." [Meaning: "That is what happened." Speaker A had expected a "no" answer.]
       A: "I'm confused. Did you study or didn't you?"
       B: "No, I didn't."

◇ **WORKBOOK:** Practice 22.

☐ **EXERCISE 14, p. A15.** *Using negative questions.*

Because negative questions are quite confusing, you should probably lead the students through this exercise. Help them understand the situation and expectation in each item.

ANSWERS:

2. A. Wasn't she in class?
   B. No. [= No, she was not in class.]

3. A: Isn't that Mrs. Robbins?
   B: Yes (, it is).

4. A: Aren't you hungry?
   B. Yes (, I am).

5. A: Didn't you sleep well last night?
   B: No (, I didn't).

6. A: Don't you feel well?
   B: No (, I don't). /
      Yes (, that's the problem).

7. A: Doesn't the sun/it rise in the east?
   B: Yes . . . .

8. A: Don't you recognize him?
   B: No (, I don't).

CHART B-4: TAG QUESTIONS

• Tag questions are an important element in English language conversation. They help establish communication because they invite a response from another person. Using the questions incorrectly can, therefore, cause confusion and disrupt communication. Students should be aware of the importance of using tag questions correctly.

• Ask the students to make sentences beginning with "I'm not sure, but I think . . . ." Have them turn each statement of opinion into an inquiry with a tag question that indicates their belief. For example: *I'm not sure, but I think we're going to have a test on question forms tomorrow.* → *We're going to have a test on question forms tomorrow, aren't we?* Another example: *I'm not sure, but I think Venus is the second closest planet to the sun.* → *Venus is the second closest planet to the sun, isn't it?*
   To elicit negatives in the main rather than tag verb, have the students begin a sentence with "It is my understanding that . . . not . . . ." For example: *It is my understanding that we're not going to have a test tomorrow.* → *We're not going to have a test tomorrow, are we?*

• Asking questions without using question word order or tags is common in everyday speech: the speaker simply uses interrogative intonation (voice rising at end). Demonstrate for the students: *Mary isn't here? She'll be here at ten? They won't be here? You can't come? You've never been to Paris? You live with your parents?* etc.

◇ **WORKBOOK:** Practice 23.

☐ **EXERCISE 15, p. A16.** *Tag questions.*

Most of the items here would typically have a rising intonation. Of course, some could be said with a falling intonation.

ANSWERS: **2.** isn't she   **3.** will they   **4.** are there   **5.** isn't it   **6.** isn't he   **7.** hasn't he [*He's learned* = "he has learned"]   **8.** doesn't/hasn't he   **9.** can she   **10.** won't she **11.** wouldn't she   **12.** are they   **13.** have you   **14.** isn't it   **15.** can't they   **16.** did they **17.** did it   **18.** aren't I/am I not

☐ **EXERCISE 16, p. A17.** *Tag questions.*

Perhaps you could tell the students which intonation to use for certain items. Or you could allow them to choose rising or falling intonation and then explain their choices. Or you could simply concentrate on the grammar and pay scant attention to intonation.

ANSWERS: **1.** isn't it?   **2.** isn't he/she?   **3.** doesn't he/she?   **4.** is there?   **5.** doesn't he/she?   **6.** didn't you?   **7.** hasn't he/she?   **8.** did you?   **9.** have they?   **10.** don't they?   **11.** can he/she/they?   **12.** is he/she?   **13.** won't it?   **14.** do they?   **15.** didn't you?   **16.** isn't there?   **17.** isn't he/she?   **18.** shouldn't you?   **19.** does he/she? **20.** didn't he/she?   **21.** don't we?   **22.** haven't you?   **23.** won't he/she?   **24.** have they? [Traditionally, the pronoun *nobody* is singular. Some grammar books, therefore, insist on the traditional tag *has he*. Usage is changing toward a preference for the plural form, however.] **25.** aren't I?/am I not?   **26.** doesn't it?

Unit C: Negatives

CHART C-1: USING *NOT* AND OTHER NEGATIVE WORDS

- A note on pronunciation of some contractions:
  1. Do not pronounce the letter "l" in *could(n't)*, *should(n't)*, *would(n't)*. They should sound like "good."
  2. Do not pronounce the first "t" in *mustn't*.
  3. Pronounce the letter "s" in *hasn't*, *isn't*, and *doesn't* like the letter "z."

◇ **WORKBOOK:** Practice 24.

☐ **EXERCISE 17, p. A18.** *Using negative words.*

The purpose of this exercise is to show students two equally correct ways to make a negative statement. The form with *no* is generally more formal. Caution students against double negatives.

ANSWERS: **2.** There wasn't any food. / There was no food.   **3.** I didn't receive any... / I received no....   **4.** I don't need any help. / I need no help.   **5.** We don't have any... / We have no....   **6.** You shouldn't have given the beggar any money. [The other alternative is less likely: *You should have given the beggar no money.*]   **7.** I don't trust anyone. / I trust no one. **8.** I didn't see anyone. / I saw no one.   **9.** There wasn't anyone... / There was no one.... **10.** She can't find anybody... / She can find no one....

CHART C-2: AVOIDING "DOUBLE NEGATIVES"

• Some native speakers of English use double negatives regularly in their speech, so students might hear double negatives and wonder if they are grammatical. Double negatives are considered to be nonstandard usage and may reflect disadvantageously on one's educational background. However, they are sometimes used for a humorous or theatrical effect.

◇ **WORKBOOK:** Practice 25.

☐ **EXERCISE 18, p. A19.** *Avoiding double negatives.*

ANSWERS:
1. I *don't* need *any* help. / I *need no* help.
2. I *didn't* see *anybody.* / I *saw nobody.*
3. I *can never . . .* / I *can't ever* understand him.
4. He *doesn't* like *either* coffee *or* tea. / He *likes neither* coffee *nor* tea.
5. I *didn't* do *anything.* / I *did nothing.*
6. I *can hardly* hear . . . [*hardly* is a negative word]
7. We *couldn't* see *anything . . .* / We *could see nothing* but sand.
8. *. . . have barely* changed (at all) . . . / *. . . haven't changed* at all . . .

CHART C-3: BEGINNING A SENTENCE WITH A NEGATIVE WORD

• This inversion is principally a literary device. Advanced students may find it interesting. Intermediate students may well ignore it.

◇ **WORKBOOK:** Practice 26.

☐ **EXERCISE 19, p. A19.** *Word order with negative words.*

ANSWERS: **2.** Seldom do I sleep . . . . **3.** Hardly ever do I agree with her. **4.** Never will I forget . . . . **5.** Never have I known Pat . . . . **6.** Scarcely ever does the mail arrive . . . . [no "s" with *arrive* because the "s" is with *does*]

Unit D: Articles

CHARTS D-1 and D-2: BASIC ARTICLE USAGE

• Articles are very difficult for students to understand and use correctly. Many languages do not have articles. Languages that do have articles use them differently from English. Articles are, in many teachers' experiences, difficult to teach. There are many nuances, complex patterns of use, and idiomatic variations. Students who are frustrated trying to understand and use articles should be reminded that articles are just a small component of English. Proficiency in using articles improves with experience; it cannot be assured overnight by learning "rules."

- The exercises point out some contrasts in usage that should help the students understand the differences among *a/an*, *the*, and the absence of any article (symbolized by Ø).

- Note the reference to Chart 5-8 in section II of Chart D-1. Chapter 5 (in Volume B) is a good place to use this unit to cover the basic uses of articles. If you are using only Book A, you might use this unit on articles at any time, and then periodically discuss the usage of articles in exercises and in the students' oral/written reponses.

- Some students may need a reminder about using *an* instead of *a*. English speakers prefer not to pronounce a vowel sound after the article *a*. Therefore, they put *n* between the two vowel sounds. For example:

    a + apple → an apple; a + old man → an old man; a + umbrella → an umbrella

    [But note that *a university* has no *n* because the *u* begins with a sort of *y* or consonant sound.]

    Also:

    a + other → another [Tradition causes this to be written as one word.]

◇ **WORKBOOK:** Practices 27 and 28.

☐ **EXERCISES 20 & 21, pp. A21—A23.** *Using articles.*

Exercise 20 is a series of dialogues. Students can work in pairs or two students can read one dialogue to the whole class.

EX. 20 ANSWERS: **3.** *a* good reason **4.** *the* reason [Both people know Jack's specific reason. Now they are deciding whether to believe it or not.] **5.** *the* washing machine [Both people know the same machine.]...*a* different shirt [no specific shirt] **6.** *a* washing machine **7.** *The* front wheel...*a* parked car...*a* big pothole...*the* car [Now both people know about the same specific car.]...*a* note...*the* owner [Each car usually has only one owner.]...*the* car...*the* note [Now both people know about this note.]...*an* apology **8.** *The* radiator [Each car has only one radiator.]...*a* leak...*the* windshield wipers...*the* leak **9.** *the* closet...*the* front hallway [specific locations that both people are familiar with]

EX. 21 ANSWERS: **4.** Ø hats [no article] **5.** *A* hat....*an* article **6.** Ø Hats...Ø articles **7.** *The* brown hat **8.** Ø problems...Ø life **9.** *a* long life **10.** *the* life [Note the difference between item 9 and item 10.] **11.** *an* engineer **12.** *an* engineer **13.** *the* name...*the* engineer...*an* infection...*the* bridge **14.** Ø people...Ø jewelry **15.** *The* jewelry **16.** *a* beautiful ring...Ø gold...Ø rubies.. *The* gold [Now it's familiar, specific.]... *The* rubies... **17.** *a* new city...*a* place...Ø newspapers...Ø advertisements...Ø apartments...*an* ad... *a* furnished apartment, *the* apartment...*a* stove...*a* refrigerator...Ø furniture...Ø beds... Ø tables...Ø chairs...*a* sofa. **18.** *a* short time...*a* furnished apartment...*The* apartment ...*a* good location...*the* stove... *The* refrigerator...*the* refrigerator door... *The* bed...*the* furniture...Ø another apartment [*another* = *an* + *other*]

Notes and Answers: Workbook

This *Guide* includes the answers only to the Guided Study Practices in the *Workbook*. (The answers to the Selfstudy Practices are in the back of the student's workbook.) In many of the Guided Study Practices, the answers depend upon the students' creativity, so no answers can be supplied here.

Chapter 1: VERB TENSES

◇ **PRACTICE 7, p. 8:** *The simple present and the present progressive.*

1. usually drinks...is drinking   **2.** takes...usually waits   **3.** is raining...is standing...is holding...is waiting   **4.** is taking...studies...has...is also taking...likes...has   **5.** are you doing...am tasting...tastes   **6.** are you writing...am making...Do you always prepare...always try   **7.** is always interrupting/always interrupts...is always asking/always asks   **8.** am preparing...don't need

◇ **PRACTICE 8, p. 10:** *Irregular verbs.*

In this exercise, the irregular verbs are grouped according to similarity of form. It is assumed that the students already know most of these irregular verbs. They can infer the forms of verbs new to their vocabulary by associating them with ones they already know.

The students can use this exercise as a worksheet, possibly in preparation for a quiz. They can check their own or each other's answers by referring to Chart 1-11 in the main text, or they can ask you to quickly check over their answers. Tell them to pay careful attention to spelling.

◇ **PRACTICE 13, p. 15:** *Simple past of irregular verbs.*

[Answers depend upon students' creativity.] Verb forms:
1. wept   **2.** spun   **3.** sought   **4.** shed   **5.** shook   **6.** spread   **7.** fled   **8.** split   **9.** crept   **10.** clung   **11.** chose   **12.** sank

◇ **PRACTICE 16, p. 17:** *The simple past and the past progressive.*

2. was...was humming   **3.** were in our living room watching...went...went...got... turned...listened...was   **4.** outwitted [= outsmarted, were more clever]... surrounded...was still inside stuffing   **5.** rang...came...were still playing...was pulling... ran...told   **6.** was looking...Did you find...took

◇ **PRACTICE 17, p. 18:** *The simple past and the past progressive.*

Expected answers:
2. took/withdrew . . . bought/purchased . . . was driving . . . collided with/hit . . . demolished/destroyed/wrecked **3.** woke/got . . . heard . . . was walking/running/crawling **4.** visited/called on . . . were doing/were washing . . . came/knocked/arrived . . . finished . . . sat . . . talked/chatted/reminisced **5.** got to/arrived at . . . was waiting/was watching . . . saw . . . waved/raised . . . said/shouted . . . were making **6.** was . . . watering/sprinkling/tending . . . began/started . . . shut/turned

◇ **PRACTICE 21, p. 21:** *The present perfect.*

You might want to give students some limit on the length of—or amount of detail in—their written answers. A lengthy or detailed answer will require use of the simple past as well as the present perfect and could serve as practice in using both tenses. In evaluating the answers, reward each correct use of the present perfect. You might choose simply to note misspellings and other errors without focusing on them.

In preparation for (or possibly instead of) writing their answers, students could discuss them in small groups. Each member of the group could give an answer as the rest of the group listens for the use of the present perfect. At the end of the speaker's answer, the others could identify (orally or in writing) the present perfect verbs s/he used. As an alternative, the group could paraphrase (orally or in writing) what the speaker said, copying or correcting the speaker's use of tenses.

Another alternative is to divide the class into five groups. Each group discusses one item. Each student writes a summary of everything that was said in his/her group or the leader of each group presents an oral summary to the rest of the class. (You might want to expand the scope of #3 to include "Why?," "Do you ever expect to do these things?," and "What are some interesting and unusual things that you have done and want to do again?")

◇ **PRACTICE 23, p. 22:** *The present perfect and the present perfect progressive.*

2. have met **3.** has been standing **4.** I have always wanted **5.** has been painting **6.** have been travel(l)ing **7.** has grown **8.** have already spent **9.** has been cooking **10.** have never heard **11.** have been waiting **12.** has been digging

◇ **PRACTICE 24, p. 23:** *Writing.*

You might want to set some limit on the length of the students' answers, which could vary from a six-sentence paragraph to a 500-word narrative.

◇ **PRACTICE 27, p. 26:** *The past perfect.*

In these sentences, point out that the earlier or first action is in the past perfect and the later or second action is in the simple past.
[Answers depend on students' creativity.] Suggestions:
1. I had never [past participle] . . . before I [simple past tense verb] . . . .
2. By the time [subject + simple past] . . . , he had already [past participle] . . . .
3. In 1987, I [simple/progressive past] . . . . Prior to that time, I had [*been* + present participle] . . . .
4. When I [simple past] . . . , someone else had already [past participle] . . . .
5. Last January, I [simple past] . . . . Before that, I had never [past participle] . . . .
6. I had never [past participle] . . . until I [simple past] . . . .
7. The movie had [past participle] . . . by the time we [simple past] . . . .
8. My [subject + simple past verb] . . . after I had already [past participle] . . . .

◇ **PRACTICE 29, p. 27:** *Writing.*

You might want to set a limit on the length of the students' answers. When you evaluate their work, reward each correct use of verb tenses. You may choose not to pay much attention to mistakes in other areas, such as spelling and word choice, in order to keep the focus on verb tenses.

◇ **PRACTICE 31, p. 28:** Will *vs.* be going to.

1. I'll ["VCR" = video cassette recorder] **2.** I'm going to **3.** is going to . . . is he going to/will he **4.** I'll **5.** I'm going to . . . I'll **6.** I'm going to **7.** I'll [*c'mon* = "come on" = Be serious/realistic!] **8.** I'll

◇ **PRACTICE 34, p. 30:** *Expressing the future in time clauses.*

The main point to remember is that a time clause (an adverb clause that begins with a time word like *after*, *until*, and *as soon as*) cannot contain a future verb form. If the students write out the sentences, have them underline the verbs.

◇ **PRACTICE 36, p. 31:** *Using the present progressive to express future time.*

Discuss situations in which the present progressive can be used to indicate future time.
3. I'm having **4.** are you doing . . . I'm studying **5.** [No change: *I'm getting it* would have a present, not future, meaning.] **6.** are they getting **7.** [No change: *You're laughing* is not a "planned event."] **8.** we're moving **9.** Is he teaching **10.** I'm not sending . . . are coming

◇ **PRACTICE 39, p. 33:** *Past and future.*

Suggest that the students use *will*; forms of *be going to* are also possible.
2. He'll shave and shower and then make
3. After he eats . . . , he'll get
4. By the time he gets . . . , he'll have drunk
5. . . . he'll dictate . . . and plan
6. . . . he'll have finished
7. . . . he'll be attending
8. He'll go . . . and have
9. After he finishes . . . , he'll take . . . before he returns
10. He'll work . . . until he goes
11. . . . he leaves . . . , he will have attended
12. . . . gets . . . will be playing
13. . . . will have been playing
14. finishes . . . , he'll take
15. will sit . . . and discuss
16. They'll watch . . . will put
17. he goes . . . Dick will have had . . . will be ready

◇ **PRACTICE 42, p. 35:** *Review of tenses.*

I. 2. I've been looking **3.** is seeing [= is meeting with] **4.** received **5.** sounds **6.** has **7.** I'll be working/I'm going to be working
II. 1. seems **2.** sent **3.** haven't received **4.** is not functioning **5.** are working **6.** will start
III. 1. haven't seen **2.** is at home recuperating **3.** hurt **4.** was playing **5.** did she hurt **6.** was trying **7.** collided **8.** fell **9.** landed **10.** twisted **11.** has been wearing **12.** hasn't been able **13.** will not/won't be **14.** Will her doctor allow/Is her doctor going to allow **15.** will have had
IV. 1. Did you enjoy **2.** I've never gone **3.** had never gone **4.** didn't know **5.** were still trying **6.** appeared **7.** started **8.** was singing **9.** was
V. 1. grew up **2.** greatly admired (possible: *had greatly admired*) **3.** had become **4.** became **5.** contained **6.** died **7.** had been working **8.** never finished **9.** has become

◇ **PRACTICE 43, p. 37:** *Review of tenses.*

1. has experienced	9. moves	17. sent
2. will experience	10. know	18. will . . . occur/is . . . going to occur
3. began	11. happened	19. have often helped
4. have occurred	12. struck	20. are studying
5. causes	13. were sitting	21. also appear
6. have developed	14. suddenly found	22. have developed
7. waves	15. died	23. will give
8. hold/are holding	16. collapsed	24. strikes

◇ **PRACTICE TEST B, p. 41:** *Verb tenses.*

1. A	6. A	11. D	16. D
2. A	7. B	12. A	17. C
3. B	8. B	13. A	18. B
4. C	9. C	14. A	19. A
5. C	10. B	15. D	20. D

Chapter 2: MODAL AUXILIARIES AND SIMILAR EXPRESSIONS

◇ **PRACTICE 4, p. 45:** *Imperatives.*

4. (Please) pass 5. Wake 6. Don't touch 7. Get 8. (Please) listen 9. (Please) read/study 10. Take 11. (Please) close/open 12. (Please) don't shout 13. Taste/Try 14. Meet 15. Help 16. (Please) turn/put 17. (Please) buy 18. Think 19. (Please) remember 20. (Please) be

◇ **PRACTICE 5, p. 45:** *Making polite requests.*

2. I see your (driver's) license 3. you give me a lift/ride 4. you check them/(take a) look at them 5. . . . changing/if we changed our appointment 6. you give me directions/draw a map for me 7. I help you . . . you show me some slacks/I see some slacks 8. if we moved/ moving to different 9. I call you 10. you please turn off the TV . . . you turn it down/lower the volume

◇ **PRACTICE 6, p. 46:** *Making polite requests.*

Assign pair work. You may not want every pair of students to work on every item. Give each pair one or two items to prepare in a time limit of 5-8 minutes. Allow each group to "perform" its best dialogue for the other students. Then everyone can discuss reasons why some dialogues were more effective than others.

This exercise could also be assigned as written homework.

◇ **PRACTICES 9 & 10, pp. 49–50.** Should, ought to, had better.

Practice 9 could be used for small-group discussion. Practice 10 could be used for pair-work writing. [Answers depend on students' ideas.]

◇ **PRACTICE 11, p. 50:** *The past form of* should.

In pairs or small groups, students can discuss their opinions about each situation. One person in each group can record their answers. Then another person can read the answers to the whole class. You should probably set a time limit for the group work (about 3–5 minutes per item) and another for each person's report (one minute).

To save time, you may want to assign only one or two items to each small group. When they report their answers, students from other groups can discuss them and add their own ideas. You should probably set a time limit for the group work and discussions.

At the end of the exercise, the class can vote to choose the best answer or the most thoughtful group.

◇ PRACTICE 12, p. 51: Be to.

You might make this a creative project. Students could produce a colorful poster for the school or classroom bulletin board, printing their list of rules on it carefully and clearly. Perhaps you could give them a different topic for their rules, such as use of the library, preparation of written homework, or care of equipment.

◇ PRACTICE 13, p. 52: *Necessity, advisability, and expectations.*

The students need to use their imaginations in this exercise; most of them probably haven't had any experience in the roles described in the given situations. You could suggest other, more familiar roles of authority (e.g., the teacher of this class), or the students could invent their own authority roles. Perhaps they could write the answers for one of the given situations and also write answers for a situation of their own devising.

Take a few minutes to discuss item #1 with the whole class. Have them add other answers, using all the rest of the modals and similar expressions in the list.

This exercise is intended as written homework but can be used for group discussion or pair work.

◇ PRACTICE 14, p. 52: Let's, why don't, shall I/we.

Item notes and possible completions:
1. ["sushi" = Japanese appetizers, small snacks]
2. we go down to the coffee house/we go to a movie ... shall we go/leave
3. we look in the suburbs ... Let's start with the North Side ... we get a newspaper?
4. [Depend on students' ideas.]
5. get out of town ... we go camping? ... stay in a motel/an inn
6. [Depend on students' ideas.]
7. [Depend on students' ideas.]
8. panic/leap to conclusions/get upset over nothing/make a mountain out of a molehill ... you call/phone her house/apartment/room? ... you just relax/take it easy?
9. you try/have some? ... go ... I call/signal/get the waiter?

◇ PRACTICE 15, p. 54: *Using* could *and* should *to make suggestions.*

[Depend on students' ideas.]

◇ PRACTICE 17, p. 55: *Degrees of certainty:* must *and* may/might/could.

Students should discuss their choices and their reasoning process.
1. A [fairly certain; logical conclusion]
2. B [uncertain]
3. C [definite]
4. B [uncertain]
5. A [fairly certain; logical conclusion]
6. C [definite]
7. B [uncertain]
8. B [uncertain]
9. C [definite]
10. C [definite]

◇ **PRACTICE 18, p. 56:** *Making conclusions:* must *and* must not.

> Students should discuss their reasons for their "best guesses."
Possible responses:
>   **3.** He must have seen this movie already.
>   **4.** She must have been tired. / She must be asleep.
>   **5.** She must not have heard them.
>   **6.** The fish must have been spoiled/bad/must not have been fresh.
>   **7.** Jeremy must like classical music.
>   **8.** Jeremy's wife must not like classical music/must like a different kind of music.
>   **9.** She must not have paid her telephone bill.
>   **10.** There must be a fire nearby.
>   **11.** She must have been to Paris.
>   **12.** The mushrooms must have been poisonous.

◇ **PRACTICE 19, p. 57:** *Degrees of certainty:* must.

> Encourage the students to make between five and ten observations and "best guesses" about their immediate environment (i.e., where they are when they are writing these sentences). Tell them to observe anything a little unusual and then play the role of a detective.
> Later, in class discussion, a student can present one of her/his observations and the rest of the class can try to figure out what "best guess" s/he made. For example:
> STUDENT A: *There was a broken egg shell in the waste can.*
> REST OF CLASS: *Who do you live with? Does he/she usually eat an egg for breakfast? Did you eat an egg for breakfast this morning? What time did you see the broken egg shell?* [And so on, until they can figure out the same conclusion that Student A made, that A's roommate must have had an egg for breakfast.]

◇ **PRACTICE 22, p. 60:** *Forms of modals.*

> **1.** might be taking   **2.** must have been watching . . . must have forgot(ten)   **3.** should have bought . . . shouldn't have waited   **4.** must have been driving   **5.** must not have planned
> **6.** must have been daydreaming . . . should have been paying . . . shouldn't have been staring
> **7.** may have borrowed . . . couldn't have borrowed   **8.** must not have been listening
> **9.** couldn't have told   **10.** must not have . . . must have been/must be sleeping   **11.** must be making/must make   **12.** must have left   **13.** should have taken . . . must be walking . . . might have decided . . . could be working/could work . . . may have called.

◇ **PRACTICE 23, p. 61:** *Degrees of certainty.*

> Encourage the class to actually go to a public place (though they can, of course, visit that place in their imaginations to complete the assignment). Perhaps the whole class could go together to a zoo or public square.
> As an alternative, show a video tape to the class. You could turn off the sound and have the class guess what the people on the tape are talking about and doing. Or you could show several minutes from the middle of a movie or TV show and have the students guess about the characters and the story.
> As another alternative, you could supply pictures for the students to write about, perhaps news photos or posters depicting people and activities. It can be fun for you to supply snapshots of your family and friends for the students to make guesses about.

◇ **PRACTICE 25, p. 62:** *Used to and* be used to.

> **1.** used to play   **2.** am used to driving   **3.** used to rely   **4.** am not used to standing
> **5.** used to come   **6.** used to think   **7.** used to like   **8.** am used to taking   **9.** are used to commuting   **10.** used to travel

◇ **PRACTICE 27, p. 64:** Would rather.

Students should be alert to signals for the present and past verbs. Item #1, for example, requires the past form of the modal (modal + *have* + past participle). [Answers depend on students' ideas.]

◇ **PRACTICE 29, p. 65:** *Modals: dialogues.*

Students might work in pairs to complete the dialogues, with one student completing A's sentences and the other completing B's. The completed dialogues can be performed, discussed by the whole class, and/or written out and handed in. (See the INTRODUCTION, p. xv–xvi, for suggestions for using completion exercises.)

◇ **PRACTICE 30, p. 67:** *Modals: dialogues.*

Assign only one dialogue to each pair. Some students may want to choose their own situations for dialogue construction. Have the pairs perform their dialogues with or without their "scripts."

◇ **PRACTICE 31, p. 68:** *Discussion using modals.*

You may need to set a time limit for these discussions. Sometimes students get rather excited about the topics and don't want to stop! To conclude the exercise, you might ask the students to rewrite or expand on a sentence as given in the textbook so that all members of the group agree with the idea. The given ideas are, for the most part, overstated generalizations of opinion that need to be qualified, explained, and supported.

If these topics are unfamiliar or uncomfortable for your students, you might add some others that are closer to their immediate interests. Topics about their school, sports, clothing fashions, etc., may be productive.

These topics can also be used for writing.

◇ **PRACTICE 32, p. 68:** *General review of verb forms.*

This entire exercise is a dialogue between two people, so you could choose two good speakers to read it. The other students should listen carefully and offer corrections or alternative answers, if appropriate.

1. had
2. happened
3. was driving
4. broke
5. did you do
6. pulled
7. got
8. started
9. shouldn't have done
10. should have stayed
11. are probably
12. started
13. had been walking/(had) walked
14. went
15. discovered
16. didn't have (BrE: hadn't)
17. can think
18. could/might have gone
19. could/might have tried
20. could/might have asked
21. asked
22. told
23. was
24. allowed
25. drove
26. must have felt
27. took
28. took
29. might get
30. will know
31. have to/have got to/had better/am going to leave
32. have to/have got to/am supposed to be
33. May/Can/Could I use
34. need
35. don't have/have no
36. I'll take

◇ **PRACTICE 33, p. 69:** *Review of modals.*

A "short paragraph" is usually about five to eight sentences in length. You might want to set a limit for your students.

In marking their papers, focus on modals and verb tenses. Reward them for correct uses of these forms.

1. A	**6.** C	**11.** D	**16.** A
2. B	**7.** A	**12.** C	**17.** B
3. A	**8.** B	**13.** A	**18.** D
4. C	**9.** C	**14.** B	**19.** C
5. D	**10.** C	**15.** C	**20.** A

Chapter 3: THE PASSIVE

◇ **PRACTICE 2, p. 75:** *Forming the passive.*

This exercise provides a review of interrogative, negative, and affirmative forms in passive voice. It requires simple transformation. It can be used as an oral exercise in class, or if written, students can correct each other's answers.

1. a. Is your house being painted by Mr. Brown?
   b. No, it isn't being painted by him.
   c. It's being painted by my uncle.
2. a. Will the dishes be washed by Steve?
   b. No, they won't be washed by him.
   c. They'll be washed by the children.
3. a. Has the meeting been planned by Sue?
   b. No, it hasn't been planned by her.
   c. It has been planned by the committee.
4. a. Is that violin played by Mr. Parr?
   b. No, it isn't played by him.
   c. It is played by his son.
5. a. Are the books going to be returned to the library by Jack?
   b. No, they aren't going to be returned by him.
   c. They're going to be returned by his sister.
6. a. Was the ancient skeleton discovered by the archeologists?
   b. No, it wasn't discovered by them.
   c. It was discovered by a farmer.
7. a. Was the food being prepared by Sally?
   b. No, it wasn't being prepared by her.
   c. It was being prepared by her mother.
8. a. Will the letters have been typed by Ms. Anderson?
   b. No, they won't have been typed by her.
   c. They will have been typed by the secretary.

◇ **PRACTICE 8, p. 80:** *Using the "by phrase."*

3. Jack is being considered for that job.
4. The Mediterranean Sea is surrounded by three continents.
5. I got upset when I was interrupted in the middle of my story.
6. ... he was embraced by each of his relatives.
7. Rome wasn't built in a day. [This is a famous saying. It means that we shouldn't expect to complete something both quickly and well. Good things take time to do well.]
8. Where is that information filed? [*They* is impersonal in the active sentence.]
9. ... the dog had been chained to ...
10. Were you annoyed (last night) by the noise from the neighbor's apartment (last night)?
11. ... the news was broadcast all over the world.
12. Are those tractors made in this country, or are they imported?
13. ... I was approached by a nice ....
14. Pencils will not be provided at the test, so ....

◇ **PRACTICE 11, p. 82:** *Active and passive.*

1. have complained ... has been done [*to date* = until now]   2. went ... had piled ... had been shoved   3. are intimidated ... buy   4. put ... sold ... was bought ... was/had been looking ... had already been sold   5. was invented ... has assisted   6. brought ... sent ...

were asked . . . was discovered . . . is still called   **7.** was recognized . . . was asked . . . took
8. occurred . . . were crossing . . . were swept . . . left . . . were found . . . were/had been seriously injured . . . took

◇ **PRACTICE 13, p. 85:**   *Present participle vs. past participle.*

> **3.** equipped   **4.** destroyed   **5.** rubbing   **6.** whispering   **7.** erased   **8.** performed
> **9.** predicting   **10.** vaccinated   **11.** rehearsing   **12.** billed [= The dentist will send him a bill.]

◇ **PRACTICE 16, p. 87:**   *Passive modals.*

> **2.** been won   **3.** scrub   **4.** been vaccinated   **5.** be taught   **6.** replied   **7.** been stopped   **8.** be revised   **9.** trade   **10.** participate   **11.** be established   **12.** eat
> **13.** be distinguished   **14.** be killed

◇ **PRACTICE 18, p. 90:**   *Stative passive.*

> **1.** is located   **2.** are summarized   **3.** is . . . listed   **4.** is forbidden   **5.** am . . . acquainted   **6.** is scheduled   **7.** is overdrawn   **8.** is cancel(l)ed [*canceled* = American; *cancelled* = British]   **9.** is wrinkled [*iron* = press]   **10.** are equipped [*automobile* = American; *motor car* = British] [Air bags are protective devices that inflate upon hard impact.]   **11.** is made   **12.** is clogged

◇ **PRACTICE 21, p. 92:**   *Present vs. past participles.*

> **3.** known for   **4.** provided with   **5.** laughing   **6.** satisfied with   **7.** connected to
> **8.** crossing   **9.** involved in   **10.** composed of   **11.** accompanying   **12.** blessed with
> **13.** limited to   **14.** annoyed at/with   **15.** blowing

◇ **PRACTICE 23, p. 94:**   *The passive with get.*

> **2.** get accepted   **3.** got cheated   **4.** got fired   **5.** got mugged [*to mug* = to rob; *scruffy* = unkempt, dirty]   **6.** get invited   **7.** get dressed   **8.** got caught   **9.** got elected   **10.** get electrocuted   **11.** got ruined   **12.** got embarrassed

◇ **PRACTICE 26, p. 97:**   *Participial adjectives.*

> **1.** printing   **2.** Experienced   **3.** intended   **4.** amusing   **5.** manufactured
> **6.** relaxing   **7.** amazing   **8.** expected   **9.** approaching   **10.** inquiring
> **11.** visiting . . . winning . . . disappointed   **12.** encouraging   **13.** invigorating
> **14.** contaminated

◇ **PRACTICE 27, p. 98:**   *Verb form review, active and passive.*

> **3.** are lost   **4.** received   **5.** are given   **6.** are discriminated . . . have been enacted
> **7.** had been offered   **8.** finish [time clause]   **9.** are returned [time clause] . . . will be given
> **10.** have been destroyed   **11.** were allowed   **12.** was not fooled   **13.** established . . . be followed   **14.** irritating . . . will be replaced   **15.** was built . . . has often been described . . . was designed . . . took   **16.** is being/will be/is going to be judged . . . will be/are going to be announced   **17.** vending . . . kicked . . . fell . . . was seriously injured . . . ended . . . is still wearing . . . vending [In fact, in the decade of the 1980s, eight people in the United States were reported to have died from a vending machine falling on them.]   **18.** proposed . . . is not being offered [also: is not/will not be/is not going to be offered]   **19.** jogged / has been jogging . . . plans/is planning   **20.** is conducted . . . are sent . . . are asked . . . is collected . . . is published . . . use

◇ PRACTICE 29, p. 101: *Writing.*

You might want to set a limit on the length of these compositions—say, 10–15 sentences. Expect that your students would have some difficulty in trying to translate explanations from another language into English; tell them to use only English reference books. If your students don't have access to reference books, perhaps they could interview a local expert, parent, or acquaintance about how some common object is made.

Another possibility is for you to invite an expert such as a ceramicist, weaver, or carpenter to speak to the class. The students can take notes as the basis for their compositions.

Another alternative is for you to photocopy a description of a process. First, discuss the process and analyze with the class the use of the passive in the passage. Then tell the students to put the passage aside and describe the process in their own words in writing.

Discuss the organization of the sample composition. It has an introduction (that announces the subject) leading to a thesis sentence ("Paper can be made . . . process."). The second paragraph discusses one topic: the mechanical process. The third paragraph is about the chemical process. The last paragraph concludes the process. The description of the process itself is in chronological order.

You may choose to ask the students to underline every example of a passive in their papers after they have finished writing and revising them. This helps you in marking their successes and errors. It also helps the students check their own use of the passive. Another possibility is for the students to read each other's compositions and underline each instance of the passive.

You might assign the first of these topics for homework and use the second one later as an in-class writing test.

◇ PRACTICE TEST B, p. 103: *The passive.*

1. C	6. A	11. D	16. A
2. B	7. B	12. A	17. C
3. A	8. A	13. C	18. C
4. B	9. C	14. A	19. A
5. B	10. C	15. C	20. D

Chapter 4: GERUNDS AND INFINITIVES

◇ PRACTICE 2, p. 106: *Gerunds as objects of prepositions.*

Students might need to consult Appendix 2 (Preposition Combinations) in the main book. Possible answers: [Depend on students' ideas.]

2. . . . for collecting dues.
3. . . . to working more than 40 hours a week.
4. . . . for being late.
5. . . . of winning a lot of money.
6. . . . to getting low marks on my tests.
7. . . . from going to the soccer match.
8. . . . in cleaning up the school yard.
9. . . . from entering this area.
10. . . . about attending the new school.
11. . . . for bringing me a newspaper.
12. . . . to hiring children.
13. . . . about having to do too much homework on weekends.

◇ PRACTICE 3, p. 106: *Verbs followed by gerunds.*

[Answers depend on students' ideas.] Note these items in particular:
5. . . . mind having to stay. . . . 6. . . . consider going swimming . . . . 8. . . . discuss going shopping . . . . 9. . . . mention having to go . . . . 13. . . . quit worrying about . . . .

◇ **PRACTICE 6, p. 109:** *Verbs followed by infinitives.*

  2. Laura reminded her roommate to set her alarm . . . .
  3. Mrs. Jones allowed each of the children to have . . . .
  4. The doctor advised my father to limit his sugar consumption.
  5. My parents often encouraged me to be independent.
  6. The children were warned not to swim . . . .
  7. The police officer ordered the reckless driver to pull over.
  8. Rose invited Gerald to come to her house Sunday . . . her parents.

◇ **PRACTICE 8, p. 110:** *Gerund vs. infinitive.*

  [Answers depend on students' creativity.]
  1. remind someone to finish **2.** postpone giving **3.** be required to have **4.** advise
  taking/advise someone to take **5.** try to learn [less likely but also possible: *try learning*]
  6. warn someone not to open **7.** like going camping/like to go camping [*go to camp*: ''camp'' =
  a noun] **8.** invite someone to go **9.** promise not to tell/promise someone not to tell
  10. not be permitted to take **11.** ask someone to tell **12.** begin blowing/begin to blow
  13. remember calling/remember to call [with different meanings] **14.** tell someone to wash
  15. be told to be **16.** avoid getting

◇ **PRACTICE 13, p. 115:** *Gerund vs. infinitive.*

  [Answers depend on students' ideas.]
  1. playing **2.** someone to save **3.** telling **4.** to get **5.** someone to take **6.** staying
  7. someone not to buy **8.** giving **9.** going **10.** travel(l)ing **11.** taking
  12. someone to go swimming **13.** being **14.** hearing **15.** to tell **16.** being
  17. eating **18.** to know **19.** to get **20.** saying **21.** seeing **22.** (someone) to give
  23. to hire someone to work **24.** to tell someone to be/telling someone to be [with different
  meanings] **25.** someone to practice speaking **26.** someone to keep trying to call

◇ **PRACTICE 14, p. 115:** *Using gerunds as subjects.*

  [Answers depend on students' creativity.]

◇ **PRACTICE 15, p. 116:** *Using* it *+ infinitive.*

  [Answers depend on students' creativity.]

◇ **PRACTICE 17, p. 117:** *Adjectives followed by infinitives.*

  Students can work in small groups, perhaps considering only three or four items. You might
ask the students to use as many different expressions in the list as they can for each item. The
group could then ''vote'' for the completion they like best, and the leader could present it to the
rest of the class. [Answers depend on students' creativity.]

◇ **PRACTICE 25, p. 123:** *Gerunds and infinitives.*

  You could ask for two or three responses to each item. Or as a special challenge, you could set
a limit on the number of words in each response; for example, not fewer than eight words nor
more than twelve, or exactly ten words. Another possibility is for the students to draw a card on
which a number is written from a stack you have prepared, or perhaps roll three dice, and then
add that exact number of words to the sentence. Making the exercise into a game can be fun and
involving for the students. Another benefit is that students understand that they can shorten (by
eliminating nonessential words), lengthen (by combining ideas into compound and complex
structures), and otherwise manipulate sentences as needed when revising their own writing.
[Answers depend on students' creativity.]

◇ **PRACTICE 27, p. 124:** *Using verbs of perception.*

Ask two or three students to write their sentences for one item on the chalkboard. Invite discussion from the class to decide which sentence they prefer and for what reasons.

Or you could copy several good students' answers for each item and give them to each student in the class. Then you can lead a discussion of why those sentences are effective. [Answers depend on students' creativity.]

◇ **PRACTICE 29, p. 125:** Let, help, *and causative verbs.*

[Answers depend on students' creativity.]

◇ **PRACTICE 30, p. 125:** *Special expressions followed by the* -ing *form of a verb.*

[Answers depend on students' creativity.]
1. remembering **2.** waiting **3.** learning **4.** thinking [also possible: *(in order) to think*]
5. playing **6.** dreaming [also possible: *(in order) to dream*] **7.** saying **8.** singing and dancing **9.** to study (with) **10.** chatting **11.** trying **12.** taking

◇ **PRACTICE 33, p. 129:** *Verb form review.*

1. to have . . . built . . . to do **2.** watch . . . practice . . . finding **3.** getting/being accepted . . . concentrating **4.** hearing . . . play . . . forgetting . . . making . . . to relax . . . enjoy **5.** to persuade . . . to give . . . to cut . . . working . . . to retire . . . take [Parallel infinitives: *to* is usually not repeated.] . . . being dedicated **6.** wasting . . . to fail . . . doing **7.** to commute . . . moving . . . to give . . . to live . . . be [parallel infinitives] . . . doing . . . doing **8.** feel . . . to get . . . feeling . . . sneezing . . . coughing . . . to ask . . . to see . . . go **9.** chewing . . . grabbing, holding, or tearing . . . swallow **10.** Attending . . . embarrassing . . . to hide . . . get [parallel infinitives] . . . leave **11.** recalling . . . being chosen . . . looking . . . laughing . . . acting . . . playing . . . being . . . achieving **12.** to get . . . running . . . having . . . sprayed **13.** being treated . . . threatening to stop working . . . to listen **14.** cleaning/to be cleaned . . . sweeping/to be swept . . . washing/to be washed . . . dusting/to be dusted . . . Reading . . . doing **15.** being . . . being . . . to be understood . . . to bridge . . . teaching **16.** having been given . . . forming . . . to accept . . . going . . . being . . . having been exposed **17.** Finding . . . to be . . . being exposed . . . staying . . . to avoid . . . to minimize . . . getting . . . to get . . . eat [parallel infinitives] . . . taking . . . to prevent catching **18.** being inconvenienced or hurt [parallel passive gerunds] . . . to remind . . . to remove . . . to turn . . . to buckle ["buckle up" = connect one's seat belt] . . . to shut . . . to fill . . . to forget to do . . . driving . . . (to) avoid making . . . being instructed . . . to perform . . . being reminded to carry

◇ **PRACTICE 35, p. 133:** *Verb forms.*

Encourage the students to use a personal experience in the introductory paragraph. You might want to set a limit (350 to 500 words). If you want a shorter composition, assign only a personal experience the writer has had that is related to one of the topics.

When marking the papers, focus on verb forms. Point out good usage as well as errors. Perhaps excerpt sentences or passages to be reproduced for class discussion.

◇ PRACTICE TEST B, p. 135:   *Gerunds and infinitives.*

1. D	**6.** C	**11.** D	**16.** C
2. D	**7.** C	**12.** A	**17.** D
3. A	**8.** C	**13.** B	**18.** C
4. B	**9.** B	**14.** D	**19.** A
5. B	**10.** A	**15.** A	**20.** D

Chapter 5: SINGULAR AND PLURAL

◇ PRACTICE 6, p. 141 (p. 161 in Vol. B):*   *Using apostrophes.*

1. bear's   2. It's . . . world's   3. actors'   4. individual's   5. heroes' encounters . . . hero's encounter   6. Children's play . . . they're . . . Adults' toys . . . children's toys

◇ PRACTICE 12, p. 144 (p. 164 in Vol. B):   *Count and noncount nouns.*

Divide the class into groups of six to ten. Each group can try to do the entire alphabet; set a time limit (15–20 minutes) and let the groups get as far in the alphabet as they can. To shorten the game, you could assign only half of the alphabet to a group.

Make sure the students focus on the correct use of *a/an* and *some.* Also tell them that items can begin with an adjective; for example, ''a bald monkey'' could be used for the letter ''B'' (but not for the letter ''M''). Explain that strange or funny answers are fine; the only requirement is that the first word (other than *a/an* or *some*) begin with the appropriate letter of the alphabet.

One way to play the game is to eliminate each player who can't remember the whole list beginning with ''A.'' The game continues until there is only one player who can recite the whole list, or until everyone left can recite the whole list from ''A'' to ''Z.'' For the classroom, however, it's better to make the game non-competitive. The purpose is for the students to have fun while they are practicing a grammar point. Tell them to try to play without taking notes, but it would be all right if they needed to jot down a few notes to jog their memory when it's their turn to speak. It would also be all right for the students to help each other remember the list and remind each other about the use of *a/an* and *some.*

◇ PRACTICE 14, p. 146 (p. 166 in Vol. B):   *Count and noncount nouns.*

2. rewards   3. Butterflies . . . caterpillars . . . insects . . . wings   4. [no plurals]
5. products . . . vegetables . . . sardines . . . vitamins . . . vitamin [no -*s*] pills   6. plenty of jobs   7. facts   8. travelers . . . suitcases . . . for three days . . . months

◇ PRACTICE 19, p. 150 (p. 170 in Vol. B):   *Using of in expressions of quantity.*

4. Ø   **5.** of   **6.** Ø . . . of   **7.** Ø   **8.** of . . . of   **9.** of OR Ø   **10.** Ø . . . Ø . . . Ø
11. Ø . . . of   **12.** Ø . . . Ø

---

*PRACTICE 6 is on page 141 in the full (or combined) edition of the *Workbook*, but on page 161 (Volume B) in the split edition.

NOTE: The *Workbook* is available in split editions (Volume A and Volume B) and in a full edition. The page numbering for Chapters 5 through 10 and for the Appendix is different between the two editions of the *Workbook.* Both sets of page numbers are given in this full edition of the *Teacher's Guide.*

◇ **PRACTICE 20, p. 151 (p. 171 in Vol. B):** *Writing.*

If you assign this as free-form writing, some students will write lyrically of their dreams, while others will list their goals and methods of attainment as though writing a marketing report. If you want the writing to take a particular shape, discuss it with the class when you make the assignment.

◇ **PRACTICE 22, p. 152 (p. 172 in Vol. B):** *Expressions of quantity.*

Discuss the importance of qualifying a generalization in order to make it accurate. The sentences in the text are examples of overgeneralizations that need expressions of quantity to make them reasonable, true, supportable statements.
[Answers depend on students' opinions.]

◇ **PRACTICE 24, p. 154 (p. 174 in Vol. B):** *Subject-verb agreement.*

2. advice *has*
3. employees *are*
4. Listening *has*
5. Many *are*
6. news *is*
7. *Doesn't* everybody *seek*
8. people *don't*
9. there *is* the possibility

10. Chinese [language] *has*
11. the Vietnamese [people] *work*
12. planes *were*
13. The number *was*
14. men *are*
15. Every girl and boy *is*
16. Politics *is*
17. people *live*

18. fish *were*
19. there *is* a reform
20. food *was*
21. *Was* there doubt
22. *are* gloves
23. *is* Kenya
24. data *is* [formal: *are*]

◇ **PRACTICE 28, p. 157 (p. 177 in Vol. B):** *Singular and plural.*

2. *Millions* of *years* ago they had *wings.* *These* wings . . . to *their* environment.
3. *Penguins'* principal food *was fish.* They . . . their *wings* evolved into *flippers* . . . .
4. Penguins *spend* most . . . in *water.* However, . . . *eggs* on *land.*
5. Emperor penguins have interesting *habits.*
6. The female *lays* one *egg* on the *ice* in . . . immediately *returns* to . . . .
7. . . . the male *takes* over. *He covers* the egg with *his* body until *it* [the egg] hatches.
8. *This* process *takes* 7 to 8 *weeks.* During *this* time, the male *doesn't* eat.
9. After the egg *hatches,* the female . . . , and the male *goes* to . . . for *himself,* his . . . .
10. . . . live in polar *regions* . . . *you* can go . . . so *you* can enjoy . . . .

◇ **PRACTICE 30, p. 159 (p. 179 in Vol. B):** *Forms of* other.

1. The others   2. the other   3. The others . . . another   4. Others . . . other . . . many others   5. the other   6. Another . . . Others [no *the* because these are not all of the important inventions]   7. Other [no *the* because these are only a few of the classes]   8. other
9. other   10. another [*a lemon* = a poorly made product]   11. another   12. others [no *the* because there may be other categories]

◇ **PRACTICE 31, p. 160 (p. 180 in Vol. B):** *Forms of* other.

Punctuation depends on the structure of students' sentences.
[Answers depend on students' ideas.]

◇ **PRACTICE 33, p. 161 (p. 181 in Vol. B):** *Error analysis.*

1. . . . was *a* child, . . . is *a* big city with tall *buildings* and many *highways.*
2. . . . quite a *few words* from *other* languages.
3. There *are* many *students* from *different* countries in my class.

4. *Thousands* of *athletes* take part in the Olympics.
5. Almost all of the *houses* in the town are white with red *roofs.*
6. . . . important *aspects* of life. *Knowledge* about . . . *helps* us . . . .
7. All of the *students'* names . . . .
8. I live in a *two-room* apartment.
9. *Many people* prefer . . . towns. Their attachment . . . *prevents* them . . . of *work.*
10. *Today's* news is . . . *yesterday's* news.
11. *Most of* the students OR *Almost all of* the students . . . .
12. . . . several *assignments* to hand in next Tuesday.
13. Today *women* work as *doctors, pilots, archeologists,* and many other *things.* [OR (possibly stylistically preferable) . . . in many other occupations.] Both my mother and father are *teachers.*
14. Every *employee* in our company *respects* Mr. Ward. OR *All (of) the employees . . . respect . . . .*
15. A child needs to learn how to get along with *other* people, how to spend his or her time wisely, and how to depend on *himself or herself.* OR [possibly stylistically preferable] *Children need* to learn how to get along with *other* people, how to spend *their* time wisely, and how to depend on *themselves.*

◇ PRACTICE 34, p. 161 (p. 181 in Vol. B): *Writing.*

One purpose of this kind of writing assignment is to reduce the students' hesitation by having them write quickly on a broad topic. This sort of practice is especially good for those students who, unsure of themselves before now, have written only laboriously, wrestling with each word, afraid of making mistakes. Assure them that mistakes are not the end of the world and that even English teachers make changes in their own paragraphs. No one can write perfectly on the first attempt. All writers need to do their own proofreading ("error analysis"), rewording, and reorganizing.

In terms of grammar, the main purpose of this exercise is to let the students see if any old habits of singular-plural misuse remain in their writing. If so, they need to be especially aware of these problems when they monitor their writing and speech. When the students correct each other's papers, ask them to look especially for errors in singular and plural. Many students tend to proofread another student's writing more assiduously than they do their own; point out that they need to apply the same care and effort to their own writing. It's simply part of the writing process.

This type of exercise, designed to develop speed and fluency as well as to improve proofreading skills, can be repeated periodically throughout the term with topics of your or the students' choosing. You can set the time limit from one to ten minutes.

◇ PRACTICE TEST B, p. 163 (p. 183 in Vol. B): *Singular and plural.*

1. C	6. C	11. C	16. D
2. B	7. D	12. D	17. A
3. A	8. A	13. B	18. C
4. C	9. D	14. B	19. B
5. B	10. B	15. C	20. B

Chapter 6: ADJECTIVE CLAUSES

◇ PRACTICE 10, p. 172 (p. 192 in Vol. B): *Writing adjective clauses.*

[Answers depend on students' creativity.] [Sometimes item 18 confuses some students. A possible completion: *When Roberto went to the hospital, the doctor (who(m)/that) he saw recommended surgery.*]

◇ **PRACTICE 11, p. 172 (p. 192 in Vol. B):** *Writing.*

You might want to set this composition at 300 to 500 words.

◇ **PRACTICE 18, p. 176 (p. 196 in Vol. B):** *Special adjective clauses.*

Students need time to think of appropriate answers. This exercise is best done as seatwork or homework to be discussed or marked later.

◇ **PRACTICE 19, p. 176 (p. 196 in Vol. B):** *Writing adjective clauses.*

3. . . . three hundred people, *some of whom* had been waiting . . . .
4. . . . the basic process *by which* raw cotton becomes cotton thread. [no comma]
5. . . . case studies of people *whose families* have . . . disease to determine . . . . [no comma]
6. . . . AIDS research, *the results of which* will be posted . . . .
7. People *who* (also possible but less common: *that*) are forced . . . sixties may . . . . [no comma]
8. My parents, *who* know how to . . . family, look forward to retirement.
9. . . . is a widespread problem *to which a solution* must and can be found. (also possible: *problem, a solution to which must* OR *problem whose solution must*)
10. . . . a new administrator *under whose direction* it will be able . . . .
11. The giant anteater, *whose tongue* is . . . (12 inches), licks up ants for its dinner.
12. The anteater's tongue, *which* can go . . . minute, is sticky.

◇ **PRACTICE 23, p. 179 (p. 199 in Vol. B):** *Adjective phrases.*

2. *Food passing* from the mouth . . . through a *tube called* the esophagus.
3. *Animals born* in a zoo . . . than *those captured* in the wild.
4. . . . movie *program consisting* of *cartoons featuring* Donald Duck . . . .
5. . . . is *flour, a fine powder made* by grinding wheat or other grains.
6. My uncle *Elias, a restaurant owner*, often . . . from *boats docked* at the local pier. Customers come . . . seafood *feast considered* to be the best . . . .
7. . . . reinforce *firefighters trying* to save a *settlement threatened* by a forest fire . . . . started by *oil leaking* from a *machine used* to cut timber.
8. . . . a way . . . glow in the *dark, a technique* (that) scientists can use . . . activity of *cells within* plants and animals. This *development, announced* by the *National Science Foundation, the sponsor* of the research, should prove useful to *scientists studying* the basic . . . .
9. . . . occurs when *something existing* in nature is recognized for the first time . . . . An invention is *something made* for the first time by a creator . . . . *The telephone and the automobile, two examples* of important twentieth-century inventions, can be used to illustrate how . . . .

◇ **PRACTICE 24, p. 180 (p. 200 in Vol. B):** *Speaking and writing.*

The purpose of this practice is to encourage students to express their own knowledge and opinions while they are using many of the English structures they have learned. If the students discuss the questions in groups, the groups could later compare their lists of inventions and report their conclusions to the rest of the class.

The questions are just suggestions to stimulate the discussion or writing. It is not necessary to answer the questions in sequence or to answer every one of them.

In class, students could make a list of twentieth-century inventions, then rate them by answering item #1. After discussing their lists and ratings, they could complete the exercise in writing as seatwork or homework. In their writing, they should use several adjective clauses and phrases in their definitions, descriptions, and explanations. (Students may have a little difficulty with conditional verbs in item #5.)

[Answers depend on students' ideas.]

◇ **PRACTICE 25, p. 180 (p. 200 in Vol. B):** *Adjective clauses and phrases.*

[*choppy* sentences = short and not connected smoothly]

POSSIBLE ANSWERS:

2. Disney World, *an amusement park located* in Orlando, Florida, covers a large area of *land including* lakes, golf courses, campsites, hotels, and a wildlife preserve.
3. Jamaica, *the third largest island in the Caribbean Sea*, is one of the world's leading producers of *bauxite, an ore from which* aluminum is made.
4. Robert Ballard, *an oceanographer*, made headlines in *1985 when he discovered* the remains of the *Titanic, the "unsinkable" passenger ship that has rested* [possible but not preferred in formal style: *which has rested*; also possible: *ship resting*] on the floor of the Atlantic Ocean since *1912 when it* struck an iceberg [OR *since it struck an iceberg in 1912*] and sank.
5. William Shakespeare's *father, John (Shakespeare)*, was *a glove maker and a town official who owned* a shop in *Stratford-upon-Avon, a town* about 75 miles (120 kilometers) northwest of London. [The *who* -clause could follow *John* (with commas), but that would create a somewhat awkward sentence that is unnecessarily complex. Also: *who owned* can't be reduced to an adjective phrase (*owning*); the present participle in modifying phrases often gives a progressive notion or describes a progressive situation. *Who owned* is not a progressive notion here.]
6. The Yemen Arab *Republic, located* at the southwestern tip of the Arabian Peninsula, is an ancient *land that* [possible but not preferred: *which*] *has been host* to many prosperous *civilizations*, including the Kingdom of Sheba and various Islamic empires. [The *located* -phrase shouldn't follow *land*: "an ancient land located at the southwestern tip of the Arabian Peninsula that has been host . . ."; "that has been host . . ." is too far from "an ancient land" and may be mistakenly thought to refer to "Peninsula.")

◇ **PRACTICE 27, p. 181 (p. 201 in Vol. B):** *Error analysis.*

1. Last Saturday, I attended a party *given* by one of my friends. My friend, *whose* apartment is in another town, was very glad that I could come. OR . . . by one of my friends *whose* apartment is in another town, [comma is not required] *and who* was very glad that I could come.
2. Dr. Darnell was the only person *who(m)/that/Ø* I wanted to see.
3. There are eighty *students from* all over the *world studying* English at this school. OR . . . students from all over the world *who study* . . . . [no commas]
4. The *people who(m)/that/Ø we met* on our trip last May are going to visit us in October.
5. Dianne *Jones, who used to teach Spanish, has* organized a tour of . . . .
6. There is an old legend (that is) *told* among people in my country about *a man living in the seventeenth century who saved* a village from destruction. OR . . . *a man who lived* in the seventeenth century *and (who) saved* a village from destruction.
7. . . . since I came *here, some of whom* are from my country. OR . . . *here. Some of them* . . . .
8. The old man *(who was) fishing* next to me on the pier and (was) muttering to himself. OR The old man was fishing next to me on the pier and (was) muttering to himself.
9. People *who* (also possible but not preferred: *that*] can speak English can be . . . .
10. . . . afraid of the *beggars who* (also possible but not preferred: *that*) *went* from . . . .
11. The path (that) *we took* [no *it*] through the forest [no comma, no *it*] was narrow and steep.
12. At the national park, there is a path *that* [also possible but not preferred: *which*] *leads* to a spectacular waterfall. OR . . . a path *leading* to . . . . OR At the national park, [no *there is*] a path leads to a spectacular waterfall.

◇ **PRACTICE 28, p. 182 (p. 202 in Vol. B):** *Writing game.*

Once they get control of adjective clauses, some students tend to overuse them for a while. This exercise is a way of pointing out that it is possible to use too many adjective clauses. At the same time, the students should have fun playing with the structures they now control.

◇ PRACTICE 29, p. 182 (p. 202 in Vol. B):   *Writing.*

Students should now feel relatively comfortable using adjective clauses and phrases in their written sentences. However, you should perhaps assure them that it is neither necessary nor appropriate to have such structures in **every** sentence. Reward their successful sentences, especially those with good adjective clauses or phrases. You might want to set a limit on how long or short the essay(s) should be.

◇ PRACTICE Test B, p. 184 (p. 204 in Vol. B):   *Adjective clauses.*

1. C	**6.** B	**11.** D	**16.** C
2. B	**7.** D	**12.** B	**17.** D
3. A	**8.** D	**13.** C	**18.** C
4. A	**9.** B	**14.** B	**19.** A
5. C	**10.** C	**15.** A	**20.** B

Chapter 7: NOUN CLAUSES

◇ PRACTICE 5, p. 190 (p. 210 in Vol. B):   *Information questions and noun clauses.*

Take some time to explain this exercise. The idea is to practice a realistic conversational exchange between two speakers. Students may want to complete the conversation naturally, as in this example:
STUDENT A: Who is your roommate?
STUDENT B: You want to know who my roommate is. [Intonation may rise at the end, like a question.]
STUDENT A: That's right./Yes./Right.
STUDENT B: His/her name is (. . .).
[Answers depend on students' creativity.]

◇ PRACTICE 9, p. 193 (p. 213 in Vol. B):   *"That" clauses.*

[Answers depend on students' creativity.]

◇ PRACTICE 15, p. 199 (p. 219 in Vol. B):   *Reported speech.*

Students' answers will vary. They can read each other's to discover the variations and to help check for mistakes. Possible answers follow:
1. Alex asked me what I was doing. I replied that I was drawing a picture.
2. Ann asked Sue if she wanted to go to a movie Sunday night. Sue said that she would like to but that she had to study.
3. The little boy asked Mrs. Robinson how old she was. She told him that it was not polite to ask people their age.
4. My sister asked me if there was anything I especially wanted to watch on TV. I replied that there was a show at 8:00 that I had been waiting to see for a long time. She asked me what it was. When I told her that it was a documentary about green sea turtles, she wondered why I wanted to see that. I explained that I was doing a research paper on sea turtles and thought I might be able to get some good information from the documentary. I suggested that she watch [subjunctive] it with me. She declined and said she would rather do her math homework than watch a show on green sea turtles.

◇ **PRACTICE 16, p. 200 (p. 220 in Vol. B):** *Reporting speech.*

The written reports can be quite short and succinct. Also, you or the class can provide other topics for discussion.

◇ **PRACTICE 17, p. 200 (p. 220 in Vol. B):** *Reporting speech.*

The interviewee can be a member of your family, a faculty member, a community leader, your next-door neighbor—students enjoy interviewing any native speaker. Whoever the interviewee, prepare the class. Give them information about the person and ask them to prepare questions before they come to class on the day of the interview. Record the interview (on audio or video tape) so that the accuracy of quotations can be checked (and students can proudly hear their own public English).

All students will interview the same person, so their written reports will be similar. Therefore, you might choose the best one for ''publication.'' As an alternative, you could arrange for several people to be available for interviews and divide the class into groups. Then students' reports will differ, and you could publish more than one.

◇ **PRACTICE 19, p. 201 (p. 221 in Vol. B):** *Error analysis.*

1. I didn't know where I *was* supposed to . . . science *museum was/is*. She *told* me the name of the street. She said she *would* tell me *when I should* get off the bus.
2. Studying . . . realize [no *that*] what kind of career [no *did*] I *wanted* to have.
3. My mother said, [comma] ''[quotation mark] Don't [capital ''D''] forget our family when you're far away from home.'' [quotation mark] OR My mother *told me not to forget my* family when *I was* far away from home.
4. When I asked the taxi driver to drive faster, [comma] he said, [comma] ''[quotation mark] I will drive faster if you pay me more.''[quotation mark] At that time [optional comma], I didn't care how much *it would* cost, so I told him to go as fast as he *could*. OR . . . faster, he said (that) [no punctuation] he would drive faster if I paid him more. At that time . . . .
5. My mother did not live with us. When other children asked me where *my mother was*, I told them she *was* going to come to visit me very soon. OR . . . *mother was*, I told them, [comma] ''[quotation mark] She [capital ''S''] is going to come to visit me very soon.'' [quotation mark]
6. *When* I asked him what kind of movies *he liked*, he *told* me [OR *said to* me], ''I like romantic movies.'' OR I asked him what kind of movies he *liked*. *He* told *me he liked* romantic movies/*ones*.

◇ **PRACTICE TEST B, p. 204 (p. 224 in Vol. B):** *Noun clauses.*

1. A	6. B	11. D	16. D
2. C	7. B	12. D	17. B
3. D	8. C	13. B	18. C
4. D	9. C	14. D	19. A
5. C	10. A	15. A	20. C

Chapter 8: SHOWING RELATIONSHIPS BETWEEN IDEAS—PART I

◇ **PRACTICE 5, p. 208 (p. 228 in Vol. B):** *Parallel structure.*

2. past verb (phrase)   3. past progressive verb (phrase) [omit *was*]   4. adjective   5. simple verb (phrase) . . . simple verb (phrase)   6. gerund (phrase)   7. infinitive (phrase)   8. present tense verb (phrase)   9. gerund (phrase)   10. infinitive [no *to*] (phrase) . . . adjective . . . infinitive [no *to*] (phrase)   11. manner or time phrases [e.g., *by mail or in person; this week or next (week)*]   12. noun (phrases)

◇ **PRACTICE 6, p. 209 (p. 229 in Vol. B):** *Parallel structure.*

2. missed   **3.** running   **4.** cautiously   **5.** making   **6.** sensitive   **7.** close   **8.** to get
9. use . . . by spitting   **10.** scary . . . good luck . . . harmless . . . tangle . . . are . . . other dread
diseases . . . spreading seeds, and eating insects . . . can destroy . . . gentle

◇ **PRACTICE 8, p. 210 (p. 230 in Vol. B):** *Using parallel structure.*

You can use this exercise to teach the students about the writing process. In a first draft, people often write as though they were speaking to their reader. The students should write their initial ideas and let their first draft sit for at least 24 hours. On second look, they should cross out, insert, and reword, as well as check spelling and grammar. Then they rewrite. Their revisions should be shorter and more concise than the first drafts. Ask the students to hand in both drafts. If necessary, suggest further ways the writers can effectively use parallel structure and ask for third drafts.

One of the purposes of this exercise is to demonstrate that revision is a necessary and integral part of the writing process. Another purpose is to show how parallel structure allows writers to express their ideas concisely.

◇ **PRACTICE 11, p. 211 (p. 231 in Vol. B):** *Periods and commas.*

Points at which punctuation is needed are underlined.
1. Mr. Hood is admired because he dedicated his life to helping the poor. He is well known for his work on behalf of homeless people.
2. Greg Adams has been blind since he was two years old. Today he is a key scientist in a computer company. He is able to design complex electronic equipment because he can depend on a computer that reads, writes, and speaks out loud. His blindness neither helps nor hinders him. It is largely irrelevant to how well he does his job.
3. Microscopes, automobile dashboards, and cameras are awkward for lefthanded people to use. They are designed for righthanded people. When ''lefties'' use these items, they have to use their right hand to do the things that they would normally do with their left hand.
4. When you speak to someone who is hard of hearing, you do not have to shout. It is important to face the person directly and to speak clearly. My father, who is hard of hearing and wears a hearing aid, can understand me if I speak distinctly. As long as I enunciate clearly, I do not need to shout when I speak to him.

◇ **PRACTICE 13, p. 213 (p. 233 in Vol. B):** *Verb tenses in adverb clauses of time.*

1. B	**5.** D	**9.** B	**13.** D
2. D	**6.** A	**10.** B	**14.** B
3. C	**7.** B	**11.** B	**15.** A
4. D	**8.** C	**12.** A	

◇ **PRACTICE 15, p. 215 (p. 235 in Vol. B):** *Using adverb clauses to show time relationships.*

Encourage students to use a variety of verb tenses. [Answers depend on students' creativity.]

◇ **PRACTICE 19, p. 217 (p. 237 in Vol. B):** *Using because and therefore.*

[Only one possible answer is given.]
2. (a) Angela ate a sandwich because she was hungry.
   (b) Angela was hungry. Therefore, she ate a sandwich.
3. (a) We need to eat nutritious food because good health is important.
   (b) Good health is important. Therefore, we need to eat nutritious food.

4. (a) Because Edward missed the final exam, he failed the course.

   (b) Edward missed the final exam. Therefore, he failed the course.

5. (a) Jessica secured a good job in international business because she is bilingual.

   (b) Jessica is bilingual. Therefore, she secured a good job in international business.

◇ **PRACTICE 23, p. 220 (p. 240 in Vol. B):**   *Using such . . . that and so . . . that.*

[Completions depend on students' creativity.]

1. so	**5.** so	**9.** such	**13.** so
2. so	**6.** such	**10.** so	**14.** so
3. such	**7.** So	**11.** so	
4. so	**8.** so	**12.** such	

◇ **PRACTICE 25, p. 222 (p. 242 in Vol. B):**   *Using so that.*

[Answers depend on students' creativity.]

◇ **PRACTICE 26, p. 222 (p. 242 in Vol. B):**   *Cause and effect.*

1. A, B	**5.** B	**9.** A, C	**13.** A, B, D
2. A, D	**6.** A, D	**10.** C	**14.** B
3. B, C	**7.** C	**11.** B	
4. A, B, D	**8.** D	**12.** C	

◇ **PRACTICE 32, p. 227 (p. 247 in Vol. B):**   *Modifying phrases.*

1. + G Having sticky pads on their feet, flies can easily walk on the ceiling.

2. + J Having worked with computers for many years, Robert has an excellent . . . .

3. + I Having been born two months premature, Mary needed special care . . . .

4. + D Having done everything he could for the patient, the doctor left to attend to other people.

5. + A Never having eaten Thai food before, Sally didn't know what to expect when she went . . . .

6. + H Having no one to turn to for help, Sam was forced to work out the problem by himself.

7. + C (Being) an endangered species, rhinos are protected by law from poachers who kill . . . .

8. + B (Being) able to crawl into very small spaces, mice can hide in almost any part of a house.

9. + E Having done very well . . . and being nearly finished, Nancy expects to be hired . . . .

10. + F (Being) extremely hard and nearly indestructible, diamonds are used extensively in industry . . . .

◇ **PRACTICE 35, p. 229 (p. 249 in Vol. B):**   *Modifying phrases.*

1. Alexander Graham Bell, . . . One day in 1875, *(while) running* a test . . . I want you." *Upon hearing* words coming from the machine, *Watson* immediately . . . . OR *Hearing* words . . . , *Watson* . . . . [*Upon* expresses a time relationship; *hearing* (without *upon*) expresses a cause and effect relationship. Both make sense here.]

   After successfully testing/After having successfully tested OR *Having successfully tested* [*After* expresses time; omitting *after* expresses cause and effect. Both are viable in this instance.] . . . . *Believing* the telephone was a toy . . . , most people . . . .

2. Wolves are much misunderstood animals. *Believing* that wolves eagerly kill human beings, *many people* fear them . . . . [*the lower 48 states* = the United States without Alaska or Hawaii]

   (Being) strictly carnivorous, wolves hunt . . . .

   (Having been) relentlessly poisoned . . . , the timber wolf . . . . In the 1970s, *realizing/having realized* a mistake had been made, U.S. lawmakers passed laws to protect wolves.

   . . . Today, *(after) having been/after being unremittingly destroyed* for centuries, wolves are found . . . .

◇ **PRACTICE 38, p. 232 (p. 252 in Vol. B):** *Speaking.*

Obviously, students may or may not use the grammar points from this chapter in their skits. However, if you hear some natural use of a recently learned structure, you might point it out to the class and praise them for their achievement. The main purpose of this exercise is to get the students involved in a fun activity while preparing them for the writing assignment that follows. Discuss how emotions are communicated in speech, including relevant gestures, facial expressions, and tone of voice. Then discuss how emotions are communicated in writing by involving the readers in the narrator's situation to allow them to experience what the narrator experienced.

◇ **PRACTICE 39, p. 232 (p. 252 in Vol. B):** *Writing.*

Suggest that the students write a first-person narrative in chronological order. Tell them their task is to draw their readers into the experience and make them feel, or at least understand, the emotion. Discuss the use of concrete, specific detail to place the reader in the narrator's circumstance. Encourage the use of dialogue (quoted speech).

◇ **PRACTICE TEST B, p. 233 (p. 253 in Vol. B):** *Showing relationships between ideas.*

1. C	6. A	11. A	16. C
2. D	7. D	12. D	17. B
3. C	8. B	13. D	18. A
4. B	9. C	14. A	19. D
5. C	10. D	15. B	20. C

Chapter 9: SHOWING RELATIONSHIPS BETWEEN IDEAS—PART II

◇ **PRACTICE 2, p. 236 (p. 256 in Vol. B):** *Using* even though *vs.* because.

[Answers depend on students' creativity.] [In item 8: *my feet are killing me* = my feet hurt; *my head is pounding* = I have a headache.]

◇ **PRACTICE 8, p. 240 (p. 260 in Vol. B):** *Direct opposition.*

[Answers depend on students' creativity.] [In item 4: *keeps to herself* = doesn't share her thoughts and feelings with others.]

◇ **PRACTICE 10, p. 242 (p. 262 in Vol. B):** *Cause/effect and opposition.*

3. even though/although [*Because* would indicate a mischievous or spiteful gardener!]
4. Nevertheless/However **5.** Even though/Although **6.** In spite of/Despite [*Due to/Because of* indicates a relationship that is probably untrue; many ancient games have not survived.]
7. Therefore **8.** on the other hand/however [*Nevertheless* indicates that adults usually influence children's opinions, which might be true.] **9.** because of/due to **10.** Although/Even though **11.** because/since **12.** Even though/Although **13.** because of/due to **14.** Therefore **15.** Although/Even though [also possible: *While*] **16.** Because/Since

◇ **PRACTICE 11, p. 243 (p. 263 in Vol. B):** *"If" clauses.*

3. If I *have* free time, I [+ simple present tense] . . . .
4. If I *have* some free time tomorrow, I'll/I'm going to . . . .
5. If I *can't come* [also possible: *am unable/am not able* to come], . . .
6. If I *can't attend* a meeting at my office, . . .
7. If you *are* too tired . . . ,

8. If I *can't get* [also possible: *am unable/am not able* to get] . . . ,

9. If we *don't have* enough money, . . .

10. If people *continue* to destroy . . . ,

◇ PRACTICE 12, p. 243 (p. 263 in Vol. B):   *Using* whether or not *and* even if.

[Answers depend on students' creativity.]

◇ PRACTICE 17, p. 246 (p. 266 in Vol. B):   *Expressing conditions.*

[Answers depend on students' creativity.]

◇ PRACTICE 20, p. 248 (p. 268 in Vol. B):   *Summary of relationship words.*

[Answers depend students' creativity.]

EXPANSION: After B completes A's sentence, A should paraphrase the whole sentence using a different connecting word/expression (e.g., ''You wanted to fly a kite, but you went to class so you could improve your English.'').

◇ PRACTICE 22, p. 250 (p. 270 in Vol. B):   *Summary of relationship words.*

[Answers depend on students' creativity.]

EXPANSION: Choose one item. Tell each group to make the longest grammatically correct sentence they can. Ask that the sentences be written on the board with the number of words counted. Give the group with the longest correct one a ''prize'' (e.g., applause, one-minute early dismissal from class, a small piece of candy apiece). This is just a word game whose main purpose is fun. If your students seem too competitive already, don't award a prize. Instead, praise each group's efforts equally. (When setting up a ''make-the-longest-correct-sentence word game,'' limit the number of adjectives to ten.)

◇ PRACTICE 23, p. 250 (p. 270 in Vol. B):   *Summary of relationship words.*

Partial notes on punctuation:
1. comma before *but*   **5.** punctuation before and after *therefore*   **7.** comma after *month*
9. punctuation before and after *however*   **10.** comma after *color*   **12.** punctuation before and after *nevertheless*   **13.** add subjects to each clause, punctuation before and after *on the other hand*   **14.** comma after *weeks*   **15.** comma after the *since*-clause   **17.** punctuation before and after *consequently*   **18.** comma before *so* [unless it is part of *so . . . that* or *so that*]   **19.** so rapidly *that*

◇ PRACTICE 24, p. 251 (p. 271 in Vol. B):   *Punctuation.*

The points at which punctuation (and possibly capitalization) is needed are underlined.
2. Although a computer has tremendous power and speed, it cannot think for itself. A human operator is needed to give a computer instructions, for it cannot initially tell itself what to do.
3. Being a lawyer in private practice, I work hard, but I do not go into my office on either Saturday or Sunday. If clients insist upon seeing me, they have to come to my home.
4. Whenever my father goes fishing, we know we will have fish to eat for dinner, for even if he doesn't catch any, he stops at the fish market on his way home and buys some.
5. The goatherd who supposedly discovered coffee is a legendary rather than historical figure. No one knows for sure that the first coffee was discovered when an Ethiopian goatherd noticed that his goats did not fall asleep all night long after they had eaten the leaves and berries of coffee plants.
6. Whenever the weather is nice, I walk to school, but when it is cold or wet, I either take the bus or get a ride with one of my friends. Even though my brother has a car, I never ask him to take

me to school because he is very busy. He has a new job and has recently gotten married, so he doesn't have time to drive me to and from school anymore. I know he would give me a ride if I asked him to; however, I don't want to bother him.

7. The common cold, which is the most widespread of all diseases, continues to plague humanity despite the efforts of scientists to find its prevention and cure. Even though colds are minor illnesses, they are one of the principal causes of absence from school and work. People of all ages get colds, but children and adults who live with children get the most. Colds can be dangerous for elderly people because they can lead to other infections. I have had three colds so far this year. I eat the right kinds of food, get enough rest, and exercise regularly. Nevertheless, I still get at least one cold a year.

◇ PRACTICE 25, p. 252 (p. 272 in Vol. B): *Showing relationships.*

1. If you really mean what you say, I'll give you one more chance, but you have to give me your best effort. Otherwise, you'll lose your job.
2. Due to the bad weather, I'm going to stay home. Even if the weather changes, I don't want to go to the picnic.
3. Even though the children had eaten lunch, they got hungry in the middle of the afternoon. Therefore, I took them to the market so that they could get some fruit for a snack before we went home for dinner.
4. Whereas Robert is totally exhausted after playing tennis, Marge isn't even tired in spite of the fact that she ran around a lot more during the game.
5. Even though my boss promised me that I could have two full weeks, it seems that I can't take my vacation after all because I have to train the new personnel this summer. If I don't/can't get a vacation in the fall either, I will be angry.
6. In the event that Paul finishes his deliveries early this evening, he'll join us just in time for dinner. Therefore, you should make a reservation for him. Otherwise, the restaurant may not be able to accommodate all of us at the last minute.
7. Inasmuch as education, business, and government are all becoming more dependent on computers, it is advisable for all students to have basic computer skills before they graduate from high school and enter the work force or college. Therefore, a course called "Computer Literacy" has recently become a requirement for graduation from Westside High School. If you want more information about this course, you can call the academic counselor at the high school.
8. While many animals are most vulnerable to predators when they are grazing, giraffes are most vulnerable when they are drinking. They must spread their legs awkwardly to lower their long necks to the water in front of them; consequently, it is difficult and time-consuming for them to stand up straight again to escape a predator. However, once they are up and running, they are faster than most of their predators.

◇ PRACTICES 26 & 27, p. 254 (p. 274 in Vol. B): *Showing relationships; Giving examples.*

[Answers depend on students' creativity.]

◇ PRACTICE 29, p. 256 (p. 276 in Vol. B): *Error analysis.*

This is a summary review exercise containing grammar covered in Chapters 1 through 9. It intends to challenge the proofreading skills that students have acquired during the course. Students need out-of-class time to edit these sentences. Possible answers:
1. We went shopping after we ate/after eating dinner, but the stores were closed. Therefore, we had to go back home even though we hadn't found what we were looking for.
2. I want to explain that I know a lot of grammar, but my problem is that I don't have/haven't a large enough vocabulary. OR I know a lot about grammar, but I don't know enough vocabulary to express my ideas. [You might explain that even a student who has "enough vocabularies" but not "alot of grammars" has many problems communicating accurately.]

3. When I got lost in/at the bus station, a kind man helped me. He explained (to me) how to read the huge bus schedule on the wall, took me to the window to buy a ticket, and showed me where my bus was. I will always appreciate his kindness.

4. I (had) never understood the importance of knowing English/the English language until I worked at a large international company.

5. When I was young, my father found an American woman to teach my brothers and me English, but when we moved to another town, my father wasn't able to find another teacher for five more years.

6. I was surprised to see the room that I was given in the dormitory because there was no furniture and it was dirty.

7. When I met Mr. Lee for the first time, we played ping pong at the student center. Even though we couldn't communicate very well, we had a good time.

8. Because the United States is a big country, it has a diverse population.

9. My grammar class started at 10:35. When the teacher came to class, she returned the last quiz to my classmates and me. Then/After that, we had another quiz.

10. The first time I went skiing, I was afraid to go down the hill, but somewhere from a little corner of my head a voice kept shouting, "Why not? Give it a try! You'll make it!" After standing around a couple of minutes more with my (index) finger in my mouth, I finally decided to go down that hill.

11. If a wife has a job, her husband should share the housework with her. If both of them help, the housework can be finished much faster.

12. This is a story about a man who had a big garden. One day he was sleeping there. When he woke up, he ate some fruit, picked some apples, and walked to a small river where he saw a beautiful woman on the other side. He gave her some apples, she gave him a loaf of bread, and the two of them walked back to the garden. Some children came and played games with him. Everyone was laughing and smiling until one child destroyed a flower. The man became angry and told them to get out of there, so the children and the beautiful woman left. After that, the man built a wall around his garden and would not let anyone in. He stayed in it alone for the rest of his life.

◇ PRACTICE TEST B, p. 258 (p. 278 in Vol. B): *Showing relationships between ideas.*

1. B	6. A	11. A	16. B
2. B	7. D	12. B	17. B
3. D	8. C	13. D	18. D
4. C	9. D	14. A	19. B
5. C	10. A	15. A	20. D

Chapter 10: CONDITIONAL SENTENCES

◇ PRACTICE 6, p. 264 (p. 284 in Vol. B): *Conditional sentences.*

1. If I had been absent . . . .
2. If I had enough energy . . . .
3. If ocean water weren't salty, . . .
4. If our teacher didn't like his/her job, . . .
5. If I knew how to swim, . . .
6. If you had asked for my opinion, I would have . . . .
7. If water were/was not heavier than air, . . .
8. If most nations didn't support world trade agreements, . . .

◇ **PRACTICE 7, p. 265 (p. 285 in Vol. B):** *Conditional sentences.*

You could use this as a books-closed oral exercise to stimulate discussion. Student A could make a true statement. Student B could make a conditional sentence about that statement. [Answers depend on students' creativity.]

◇ **PRACTICE 10, p. 266 (p. 286 in Vol. B):** *Using* could, might, *and* should *in conditional sentences.*

Discuss the meanings of the modal auxiliaries. [Answers depend on students' creativity.]

◇ **PRACTICE 12, p. 268 (p. 288 in Vol. B):** *Omitting* if.

1. Were she ever in . . . .   2. Should Bob show . . . .   3. Had my uncle stood . . . .
4. Should you hear . . . .   5. Were I the greatest . . . .   6. Had you not lent . . . . [*Had* isn't contracted with *not* in this pattern.]   7. Should the president question . . . .   8. Had my roommate not mentioned . . . .

◇ **PRACTICE 15, p. 271 (p. 291 in Vol. B):** *Expressing conditions.*

Possible answers:
1. If Ron didn't have a meeting with his son's math teacher, he could/would go to the ball game with Jim after work tonight. If Jim asks Ron to go to another ball game some other time, Ron might go.
2. Tommy wouldn't have got(ten) into a lot of trouble if he hadn't taken his pet mouse to school/if he hadn't let his friend Jimmy put the mouse in the teacher's desk drawer. If the teacher hadn't opened her desk drawer, she would/might not have found the mouse. Etc.
3. If they had hired professional movers, they would have saved a lot of money. If the driver hadn't turned around to look in the back, the truck might not have crashed into a police car. Etc.
4. If I hadn't lost the saw that I borrowed, I wouldn't be embarrassed (now) to borrow the ax. If I had been more careful, I wouldn't have lost the saw. If I ask to borrow the ax, my neighbor might not lend it to me because I lost the saw. Etc.

◇ **PRACTICE 16, p. 272 (p. 292 in Vol. B):** *Conditional sentences.*

Encourage the students to produce the different conditional verb forms they have been studying. [Answers depend on students' creativity.]

◇ **PRACTICE 17, p. 272 (p. 292 in Vol. B):** *Conditional sentences.*

These questions can spur spontaneous use of conditional sentences in a lively class discussion. Encourage diversity of opinion. [Answers depend on students' creativity.]

◇ **PRACTICE 20, p. 274 (p. 294 in Vol. B):** *Using* wish.

[Answers depend on students' creativity.] [In item 6, the word "teleportation" may not be in the students' dictionaries. It is a sci-fi (science fiction) term generally meaning transmission of any physical matter to a receiving unit over any distance through molecular breakdown and subsequent reassembly.]

◇ **PRACTICE 22, p. 275 (p. 295 in Vol. B):** *As if/as though.*

[Answers depend on students' creativity.]

◇ PRACTICE 23, p. 276 (p. 296 in Vol. B): *Conditionals.*

1. had been run   **2.** would look   **3.** had had   **4.** hadn't been driving   **5.** wouldn't have slid   **6.** step [*step on the gas* = accelerate the car]   **7.** hadn't taken   **8.** wouldn't have lost **9.** hadn't lost   **10.** would have had   **11.** had had   **12.** wouldn't have to pay   **13.** hadn't been driving   **14.** wouldn't have run into   **15.** wouldn't be   **16.** were/was   **17.** would take   **18.** stay   **19.** would stay   **20.** weren't/wasn't   **21.** could go   **22.** I'll fly **23.** I'll take   **24.** could drive   **25.** would be

◇ PRACTICE TEST B, p. 278 (p. 298 in Vol. B): *Conditional sentences.*

1. D	**6.** A	**11.** D	**16.** A
2. D	**7.** D	**12.** B	**17.** B
3. A	**8.** B	**13.** D	**18.** D
4. C	**9.** A	**14.** C	**19.** C
5. B	**10.** C	**15.** B	**20.** A

Appendix 1: SUPPLEMENTARY GRAMMAR UNITS

◇ PRACTICE 10, p. 285 (p. 141 in Vol. A): *Nouns, verbs, adjectives, adverbs, prepositions.*

This exercise can be used in class discussion to make sure that the students understand the basic terminology used in the textbook. The exercise can be expanded by asking them to identify words in addition to those that are underlined. The material can also be used to discuss sentence structure; you could focus on the elements of a simple sentence or preview the compound-complex structures covered in Chapters 6–9. (Some teachers like to diagram sentences for their students.) In addition, you could ask the class to discuss punctuation and capitalization.

2. whales = NOUN . . . mammals = NOUN . . . breathe = VERB [Point out the spelling and pronunciation of *breathe* (verb) and *breath* (noun).] . . . air = NOUN [Note that in this sentence *live* is an adjective and *young* is a noun. You might ask students to find these particular uses of these two words in their dictionaries. Mention that it can be helpful to determine the grammatical function of a word in order to know which definition to look at in a dictionary.]

3. highly = ADVERB . . . trainable = ADJECTIVE . . . intelligent, sensitive = ADJECTIVES . . . refused = VERB . . . Finally = ADVERB . . . immediately = ADVERB . . . took, shared = VERBS

4. dive = VERB . . . deeply = ADVERB . . . beneath = PREPOSITION . . . surface = NOUN . . . under = PREPOSITION . . . water = NOUN . . . for = PREPOSITION

5. migrations = NOUN . . . among = PREPOSITION . . . swim = VERB . . . from = PREPOSITION . . . to = PREPOSITION . . . icy = ADJECTIVE

6. with = PREPOSITION . . . wide = ADJECTIVE . . . clicks, whistles, songs = NOUNS . . . gather = VERB . . . around = PREPOSITION . . . communicate = VERB . . . through = PREPOSITION

◇ PRACTICE 17, p. 292 (p. 148 in Vol. A): *Information questions.*

Practice 17 is a transformation exercise whose purpose is to review question words and forms. The questions the students make should produce the words in parentheses as short answers. Student A could ask the question, and Student B could say the short answer.

As an expansion of the exercise, the class could provide other possible answers to the questions. For example, in item #1:

A: *How do you take your coffee?*
B: *Black.* OR *With milk.* OR *With cream and sugar.*

2. What kind of dictionary do you have? [have you?/have you got?] [Answer: English-English. OR Bilingual. OR Spanish-English, etc.]

3. What does he do for a living? [Answer: Runs a grocery store, etc.]

4. Who was Margaret talking to?/To whom was Margaret talking? [Answer: Her uncle, etc.]

5. How many people showed up for the meeting?

6. Why could none of the planes take off?

7. What was she thinking about?/About what was she thinking?

8. How fast/How many miles per hour [OR an hour] were you driving when the policeman stopped you? [Point out that the subject-verb inversion occurs in the main clause, not the dependent (adverbial) clause.]

9. What kind of food do you like best?

10. Which apartment is yours?/Where is your apartment?

11. What is Oscar like? [Possibly: What kind of person/man is Oscar?]

12. What does Oscar look like?

13. Whose book fell to the floor?

14. Why isn't Abby here?

15. When will all of the students in the class be informed of their final grades? [Point out that even when there is a long subject, only the first auxiliary precedes it. The rest of the verb follows the complete subject.]

16. How do you feel?

17. Which book did you prefer?

18. What kind of music do you like?

19. How late is the plane expected to be?

20. Why did the driver of the stalled car light a flare?

21. Which pen do you want?

22. What's the weather like in July?

23. How do you like your steak?

24. How did you do on the test?

25. How many seconds are there in a year? [For fun, ask the students to figure out how many minutes (525,600) and hours (8760) there are in a year.]

◇ PRACTICE 18, p. 292 (p. 148 in Vol. A): *Information questions.*

Students can practice in pairs. If the exercise is used in class discussion, you should model spoken contractions for the students [e.g., ''when're,'' ''what color're,'' ''what kind of tea's that,'' ''what'd ya''].

3. Who is/Who's that letter from?   4. Who wrote that letter?   5. Whose coat is that?
6. When are Alice and John going to get married?   7. Which/Whose team won?   8. What color are her eyes?   9. What color is her hair?   10. What kind of tea is that?   11. What do you usually drink with your breakfast?   12. How long does it usually take you to eat breakfast? [Less likely: *How many minutes . . .?*]   13. How did you get to the airport?   14. How many brothers and sisters do you have/have you?   15. Where did you grow up?   16. How long does it take to get there by plane?   17. What kind of novels/books do you like to read?
18. Which chapters/What chapters/What will the test cover? [*cover* = include, comprise]
19. Why did Frank quit school?/How come Frank quit school?   20. How long has she been sick?   21. How many (people) are you going to invite?   22. Which camera should I buy?
23. Who discovered radium?   24. What are you doing?   25. How is/How's everything going?

◇ PRACTICE 19, p. 293 (p. 149 in Vol. A): *Information questions.*

Students can make up questions in class discussion or write dialogues to hand in. If the exercise is written, have the students write both the question and the answer.

Examples: 6: How do you spell *sitting*?   15. Where are you from? Where is Saudi Arabia located? What is the population? What is the major religion? What is its principal product? What is the capital?

◇ PRACTICE 20, p. 294 (p. 150 in Vol. A): *Asking questions.*

[Answers depend on students' creativity.] In item #**4**, the interviewer (Speaker A) says: "Mr./Ms. _____, isn't it?" This means that the interviewer is identifying the other person with the name that is on the job application paper.

◇ PRACTICE 21, p. 294 (p. 150 in Vol. A): *Shortened yes/no questions.*

This can be done quickly as a group or class exercise. Two students can read the dialogue aloud from the book, then another student can give the complete form of the question that has been shortened.

1. *Do you* need some help? **2.** *Are you* expecting someone? **3.** *Did you* stay up late last night? [*Yup* = Yes (very informal)] **4.** *Have you* ever been there before? **5.** *Are you* nervous? [*Who me?* = (surprised) Are you talking about me? Do you think I'm nervous?] **6.** *Do you* want a cup of coffee? [*Only if it's already made.* = Don't make a new pot of coffee just for me.] **7.** *Have you* heard any news...? **8.** A: *Are you* hungry? B:...*Are you* hungry?

◇ PRACTICE 28, p. 299 (p. 155 in Vol. A): *Using articles.*

If you ask students to write this exercise on paper for homework, they should underline the articles. This makes it easy for you to check.

If you do this exercise orally, it can be difficult for the students to hear the articles accurately. Try this technique: Give each student four cards or pieces of paper about 5″ (12.5 cm) square. On each card they should write one article (*a, an, the,* or Ø) in large letters. You should do the same. Then a student (or you) can read a sentence aloud. When the space for an article occurs, everybody holds up the card with the necessary article so that you can see it. Then you hold up the same word so the whole class can see it. Sometimes this creates a little confusion and laughter as students pick out their cards, but it keeps everyone actively involved in the lesson. Discuss any questions that arise.

1. ...*a* teacher...*a* computer programmer...*an* architect...*an* apartment...*a* house.
2. ...*the* name of *a* famous architect...*the* architect...*a* hotel in Tokyo...*The* hotel...Ø earthquakes.
3. ...*a* sandy shore...Ø animals...*the* surface...Ø life...Ø crabs, Ø shrimp [*Shrimp* is plural here; it has the same form in both singular and plural, like *deer* or *sheep*.], Ø worms, Ø snails, and Ø other kinds of Ø marine animals
4. ...*the* sand [of that beach]...Ø animals...*a* crab...*The* crab...*a* good time at *the* beach
5. ...Ø stones, Ø glass, and Ø keys...*a* person
6. ...*a* recent newspaper article...*an* Australian swimmer...*a* shark...*a* group...*the* shark...*the* swimmer, *the* dolphins...*the* swimmer's life
7. ...Ø evidence...Ø dolphins...Ø nature...*an* average...Ø suicide
8. ...*a* committee...*The* committee...*the* following proposals...*a* new sewage disposal plant...*a* new park...*the* present proposal, *the* new park...*a* swimming pool
9. ...*the* southeast corner...*a* landmark...*a* bolt...
10. ...Ø old cars...*a* 1922 automobile...*an* antique car
11. ...Ø power windows...*a* cassette player...*a* multi-adjustable driver's seat
12. ...Ø jokes...*a* frog...*a* lunchbox...*a* table...*the* school lunchroom [Other articles are possible. The given answers assume there is more than one table in a school lunchroom and that there's only one lunchroom in a school.]
13. Ø Most mirrors...Ø glass...*a* thin layer...Ø silver...Ø aluminum
14. ...*the* sun...*the* hours...*A* person's...Ø cancer
15. Ø Phonograph records...Ø compact discs
16. ...*a* coat hanger...*the* lock...*the* window...*the* driver's seat...*the* door...*the* police...*a* taxi...*the* car
17. ...*a* fly...*the* ceiling...*the* fly...*the* last second...*the* ceiling
18. ...*the* last sentence...*the* end